Linking Learning and Performance

IMPROVING
HUMAN
PERFORMANCE
SERIES

Series Editor: Jack J. Phillips, Ph.D.

Linking Learning and Performance

Toni Krucky Hodges

BUTTERWORTH
HEINEMANN

Boston   Oxford   Auckland   Johannesburg   Melbourne   New Delhi

Library of Congress Cataloging-in-Publication Data

Hodges, Toni Krucky
   Linking learning and performance: a practical guide to measuring learning and on-the-job performance / Toni Krucky Hodges.
      p. cm.
   Includes index.
   ISBN 0-7506-7412-1
   1. Employees--Training of. 2. Performance standards. I. Title.

HF5549.5.T7 H593 2001
658.3´12404--dc21

                                                                      2001052461

British Library Cataloging-in-Publication Data
A catalogue record for this book is available from the British Library.

The publisher offers special discounts on bulk orders of this book.
For information, please contact:

Manager of Special Sales
Butterworth–Heinemann
225 Wildwood Avenue
Woburn, MA 01801–2041
Tel: 781–904–2500
Fax: 781–904–2620

For information on all Butterworth–Heinemann publications available, contact our World Wide Web home page at: http://www.bh.com

10 9 8 7 6 5 4 3 2 1
Printed in the United States of America

THIS BOOK IS DEDICATED TO MY FATHER,
ANTON KRUCKY, JR.

Contents

About the Author

For the past 20 years, Toni Hodges has concentrated on measuring human performance. She has conducted and managed operations, systems, and group evaluations for corporate, defense contracting, and government organizations. Her work has included the development of individual assessment tools, and of large organizational tracking tools, all aimed at measuring the performance and monetary value of human resource and systems intervention programs.

Most recently Hodges managed measurement and evaluation for Verizon's Workforce Development Group. At Bell Atlantic she created and managed a measurement and evaluation program that, in 1999, was chosen as a best practice from among programs at over 200 companies. She was also selected as one of nine "Training's New Guard—2001" by the American Society for Training and Development (ASTD), and she was featured in the May 2001 issue of *Training and Development* magazine.

In 2000 the ROI Network™ named Hodges "Practitioner of the Year." She currently serves as Chairperson for the ASTD Publishing Review Committee and as President of the ROI Network, and she is in frequent, worldwide demand as a conference speaker. She has published numerous articles, and she was editor of the best-selling ASTD In Action series, *Measuring Learning and Performance*. Ms. Hodges can be reached at tonihodges@mindspring.com.

Preface

This book is for those of you who, after I have spoken at a conference or workshop, have come up to me (or called me later) with a sense of panic in your expression or voice to say, "Help!" Many of you do not have an extensive background in evaluation, yet you must play the role of the evaluator in your organization. You may be a trainer or HRD program designer by profession or a manager in the HR department, and you feel intimidated by the mounds of literature on measurement and evaluation. For you, this book will offer practical guidance and ideas from current practitioners. If you are a more experienced evaluator, you may want to investigate some tools and techniques offered here that other practitioners are using successfully.

I have tried to use as little discussion of theory as possible and focus on application. The book offers tips for the design of learning measures and the development of job performance data collection instruments. These tips are based on literature, my own experience, and the experience of practitioners I know. Each chapter ends with a checklist, so you can keep yourself honest at each step along the way. The case studies in progress are typical HRD programs that illustrate the techniques and tools described in each chapter. When you get to the last chapter, you will feel as if you have thoroughly and successfully evaluated each program and presented the results yourself. You may have an immediate need to evaluate a program and can replicate the case study evaluation that most resembles your own.

The information provided is sufficient to allow you to develop good learning-measures and analyze the data you collect from those measures. You will be able to develop effective job performance instruments and analyze the data you collect from them. You will be able to draw conclusions from the results of your analysis, make meaningful recommendations based on those conclusions, and determine how best to present the results to your particular audience. If that is not enough, additional resources are provided.

Think of evaluation as growing a tree. The roots of the tree are the needs for the program. A needs-assessment will determine what kind of tree needs to be planted—will it be large or small, and of what variety? The roots will need to be fertilized with usability and quality testing to ensure proper growth and longevity. The tree trunk that grows from the roots represents the objectives for the program. Without the objectives, the rest of the tree cannot be defined and will thus not grow. From the tree trunk grow the branches that represent the skills and knowledge for your program. They must be tested to ensure strength and continued growth. From each branch, leaves form, representing the individual job performances resulting from the skills and/or knowledge learned. If the leaves are healthy and plentiful, fruit will grow. The fruit that the tree bears represents the final benefits of the program. The benefits may include increased employee motivation, more productive meetings, or fewer ware-house accidents. By comparing the resulting fruits to the cost of the efforts to plant, fertilize, monitor, and grow the tree, the actual Return on Investment (ROI) can be determined. The program evalu-ator is in the perfect position to ensure that this program tree does indeed bear fruit. So put on your evaluator sun hat, roll up your sleeves, and get ready to get your hands filled with rich soil.

Foreword

Jack J. Phillips, Ph.D.

The Jack Phillips Center for Research, a Division of Franklin Covey Company

You'd have to be living underground not to be aware of the tremendous trend to increased evaluation and measurement for training and development. Everywhere we turn, there's increased pressure for accountability and a need to show the impact of training in a variety of ways, using different types of measures.

When we conduct our workshops on Measuring Return on Investment (over 500 have been conducted in thirty-two countries, with 10,000 participants), many frequently asked questions involve the measurement at other levels in addition to ROI. Though we stress that organizations measure a variety of issues, including ROI, most participants ask, "Although I understand the need for ROI, how can I measure the actual learning that takes place and how it is being applied on the job?" Practitioners need to know how to measure, at all levels from reaction and satisfaction to learning, application, business impact, and ROI. These days, practitioners are desperately seeking help with measuring learning and application—the focus of this book.

Though excellent progress has been made in measuring reaction and satisfaction, many practitioners are struggling with efficient and effective ways to measure learning and application. They also recognize that, from the client's perspective, data on learning and application are more valuable than reaction data. This book focuses on these two critical issues: measuring learning and application. Author Toni Hodges brings a wealth of experience to this exploration, as she has struggled with these issues in her own work.

In this new book, Toni presents practical approaches proven in workplaces, using sound methodology based on valid and reliable approaches. Though measuring learning and application is not easy, she succeeds in simplifying the process by tackling issues one step at a time, showing many "how to's" and offering advice and tips along the way. She leaves the reader with a sense of, "Yes, I can do this. This is what I need now in my work!"

When individuals are involved in a learning solution, a chain of impact should occur as training yields results. Participants react favorably to the learning process, learn new skills and knowledge, apply them successfully on the job, influence business measures, and, hopefully, have a positive ROI. Perhaps the most critical linkage in this chain of impact is the portion connecting what occurs in the learning activity (measuring learning) to the actual transfer to job performance (measuring application).

Toni's book, *Linking Learning and Performance,* tries to unravel this critical mystery and establish this important linkage.

Toni's original title for this work was "But Did They Get It?," which underscores the key focus of this book. While it's one thing to make sure that participants have attended training and reacted favorably, it's more important to know that they have actually learned something and translated it into improved job performance. This is the important focus of this work.

This book follows Toni's very successful casebook, *Measuring Learning and Performance*, published by the American Society for Training and Development. This best-seller has generated a tremendous amount of interest. Many of the readers and users of the casebook wanted more details, organized as a specific body of knowledge. Consequently, Toni developed this important new contribution to our Improving Human Performance series.

I think you will find this book extremely valuable and an excellent reference as you make progress in the journey toward developing the payoff of the investment in human resource development. Please enjoy this book and provide Toni with your feedback.

CHAPTER 1

Why It Is So Important to Measure Learning and Performance

Since the mid 1990s there has been a surge of interest in determining the business impact of Human Resource Development (HRD) programs. This is exciting because it demonstrates the importance of showing the value of development programs in language that stakeholders understand. Due to this interest, a flurry of activity and resources is focusing on Return on Investment (ROI) analyses. Though significant and important, the focus of ROI activity often leaves some of the more basic and fundamental evaluation methodologies sitting on the sidelines.

Two players often left on the bench are *learning* and *performance evaluations*. This is unfortunate because these are the two types of evaluation that offer the best opportunity to uncover the reasons for an HRD program's struggle or failure. For example, if an evaluator finds a negative ROI, measuring learning and job performance can determine the reason. These are the evaluations that can answer questions such as:

- Is the problem that the program participants never applied the skills or knowledge on the job, or is it that they never learned them to begin with?
- If the skills or knowledge were learned but not applied, what is inhibiting the application?
- What should be done? Should the HRD manager cancel the program?
- Should the manager select a new vendor?
- Is the program more suitable for a different audience?

1

- Should the program designers attempt to improve the program?
- If improvement is sought, what specific type of improvement is needed?
- What lessons learned can the HRD department apply to future programs?

Now, while executives have an appetite for determining the impact of the HRD programs in which they are investing, the evaluator must ensure they can answer questions such as these. If they cannot, measuring business impact will be a trend that will quickly pass. The evaluator must determine how effective the program is in teaching skills and knowledge and in ensuring those skills and knowledge are transferred to the participants' work environment. But the evaluator today is most often working in a fast-paced environment where lengthy, time-consuming studies are just not practical. So the challenge is to design instruments for measuring learning and job performance and to analyze the data acquired from these instruments in a comprehensive, yet practical, way.

PROGRAM EVALUATION OVERVIEW

Before beginning the focus on measuring learning and job performance, let's look at how they fit in the overall evaluation process. Figure 1-1 depicts the different components for program evaluation.

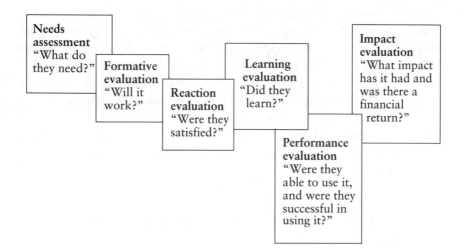

Figure 1-1. Components for HRD evaluation (Hodges 1999).

Each component is an area of expertise unto itself. A *needs-assessment* produces the clear definition of the objectives for the program. Program planners identify potential barriers to performance and begin to develop transfer enablers (Sullivan 1998). During the *formative evaluation* component, a prototype program undergoes the rigors of usability engineering and quality-assurance testing. Usability engineering involves activities throughout the product lifecycle and has as its goal the design of an interface that leads to productivity and ease of use. For electronic training products (CBT, multimedia, EPSS, WWW, etc.), the evaluation of the human-computer interface is very important. As the title for this type of evaluation suggests, the focus is on both the user of the technology and the technology itself. Quality assurance focuses on the actual functioning of the product, ensuring that it has been designed according to requirements and that no technical errors occur during its use. For instructor-led programs, designers check the program material to ensure it meets established standards. After quality-assurance testing, the evaluator tests the program in a pilot and recommends any necessary final revisions. The program delivery team then implements the program.

The remaining components constitute the *summative evaluation*. These include:

Reaction evaluation. Once implemented, the evaluator determines if the participants were satisfied with the learning-event. Often they are asked if they expect that they will be able to successfully use the knowledge or skills taught. The evaluator can use surveys and/or conduct interviews or focus groups at the completion of program modules or at the end of the entire program.

Learning evaluation. The purpose for this evaluation is to determine the extent to which the program has met its learning objectives. The evaluator tests the students to determine the extent to which they acquired the knowledge or skills specified in the program objectives.

Performance evaluation. The purpose for performance evaluation is to determine the extent to which the program has met its performance objectives. The evaluation will determine the extent to which program participants have been able to apply or transfer the knowledge gained, or skills acquired, to the job.

Impact evaluation. The purpose for the impact evaluation is to determine the degree to which the program has met its business objectives and the degree to which the expectations of client (the stakeholder for the program) have been met. This is done depending upon the objective(s) and could include measuring output increases, cost savings, timesaving, and quality improvement (Phillips 1997). The evaluator may conduct an ROI analysis as part of this evaluation.

The evaluator can assess a program at any stage of design or implementation. Some might suggest, however, that the evaluator completes the components that constitute a summative evaluation in sequence. That is, the reaction evaluation should be conducted before the learning evaluation, which should be conducted before the performance evaluation, which should be conducted before the impact evaluation. There is merit to this suggestion because an analyst can often find linkages between the components if the evaluation data from each are available. Figure 1-2 depicts the flow for such a linkage.

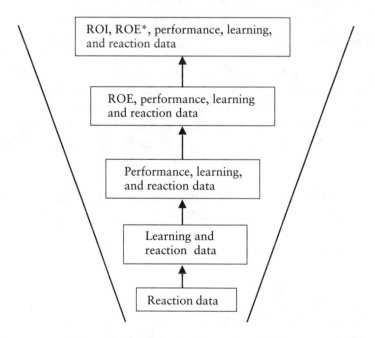

Figure 1-2. Correlation pyramid.

* ROE (Return on Expectation) is a method used to acquire data on the extent to which the program met the client's expectation (Hodges 1998). It is discussed in detail in chapter 7.

This pyramid is inverted to depict how the most simplistic evaluation data (reaction data) can be used to build upon progressively more complex evaluation data. In this way, if the evaluator finds negative results in an ROI analysis, they can use these different sources of data to investigate the reason(s) for those results and answer the questions posed in the beginning of this chapter. Let's walk through such an investigation.

USING SUMMATIVE EVALUATION DATA TO INVESTIGATE

Why is the ROI Negative?

When the evaluator conducts an impact evaluation and finds a negative ROI or that the business objectives have not been met, the question that the program stakeholders are likely to ask is, "What happened?" They have, most likely, spent a great deal of money and other resources on this program, so the question is a fair one. Anecdotal information may provide some clues, but probably does not provide the information to substantiate the cancellation of a program or to take the steps necessary to enhance the program. An investigation is needed.

The evaluator can conduct a Return on Expectation (ROE) evaluation to determine the extent to which the client's expectations have been met. This evaluation may show that the client has a good sense of what is working and what is not, and is in a good position to determine the reasons for some of this. The client is normally used to talking about fina ncial issues and can often provide good estimates of business impact.

Why is the ROE Negative?

If the ROE evaluation is negative or marginal, the evaluator can take the next critical step to determine if the performance objectives were met—were the program participants able to perform on the job as intended? If they were, at what level of proficiency were they able to perform? If the performance did not take place or the proficiency level was low, then it is not surprising that the evaluator found a negative ROI or that the business objectives were not fully met. If, when conducting the performance evaluation, the analyst determines that the performance was low, the organization will want to know that this was the case, so that they can take steps to enhance the program or improve the participants' work environment.

Why Isn't Performance Taking Place?

There are many possibilities for poor performance. The participants may have learned the skills, but they do not have the systems or other resources they need to do the job. They may not have the reinforcement that they need from their supervisors. One can think of many such barriers as these that could prevent successful performance from taking place. These can be determined from a performance evaluation. But what if they never learned the skills to begin with? A learning evaluation will determine if this is the case.

If the learning evaluation demonstrates that the program participants did not learn what was intended and the program objectives, therefore, were not met, the program participants should not be expected to apply the skills on the job.

Why Isn't Learning Taking Place?

The program may have been too difficult for this particular audience. The program may not have been presented using the best delivery method. Or the participants were forced to attend the class, and their resentment interfered with their learning. The participants may not have the prerequisite knowledge or skills to take the course to begin with. The instructor may not have presented the material in an organized fashion, the instruction may not have been clear, or the content may not reflect what truly happens on the job. One way to determine which of these possibilities is the culprit is to have reaction data.

So there is value in measuring at each level of the pyramid. Most organizations measure reaction. And many are attempting to conduct ROI studies. But, although they are important, little meaningful or useful information can be gained from these. The really rich sources of information are found in measuring if the participants got it (learning evaluation) and if they can use it (performance evaluation). If the program has gone astray or is not maximizing the return on the investment made, these are the two opportunities to determine the reason and what can be done to fix the problems. And these are the two types of evaluations that can identify and prevent potential barriers to performance.

CASE STUDIES OF TYPICAL HRD PROGRAMS

This book presents three different types of HRD program examples throughout to illustrate the methodologies discussed in each chapter: a technical training program, a sales/customer service training program, and a leadership development program. They are called "case studies in progress" because, after each chapter discussion, the case studies walk through, step-by-step, the processes and techniques described in that chapter, so the reader can see actual applications. The case studies progress until each has been evaluated, reported, and presented. In addition to these fictional programs, the chapters provide examples of tools and methodologies from actual programs conducted among various organizations.

REFERENCES

1. Hodges, T. K. 1998. "Measuring Training Throughout the Bell Atlantic Organization," In *In Action: Implementing Evaluation Systems and Processes,* series editor, J. J. Phillips, American Society for Training and Development, Alexandria, Va.
2. Hodges, T. K. 1999. "The Value of Measuring Learning and Performance," In *In Action: Measuring Learning and Performance,* American Society for Training and Development. ed., T. K. Hodges, Alexandria, Va.
3. Phillips, J. J. 1997. *Return on Investment.* Houston, Tex.: Gulf Publishing Company.
4. Sullivan, R. L. 1998. *Info-line: The Transfer of Skills Training.* Alexandria, Va.: American Society for Training and Development.

CHAPTER 2

How to Develop Objectives and Plan for the Evaluation

Today's evaluator has the opportunity not just to determine the outcome of an HRD program but to *influence* the program outcome. If involved in the planning phases of the program, the evaluator can use historical company data, for example, to eliminate potential barriers to the effective transfer of the skills and/or knowledge provided. Or the evaluator can identify techniques that can be used as part of the program itself to serve not only as an evaluation tool but also as a method for learning retention and transfer. Early involvement is the key.

PLANNING FOR THE PROGRAM EVALUATION

It is a missed opportunity if the evaluation is thought of only as an "after the fact" task. Evaluation needs to be integrated into the organization. To determine how an organization is doing overall, the evaluator can put into place systems to ascertain reaction and learning for all of its HRD programs. This determines, for example, the most successful media types or areas of content. The company can use this information to make decisions about future programs and to intervene for those programs that are falling short of an established standard. In addition to this type of organization-wide evaluation, the evaluator has the opportunity to become integrated into the planning, design, and implementation of specific programs—programs that are expected to impact many employees and those that are expensive or

8

significant in meeting company goals. In these instances, the evaluator can take steps to help ensure program success by using evaluation tools to plan, develop, execute, and evaluate the program. And the evaluator can ensure that the results of the evaluation are presented in a manner that provides clear direction for continuous improvement or for making key decisions.

Putting Together a Program Task Force

When planning for the program evaluation, the evaluator can take the lead to put together a task force of the key players for the program. The players' identities would depend on the program as well as the way the organization is structured. But a task force for initial planning would include the following functional areas:

- The stakeholder or client—the person(s) who has determined there is a need for some type of intervention or solution and who may be the same person paying for the program
- A design representative—the person(s) who is responsible for the development of the solution and who may be the same person responsible for conducting a needs-assessment
- A delivery representative—the person(s) who is responsible for implementing the program and may include a representative(s) from the training staff
- A field representative—the person(s) who fully understands the environment in which the program participants will be attempting to apply the skills or knowledge acquired from the program
- The evaluator—the person responsible for the evaluation of the program and who also may be one of the above or someone designated exclusively for the evaluation component

Putting together this team at the beginning stages of the program will ensure:

1. Some type of needs-assessment is conducted to identify a solution(s).
2. The solution identified takes into account potential field barriers to performance, so that steps can be taken to determine strategies for removing those barriers.
3. Potential enablers for successful performance are identified, so that steps can be taken to ensure those enablers are put into place.

4. The solution is practical and feasible to develop and implement.
5. The evaluation strategy is identified, so that tools and processes required, such as the establishment of a control group, can be put into place as needed.
6. Everyone understands the expectations for the program.
7. Everyone feels ownership in the process, so they are more likely to participate at key critical times throughout the program planning, design, implementation, and evaluation.
8. The method for communicating the results of the evaluation has been planned.

An initial face-to-face meeting or conference call with all these players when the stakeholder first indicates a need is ideal. It may be that the stakeholder and a subject matter expert have determined that the solution is some type of training program and it is at that point that the task force is convened. But the evaluator can facilitate this early dialogue by asking the key questions that will set the stage for a successful program. If this initial dialogue is established and continues throughout the program design, delivery, and summative evaluation stages, the program has a far greater chance for success.

Defining Objectives from a Needs-Assessment

The first key question the evaluator must ask, which will drive how the program will be designed and evaluated, is, "What is the problem that needs a solution?" When there is clarity around this, the program objectives can be determined.

The objectives for any HRD program serve as the foundation for further development and measurement. Developing appropriate objectives can be the most difficult of all the steps and is the step most program developers skip. One reason for this could be that no one conducted a needs- assessment or analysis to identify clear program objectives.

People's eyes tend to glaze over at the mention of conducting a needs-assessment. But companies have developed practical ways to conduct timely and cost effective assessments of needs. Rossett (1987) recommends a process that identifies the people who can provide the information and the type of facilitation required to conduct effective interviews with those people to obtain necessary data in a timely manner. The program task force that the evaluator convened may be the first step in this process. Robinson and Robinson (1989) recommend that the analyst become proactive in identifying systems or problems that may require some type of intervention. They suggest that HRD professionals constantly perform environmental scans of their own organizations. They can do this by:

- Reading journals associated with their industry to spot trends
- Reviewing organizational performance indicators and information to determine how the organization is doing
- Taking line managers to lunch or just seeing them at meetings and asking questions about the state of their business
- Volunteering to serve on task forces or committees that put them in contact with line managers and in a position to hear of potential business needs
- Reading and asking questions about the organization's vision, strategic plan, and new ventures and challenges, and searching out the implications for training
- Questioning workshop participants at breaks and at lunch to find out the business challenges they are facing

Apple Computer utilizes a timesaving approach to conduct gap analyses (Burkett 2000). This is necessary because they do not have the time or money to invest in what can be lengthy needs-assessments. Franklin Covey uses a "baseline evaluation" to start their process for workshop evaluations (Peterson and Bothell 1999). They ask their clients to complete a questionnaire, part of which includes the questions:

1. Why does your company or organization want the training?
2. What is the problem or opportunity?
3. Which three or four key business results does your company want to change? (They provide a prompt that lists potential results with this question.)
4. How will you know if you have been successful?
5. Which key business results would you like to measure?

More often than not, an evaluation must be conducted on an existing program on which a needs-assessment or gap analysis has not been conducted. AT&T developed business and job performance objectives for a program that had been running for many years (Fawson 1999). In this case, the analyst needed to "infer" business and job performance objectives from the course content and from other promotional materials about the program. After several iterations, the company's district manager and the evaluation manager agreed upon the objectives that were then used for evaluation.

The Evaluation Plan

The evaluation plan is started after the needs-assessment has established the program objectives. The plan includes:

1. Identification of the Program Task Force members.
2. The background of the user group and the problem leading to the program solution.
3. The business and performance objectives.
4. The beginning of a specific measurement or data collection strategy or plan (chapter 7).
5. The way in which the results of the evaluation will be used.

As the program moves forward, the members of the task force develop the performance and learning objectives. They identify program enablers and barriers, and the evaluator further develops the measurement or data collection strategy. This plan serves as a driver for developing the critical objectives for evaluation as well as for identifying the steps necessary for a successful program design and implementation.

A second reason that clear objectives are not normally well defined may be because the "how to" for developing objectives does not fall within the framework of any one discipline, yet crosses all the disciplines and functions necessary for the development of an effective program solution.

DEFINING PROGRAM OBJECTIVES

When thinking of program objectives, instructional designers think most often of learning or course objectives, and this is what they are taught to develop. But before they develop learning objectives, they must have a clear understanding of the job behaviors or performances required. To identify those job behaviors or performance requirements, program planners must know the expected business results from successful performance. Rather than having the program designers begin developing learning objectives, therefore, the evaluator must facilitate a discussion to identify the business objectives first. These will drive the identification of the job performance objectives. Only after the performance objectives are listed can relevant and targeted learning objectives be established.

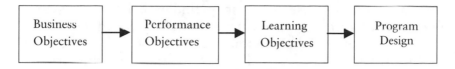

Figure 2-1. Sequence for developing objectives.

The business objectives uncovered during the needs-assessment reflect the client's expectations and are stated initially in business terminology. From these business objectives, program planners develop the performance-based objectives, stated in behavioral terminology. And from these performance-based objectives, the program designers develop the course or learning objectives, stated in instructional design terminology (Figure 2-1). Finally, from these learning objectives, the HRD program design begins.

Following are the definitions of the three different types of HRD program objectives and examples for each type.

The *business objectives* specify what the participants will accomplish in business unit performance measures as a consequence of the application of skills and knowledge. These are expressed as outcomes in terms of hard data (i.e., output, costs, time, quality) and soft data (i.e., customer service, work habits, work climate).

Example: Annual sales will be increased by 30 percent.

The *performance objectives* provide precise, measurable statements of the behaviors that participants will be able to demonstrate on the job. They often specify the conditions under which the behaviors will be demonstrated as well as the criteria for acceptable performance.

Example: Sales representatives will ask customers to consider at least two products using the product suggestions from the Sales Software tool on each call.

The *learning objectives* describe what learners will be able to do at the end of their training or intervention program. Learning objectives should match the performance objectives as closely as possible.

Example: Students will be able to access the Sales Software tool on the correct computer platform for each role-play exercise.

In addition to these, some may find it helpful to establish *preference objectives* that measure the extent to which the program participants believed the program successfully provided them with the instruction they needed, whether that be the program administration, instruction, content, media, or material (Phillips, Stone, and Phillips 2000). Evaluators gather this data immediately after the program. Some evaluations ask the participants to "predict" the extent to which they learned the skills and/or knowledge taught in the course or even the extent to which they will *use* them. Reaction or preference objectives may be based on overall company trends or on individual components of the program. Instructor questions, for example, may have higher standards than other program components because questions regarding the instructor typically receive higher scores.

Example: On a five-point scale, with 5 being the most satisfied and 1 being the least satisfied, the participants will rate all categories 4.0 or greater.

Objectives are the link between the needs found in the needs-assessment and the evaluation strategy. Figure 2-2 provides an example of linking needs-assessment with the evaluation of an HR program. Notice in this example the critical nature of the program objectives.

Objective Components

It is important that each of the program objectives is defined clearly and stated in measurable terminology. Course designers normally have been taught the essential components of a good learning objective, such as those in Table 2-1.

Performance and business objectives can be defined using the same components for developing learning objectives. Business objectives normally define a required change in some type of business measure so these definitions may not be applicable, but they may be helpful in establishing performance objectives because they are behaviorally described in measurable terminology. Following are tips offered for developing clearly defined and measurable performance and learning objectives.

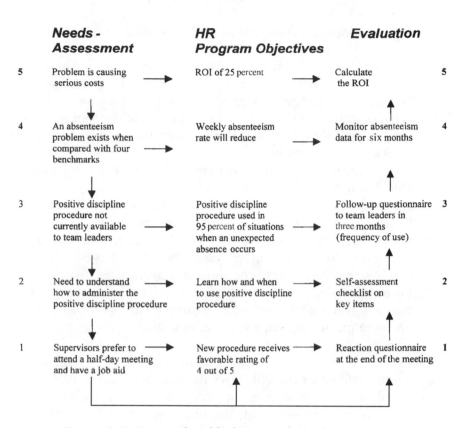

Figure 2-2. Example of linking needs with evaluation (Phillips, Stone, and Phillips 2001).

Table 2-1

Essential Components of a Good Learning Objective

Component	Example
The *learner* component: who the learner is	The *Participant*
The *performance* component: the observable behavior, action, or outcome the trainee will be able to perform	The Participant will be able to *ride* the unicycle
The *condition* component: the conditions under which the student will perform the behavior, action or outcome	Given a *unicycle and an obstacle course*, the student will be able to ride the unicycle through an obstacle course
The *criterion* component: the criteria that you use to determine their successful performance (if less than 100 percent)	Given a unicycle and an obstacle course, the student will be able to ride the unicycle through an obstacle course *without falling off the bike*

Tips for Developing Performance and Learning Objectives

1. State objectives in terms of participant behavior, not in terms of learning activities or purposes of the instructor. Example: *Distinguish between . . .* versus *to learn the importance of . . .*
2. Begin objectives with active verbs that indicate the behavior that a participant should show in dealing with the content. Example: *Define . . .* versus *know . . .*
3. State objectives in terms of participant behavior that is measurable. Example: *Selecting* the correct procedure . . .
4. State objectives precisely, using terms that have uniform meaning. Example: *Listing* the rules . . . versus *understanding* the rules.
5. Ensure the objectives are unitary; each statement is related to only one process. Example: *Select* the correct procedure . . . versus *select* the correct procedure and *operate* the switch . . .
6. Ensure the objectives represent intended direct outcomes of a planned series of experiences. Example: to operate includes plugging in, turning on, accessing, and so on.

One of the most common challenges for evaluators is receiving a program to evaluate wherein the learning and performance objectives are defined in a vague manner. In order to measure the extent to which objectives have been met, the objectives must be written in measurable language. Table 2-2 provides some examples of recommended changes to some of the more typical ineffective objective openings.

Table 2-3 provides additional action verbs that can be used to begin measurable performance or learning objectives statements.

In most organizations, different people are responsible for the development of the different objectives. Those who have decided they have a problem that needs a solution define business objectives. They are normally the stakeholders or clients for the program. Those who clearly understand the functions of the program participants define performance objectives. They are normally the subject matter experts (SMEs) or field representatives who usually have performed or are performing the job. The learning objectives are defined by those skilled in course design. Rarely does the ability for the development of each type of objective lie in one person or group. Usually, each resides in different areas within the organization. Bringing these different people together to define these different objectives can be a challenging activity because everyone's background and perspec-

Table 2-2
**Examples of Ineffective Objective Openings and
Recommended Alternatives**

Ineffective Openings	Recommended Alternatives
Understands . . .	Defines . . .
Appreciates . . .	Gives examples of . . .
Thinks critically about . . .	Compares . . .
Is aware of . . .	Describes . . .
Feels the need for . . .	Classifies . . .
Is growing in ability to . . .	Summarizes . . .
Becomes familiar with . . .	Applies in a new situation . . .
Grasps the significance of . . .	Solves a problem in which . . .
Is interested in . . .	Expresses interest in . . .
Knows . . .	States what he would do if . . .
Enjoys . . .	Writes . . .
Believes . . .	Recites . . .

Table 2-3
**Action Verbs to Use in Beginning
Objective Statements**

Adjust	Determine	Match
Assemble	Develop	Operate
Build	Diagnose	Perform
Calculate	Discriminate	Program
Categorize	Explain	Recall
Choose	Evaluate	Repair
Count	Generate	Select
Create	Identify	State
Demonstrate	List	

tive is somewhat different. The program task force can help to facilitate this task.

Objective Mapping

Brinkerhoff and Gill (1994) developed an impact-mapping technique that creates a visual depiction of the training design process. This picture highlights the critical roles, interactions, and results needed to achieve performance improvement. A similar tool could be used to map objectives.

The Objective Mapping Process

Figure 2-3 provides the objective map template that will be used to begin the case studies in progress at the end of this chapter. The following explains how an objective mapping process works using the objective map template:

Step 1: The person(s) who believes the HRD program is needed defines the business objectives and numbers and documents them in column one. They also define the metric that would be used to determine the extent to which that objective has been met and number and document them in column two to correspond to the business objective.

Step 2: The task force then determines what potential barriers exist that may inhibit the business objectives from being met. Potential enablers to overcoming the barriers are also identified. These are documented in column three.

Step 3: The SMEs then define at least one performance objective for each business objective, that is, the performance required of the program participant in order that the business objective be met. They number each corresponding to the associated business objective and document them in column four. They then work with the evaluator to determine the most effective way(s) to measure the extent to which each performance objective has been met and number and document them in column five to correspond to the performance objective.

Step 4: The task force then determines what potential barriers exist that may inhibit the performance objectives from being met. Potential enablers to overcoming those barriers are also identified. These are documented in column six.

Step 5: The course or program designer develops at least one course objective for each performance objective, numbering them as they correspond to the performance objective and documenting them in column seven. They also determine the way that they will measure the extent to which the course objectives have been met and document those methods in column eight.

Column 1: Business Objectives	Column 2: Metric	Column 3: Enablers/ Barriers	Column 4: Performance Objectives	Column 5: Measurement Methodology	Column 6: Enablers/ Barriers	Column 7: Learning Objectives	Column 8: Measurement Methodology	Column 9: Enablers/ Barriers
1.			1a. 1b. 1c. etc.			1a1. 1a2. 1b1. 1c1. 1c2. etc.		
2.			2a. 2b. etc.			2a1. 2a2. 2a3. 2b. 2b1. 2b2. etc.		
3.			3a.			3a1. 3a2. 3a3. 3a4.		

Figure 2-3. *Objective map template.*

Step 6: The task force then determines what potential barriers exist that would inhibit the learning objectives from being met. Potential enablers to overcoming the barriers are also identified. These are documented in column nine.

This simple tool can provide the evaluator several key benefits.

Use the Objective Map for Evaluation Planning

Initializing the objective map documentation can be the first step the program task force takes to plan for the evaluation program. Once the objective columns are complete, the evaluator can begin to identify what metrics to use for determining the extent to which the business objectives have been met. The evaluator can work with the client organization to identify databases and determine collection methods. They can decide methods for converting benefits to monetary values. The evaluator can then design the measurement tools and techniques required for measuring the extent to which the peformance objectives have been met (chapter 7). And the program designers can begin to design the methods for determining the extent to which the learning objectives (chapter 3) have been met. The task force will help plan the method for communicating the results even at this early stage.

Use the Objective Map to Ensure Program Completeness and Relevancy

One of the most important contributions of the mapping process is that it can ensure that there is at least one learning objective for each performance objective and that there are no learning objectives that are not linked to at least one performance objective. This will ensure that the program is teaching *only* what it is intended to teach yet teaches *everything* it is intended to teach. The mapping process will ensure that there is at least one performance objective for each business objective and that there are no performance objectives that are not mapped to at least one business objective. This will ensure that the program is targeted to meet the business objectives and that it is time and cost effective.

Use the Objective Map to Facilitate Communication

The objective map can also serve as a communication tool. Completing the objective map could be the goal or assignment for the multi-functional task force, since its completion is critical to develop the program and evaluation plans. It also can be used as an objective development training tool for those not experienced in developing objectives.

Use the Objective Map for Accountability

Many times the course objectives are drafted or even developed prior to the time the evaluator is involved. The mapping process is effective for this situation as well, because it allows the stakeholders and the SMEs the opportunity to develop the business and performance objectives retrospectively, checking to see if the learning objectives are on track.

Use the Objective Map to Ensure Transfer

Identifying those potential barriers and enablers early in the planning phases of the program and documenting them on the map will help to keep each member of the task force focused on removing potential barriers to performance and enhancing enablers prior to the program implementation. Chapter 6 discusses more fully the role of the evaluator for ensuring transfer.

CASE STUDIES IN PROGRESS—THE BEGINNING

Three different program examples will constitute the case studies in progress that will be discussed at the end of each chapter in this book: a technical training program, a sales/customer service training program, and a leadership development program. These case studies will apply the techniques and processes offered in each chapter of this book. The beginning step is to complete the objective columns of the objective map for each program.

The Technical Training Program

The technical training program is a multimedia program designed to provide warehouse employees with the operational and safety skills needed to receive and fill customers' orders. The stakeholder believes that by improving the employees' behavior in the warehouse they will realize the following three benefits:

- Reduction in motor vehicle accidents
- Reduction in accidents on the job
- Increased customer satisfaction

These are the business objectives. In this case, a needs-assessment was conducted by the client and the field representative, so the course designer was able to work with the evaluation staff to begin the objective map for the program. Figure 2-4 provides the beginning of the objective map for the warehouse training program. To reduce motor vehicle accident, the warehouse employee must successfully perform in accordance with the eight objectives listed in the corresponding "Performance Objectives" column. To reduce accidents on the job, the employees must successfully perform in accordance with the eight behaviors listed in the corresponding "Performance Objectives" column, and so forth. After completing the steps outlined in chapters 3 through 7 in the book, the map will be completed.

Sales/Customer Service Training Program

The sales/customer service training program case study is targeted for sales/customer service representatives. The client in this case wants to:

- Improve customer satisfaction by 90 percent
- Reduce the number of escalations that reach the supervisors' desks by 80 percent

Escalation calls require the supervisors' time (averaging two hours per call) and additional administrative time (averaging one hour per call). This costs the company money.

Figure 2-5 provides the objective map for the sales/customer service training program example. After completing the steps outlined in chapters 3 through 7 in the book, the map will be completed.

Leadership Development Program

The leadership development program is designed for supervisors. The client for this program wants the supervisors to

- Reduce turnover rates by 25 percent
- Improve individual efficiency and productivity
- Improve team efficiency and productivity

Figure 2-6 provides the objective map for the leadership development program. Note that for the technical training program and the leadership development program there are overlapping learning

Business Objectives	Metrics	Enablers/Barriers	Performance Objectives	Measurement Methodology	Enablers/Barriers	Learning Objectives	Measurement Methodology	Enablers/Barriers
1. Save 80 percent of cost due to reduction in motor vehicle accidents.	Reduced motor vehicle accident reports. Associated cost savings.		1a. Use safety belt consistently. 1b. Locate blind spots. 1c. Follow defined defensive driving procedures. 1d. Maintain safe following distance. 1e. Use headlights and wipers as defined. 1f. Follow railroad-crossing rules. 1g. Follow correct rules for adverse driving conditions. 1h. Follow safe passing procedures.			1a1. and 1c1. Identify the safety devices that can protect you and your passengers in collisions. 1a2. Describe why you should wear your safety belt. 1b1. Locate blind spots. 1d1. Estimate average stopping distance. 1d2. State the rules for following distances. 1e1. and 1g1. Identify the conditions of driving and spot the hazards for each condition. 1e2. and 1g2. Identify a defensive strategy for each adverse condition. 1f1. Identify how to avoid collisions with trains. 1h1. Identify the conditions in which a pass is safe, legal, and necessary. 1h2. Identify the three maneuvers for a safe pass.		

Figure 2-4. Technical training objective map.

Business Objectives	Metrics	Enablers /Barriers	Performance Objectives	Measurement Methodology	Enablers/ Barriers	Learning Objectives	Measurement Methodology	Enablers/ Barriers
2. Reduce on-the-job accidents by 90 percent.	Cost savings due to medical treatment savings. Cost savings due to retained employees. Cost savings due to reduction in employee time off the job.		2a. Lift objects properly. 2b. Maintain correct posture when using the computer. 2c. Wear goggles and gloves when handling hazardous materials. 2d. Wear gloves when handling boxes over 15 lbs. 2e. Wear steel-toe shoes.			2a1. Identify some basic principles of ergonomics. 2a2. Identify correct movement and postures that will minimize stress while lifting and moving objects. 2a3. Identify the parts of the back. 2a4. Recognize the stress that lifting can put on the back. 2b1. Identify correct ergonomic postures and work practices. 2c1. Describe elements of the OSHA program for controlling exposure to asbestos. 2c2. Identify the two primary means of controlling lead exposure when working on a lead-sheathed cable. 2c3. Identify methods of controlling exposure and preventing creation of hazardous waste. 2c4. Identify the basic types of hazardous materials. 2c5. Identify hazardous materials you are most likely to encounter. 2c6. Identify job tasks in which hazardous material exposure is likely.		

Figure 2-4. Technical training objective map (Continued).

Business Objectives	Metrics	Enablers/Barriers	Performance Objectives	Measurement Methodology	Enablers/Barriers	Learning Objectives	Measurement Methodology	Enablers/Barriers
			2f. Drive forklift at properly defined speed. 2g. Inspect forklift prior to operation each day. 2h. Do not exceed defined height and weight restrictions while using forklift. 2i. Place load as directed properly while using forklift.			2d1. and 2e1. List required safety gear. 2f1. Explain the operations of the forklift. 2g1. Define the pre-operation inspection of the forklift. 2h1. Define operator physical requirements for using forklift. 2i1. Describe load-handling techniques.		
3. Improve customer satisfaction by 90 percent.	Reduction in customer complaints.		3a. Customer receives correct product type. 3b. Customer receives correct quantity of items. 3c. Customer receives order on time. 3d. Re-visits reduced.			3a1. Describe how a client is billed for the purchase of an item. 3a2. and 3b1. and 3c1. Use each menu option (XXX system) in support of the normal functions of the storekeeper. 3a3. and 3b2. Describe how a cycle count is conducted. 3b3. Describe how to conduct a system order entry. 3b4. Describe how to conduct a phone order entry. 3d. Prepare load for transport.		

Figure 2-4. Technical training objective map (Continued).

Business Objective	Metric	Enablers/Barriers	Performance Objective	Measurement/Methodology	Enablers/Barriers	Learning Objective	Measurement/Methodology	Enablers/Barriers
1. Improve customer satisfaction by 90 percent.	Reduction in customer complaints.		1a. Opens call with IAW-established procedures. 1b. Demonstrates interest in caller's needs. 1c. Closes call with correct understanding of actions to be taken.			1a1. Greet caller with standard company opening. 1a2. Introduces self. 1b1. Uses enthusiastic tone of voice (friendly, positive, non-monotone voice—happy, upbeat, cheery, pleasant). 1b2. Listens to customer without interrupting. 1c1. Conveys empathy. 1c2. Asks for customer's perspective. 1c3. Probes for agreement. 1c4. Restates agreed upon follow-up actions to be taken.		
2. Reduce escalations by 80 percent.	Cost savings due to reduction in time required of team leader and processing clerk.		2a. Diagnoses customer's problem or need correctly. 2b. Gains customer agreement of follow-up actions that need to be taken.			2a1. Defines purpose of call. 2a2. Communicates what the initial plan will be. 2a3. Asks customer probing questions. 2a4. Uses Company Problem Questions Checklist. 2a5. Asks what has been tried before in resolving problem. 2a6. Asks about timing issues. 2b1. Checks back with the customer to make sure rep understands issue/confirms to ensure understanding. 2b2. Summarizes call. 2b3. Probe for agreement on any follow-up steps.		

Figure 2-5. Sales/customer service training program objective map.

Business Objective	Metric	Enablers/ Barriers	Performance Objective	Measurement Methodology	Enablers/ Barriers	Learning Objective	Measurement Methodology	Enablers/ Barriers
1. Reduce turnover rate by 25 percent.	Cost savings due to reduction in turnover of subordinates.		1a. Communicate using positive language. 1b. Determine when subordinates need assistance. 1c. Conduct effective individual meetings.			1a1. and 1c1. Distinguish between negative and positive phrases. 1a2. and 1c2. Provide examples of positive responses to different real-life scenarios. 1a3. and 1b1. Recognize different learning styles and personality types in others. 1a4. and 1b2. Learn your own learning style and person-ality type. 1b3. Recognize verbal cues indicating assis-tance is required. 1b4. Recognize nonverbal cues indicating assistance is required. 1c3. and 2a1. Use active listening techniques.		
2. Increase individual effi-ciency and increase productivity.	Cost savings due to reduction in time spent in meetings. Productivity increase (percent set by each individual unit).		2a. Conduct productive team meetings. 2b. Provide personality type tests to team members effectively. 2c. Complete action plan.			2a2. Open meetings with clearly stated goals. 2a3. Encourage group participation. 2a4. Keep discussion on track. 1b5. and 2a5. Close meetings with clearly stated follow-up actions. 2b1. Administer personality indicator tests. 2b2. Explain the meaning of the results. 2b3. Explain the importance of the results for team effectiveness. 2c1. Determine areas for improvement. 2c2. List specific goals to ensure improve-ment of determined areas. 2c3. List resources required for goal completion. 2c4. List deadlines for meeting goals listed. 2c5. Communicate action plan to supervisor.		
3. Increase team efficiency.	Cost savings due to value of each team member's time.		3a. Prioritize goals and activities. 3b. Complete goals and activities in order of priority. 3c. Conduct only necessary meetings.			3a1. and 3b1. Complete weekly and daily priority lists. 3c1. Using weekly and daily priority lists, develop areas where team input is required.		

Figure 2-6. Leadership development objective map.

objectives. One learning objective can contribute to more than one performance objective. After completing the steps outlined in chapters 3 through 7 in the book, the map will be completed.

SUMMARY

If program objectives are developed correctly, the rest of the program development and evaluation effort should progress smoothly.

The checklist in Table 2-4 provides assistance for the development of business, performance, and learning objectives.

Table 2-4
Objective Development Checklist

Objective Development Checklist		
Question	YES (✓)	NO (✓)
1. Do the objectives reflect the results of a needs or gap analysis?		
2. Are the stakeholder's expectations reflected in the business objectives?		
3. Are the business objectives specific to a business unit of measure?		
4. Are the business objectives quantified where possible?		
5. Are the performance objectives stated as precise, measurable statements of behavior?		
6. Are the behaviors described in performance objectives stated in the simplest and most direct way possible?		
7. Is each learning objective mapped to at least one performance objective?		
8. Does each performance objective have at least one learning objective?		
9. Is each performance objective mapped to at least one business objective?		
10. Does each business objective have at least one performance objective?		
11. Are the objectives stated in terms that mean the same to everyone?		
12. Do the objectives reflect realistic expectations?		

REFERENCES

1. Brinkerhoff, R.O., and S.J. Gill. 1994. *The Learning Alliance: Systems Thinking in Human Resource Development*. San Francisco: Jossey-Bass Publishers.
2. Burkett, H. 2000. *ROI Network, Inc., 2000 Conference Proceedings*. Provo, Utah.
3. Fawson, T.J. 1999. "A Study of Executive Education Programs at AT&T," In *In Action: Measuring Learning and Performance*, ed. T.K. Hodges. Alexandria, Va.: American Society for Training and Development.
4. Peterson, B.D., and T.W. Bothell. 1999. "Measuring the Impact of Learning and Performance," In *In Action: Measuring Learning and Performance*, ed. T.K. Hodges. Alexandria, Va.: American Society for Training and Development.
5. Phillips, J.J., R.D. Stone, and P.P. Phillips. 2001. *The Human Resources Scorecard: Measuring the Return on Investment*. Boston: Butterworth-Heinemann.
6. Robinson, D.G., and J.C. Robinson. 1989. *Training For Impact*, San Francisco: Jossey-Bass Publishers.
7. Rossett, A. 1987. *Training Needs Assessment*. Englewood Cliffs, N.J.: Educational Technology Publications.

CHAPTER 3

How to Design Learning Measures

After developing program objectives, the next step for an effective program evaluation is to design good learning measures. To measure learning is to provide the opportunity to determine if "they GOT it!" Learning is the step upon which all other results depend. Unfortunately, designing appropriate and effective learning measures is, next to defining measurable objectives, the biggest area of neglect. Let's rectify that situation.

There are many potential factors that inhibit job performance. Some examples are:

- Unreliable or poorly designed support systems
- Little opportunity to apply the skills learned
- Little or no peer- or supervisor-coaching
- Poor job design
- Changing procedures
- Heavy workload

These barriers to performance can be complex and difficult to overcome. Isn't it just easier to blame the training? Often, that is what is done. That is why the program designer must put measures in place to determine the extent to which the program *was* effective in imparting knowledge or teaching skills. This is important not just to demonstrate that the program did its job but to help identify the many other job performance components, such as those listed above, that must be attended to in addition to the program.

Learning measures need to be practical for implementation and analysis. But rules for good test construction and validation must be adhered to, or the measures can cause ethical as well as practical problems. Ebel (1961) has outlined six requisites for the test designer:

1. Know the uses, as well as the limitations, of tests.
2. Know the criteria by which the quality of a test (or other measuring instrument) should be judged and how to secure evidence relating to these criteria.
3. Know how to develop a test and write the test questions to be included in it.
4. Know how to select a standardized test that will be effective in a particular situation.
5. Know how to administer a test properly, efficiently, and fairly.
6. Know how to interpret test scores correctly and fully, with recognition of their limitations.

These requirements can serve as guiding principles for the test designer, but one golden rule for the evaluator to remember when beginning the design and development of a learning data collection instrument is to make sure the instrument measures what it is intended to measure. This is important, so that the measure provides the data needed, yet the test-takers are treated fairly. The goal, for example, is not to test the test-takers' ability to take tests, but their knowledge and/or skill.

Constructing Good Tests

There are many types of tests that can be designed. Which type should be selected? Davis and Cerqueira (1999) believe that the type of test or assessment given should match the type of learning that is expected to take place. Davis divides his "strategy-driven assessment" process into seven training strategies. Table 3-1 summarizes the strategies and his suggested assessment types for each one.

HRD programs may utilize one or more of these strategies. Some programs use one for one phase and another for a different phase. The strategy selected depends on the objectives for each phase, but what may be more practical in most organizations would be to divide assessment types into two different categories—knowledge or attitude tests and skill or proficiency tests.

Table 3-1
Davis's Learning Assessment Strategies

Strategy	Description	Suggested Assessment	Goal
The Behavioral Strategy	Best for building skills. It draws on well-established behavioral learning theory, where participants move in small carefully reinforced steps from present performance level to a clearly operationalized goal.	Demonstration and observation. Pre- and posttest measures.	To see if the learning of specific skills has occurred.
The Cognitive Strategy	Best when participants need to understand and remember information. It draws on well-established principles from cognitive psychology, regarding the ways people attend to, process, and remember information.	Paper-and-pencil tests.	To discover how well participants understand and remember the desired information.
The Inquiry Strategy	Best used to develop abilities in critical, creative, and dialogical thinking. It draws on well-established theories about thinking processes and creativity.	Critical analysis of what someone else has written, such as a report or proposal.	To identify some of the problems in thinking.
The Mental Models Strategy	Best for training that involves problem-solving and decision-making and draws on a wide range of mental models. Mental models are used to deal with cognitive overload.	Case studies and case reports.	To see if participants can actually solve problems or make intelligent decisions.

Table 3-1
Davis's Learning Assessment Strategies (*continued*)

Strategy	Description	Suggested Assessment	Goal
The Group Dynamics Strategy	Used for improving human relations and building skills needed for teamwork. It draws on well-established theory regarding group communication and is valuable for reexamining opinions, attitudes, and beliefs and for cultivating teamwork.	Self-reports. Observations.	To see if there are attitude changes or changes in human relations or team behavior.
The Virtual Reality Strategy	Used for practice before going into real-life situations where there could be financial loss, injury, or fatality. The learning theory is based on what is known about role-play, dramatic scenarios, and simulation.	Final practice-run.	To see if the participant can demonstrate near-to-perfect behavior before entering the real world.
The Holistic Strategy	Used when there is a potentially educative experience available from which personal learning can be derived through reflection on experience. Experience-based learning is grounded in recent brain research, holistic learning theory, and constructivist psychology.	Participant feedback.	To determine the depth of understanding.

Knowledge-Based Tests

Many organizations are trying to put different labels on measures that look for knowledge or skill-gain, believing that the word *test* may sound unprofessional, particularly for management personnel. For the purpose of this discussion, the word *test* is used because it is the word that is most commonly used throughout this country and others. The tests that most are familiar with are those that measure knowledge-gain. Following are general guidelines Dixon (1990) offers for constructing knowledge-based test questions or items.

Tips for Designing Knowledge-Based Test Questions

1. Arrange the items in order of difficulty, placing easier items first, to avoid discouraging participants unnecessarily.
2. Construct each item so that it is independent of all other items. A series of items in which the correct answer to the first item becomes the condition for answering the next item can prevent the measure from providing an accurate reflection of the student's knowledge or skills.
3. Avoid constructing items by taking quotes directly from a handout, overhead transparency, or book. Direct quotes tend to encourage memorization rather than understanding, and quotations taken out of context tend to be ambiguous.
4. Avoid trick questions. The intent of a test is to determine the skills, knowledge, and attitudes of the participants, not to cause them to mark an item incorrectly.
5. Avoid negatives, especially double negatives. Such items take considerably longer to read and are often misinterpreted. If negative words must be used, underline or italicize the word or phrase to call attention to it.
6. Avoid providing clues to items in previous or subsequent items.
7. Use a variety of types of items in the test rather than limiting items to only one type. If the measure is lengthy, variety can add interest. When a variety of types of items are employed, group the items by item type so participants do not have to constantly shift response patterns or reread instructions.

Word Completion Items

The word completion item is a question or an incomplete statement requiring the test-taker to respond to the question with required statements or words or to complete the sentence. Therefore, word completion questions are used when the instructional objective requires that the test-taker recall or create the correct answer rather than simply recognize it. For example, if one of the program objectives is that the participant define solutions to particular problems, a word completion item would be an effective type of knowledge-based item. These items usually provide an objective measure of student knowledge.

One limitation to word completion items is that they often do not measure learning or program objectives that require more than simple recall of information. Also, word completion items are difficult to construct so that the desired response is clearly indicated. Often they provide irrelevant clues. Finally, they are more time-consuming to score than multiple-choice or true-false items.

Tips for Preparing Word Completion Items

1. Omit only significant words from the statement. An undesirable item would be, "Every atom has a central _____ called a nucleus." This item would be better stated, "Every atom has a central core called a(n) _____."
2. Do not omit so many words from the statement that the intended meaning is lost. An undesirable item would be, "The _____ were to Egypt as the _____ were to Persia and as _____ were to the early tribes of Israel." This item would be better phrased, "The Pharaohs were to Egypt as the _____ were to Persia and as _____ were to the early tribes of Israel."
3. Be sure there is only one correct response per blank (or blanks). For example, the following item is undesirable: "Trees that do not shed their leaves annually are _____." The item is undesirable because "conifers" and "seed-bearing" are both acceptable answers. The item could be rephrased as, "Trees that shed their leaves annually are called _____." The only correct answer is deciduous.
4. Make the blanks the same length to avoid giving cues to the correct answer.
5. When possible, delete words at the end of the statement after the student has been presented a clearly defined problem. An undesirable item would be, "_____ is the molecular weight of $KClO_3$, a chemical used to enhance plant growth." This item

would be better phrased, "The molecular weight of KClO$_3$ is
_____."

6. Limit the required response to a single key word or phrase.
7. Avoid lifting statements directly from the text, lecture, or other source.

True-False Items

The true-false test item presents test-takers with a statement and then asks them to determine whether the statement is true or false. True-false items have several advantages. First, the items can cover more material because they tend to be short. Second, they take less time to construct than word completion or other types of items. Third, scoring is easier than with completion questions.

There are also disadvantages to true-false items. For example, they tend to emphasize rote memorization. They presume the answers to questions are unequivocal. They encourage a high degree of guessing, making more items necessary. Finally, participants can score 50 percent correctly by randomly marking the answers.

Tips for Developing True-False Test Items

1. Write test directions that instruct students to *circle* the correct response.
2. Avoid using the words *always, all, never, only,* and *none* since these are almost always false.
3. Avoid using the words *sometimes, usually, maybe, often,* and *may* since statements with these words are almost always true.
4. Ensure that each statement is entirely true or entirely false without additional qualifiers such as *large, regularly, sometimes,* and *may.* An undesirable item would be, "No picture and no sound in a television set may indicate bad 5U4G tubes." A more desirable item would be, "No picture and no sound in a television set indicate bad 5U4G tubes."
5. Keep each statement relatively short.
6. Do not include two concepts in one item. An undesirable example would be, "The trend toward pop music began in the 1980s and represents a major development in the evolution of music, according to *Rolling Stone* magazine." Better phrased, the item would read, "The trend toward pop music began in the 1980s."

7. Avoid negatively stated items or those that contain double negatives. An undesirable example would be, "If a person has not had access to a patent, he or she cannot infringe the patent." More desirable would be, "If a person has had access to a patent, he or she can infringe the patent."

8. Be sure to cite the source or authority on opinion statements. An undesirable item would read, "The organization has a responsibility to aid employees who have a drug problem." A desirable item would read, "The CEO of Company X has stated that the organization has a responsibility to aid employees who have a drug problem."

9. True statements and false statements should be about the same length.

10. There should be an approximately equal number of true statements and false statements.

Matching Items

Matching items present test-takers with two lists of words or phrases and ask the test-taker to match each word or phrase on one list ("descriptors" in the left column) to a word or phrase on the other list ("options" in the right column). These items are used only to assess understanding of like (homogeneous) content: for example, types of wire, types of clouds, types of switches, and so on. Matching items most frequently take the form of a list of words to be matched with a list of definitions.

There are many advantages to matching items. One advantage is the short periods of reading and response time. Also, they provide an objective measurement of participant knowledge. They can be scored efficiently and accurately, and they are relatively easy to develop.

Limitations to matching items include the difficulty they present in measuring learning objectives requiring more than simple recall of memorized information. Additionally, if the words or phrases that appear in the left column are essentially unrelated to one another, matching items becomes extremely easy. Finally, matching items can allow participants to use the process of elimination to determine their answers if each answer is only used once.

Tips for Developing Matching Test Items

1. Include directions that clearly state the basis for matching the descriptors (left column) with the options (right column).

Indicate where to write the answer. Allow for options to be used more than once to reduce cueing. An undesirable instruction would be, "Match the following." A more desirable instruction would be, "Next to Column I, write the letter of the country in Column II that is best defined. Each country in Column II may be used more than once."

2. Use only like (homogeneous) material in matching items. For example, a list that contains names of authors, types of sweaters, and flavors of gum will be easier to match to a corresponding "B" list that contains only names of the different types of cows.

3. Keep matching items brief. Limit them to less than ten.

4. Include more options than descriptors or allow options to be used more than once to prevent answering through process of elimination.

5. Reduce the amount of reading time by including only short phrases or single words in the descriptor list.

6. Arrange the options list in some logical order, for example, chronologically or alphabetically. This way the test-takers won't get clues from the order in which the responses appear.

7. Place the list of descriptors and options on the same page.

Multiple-Choice Items

The multiple-choice item presents test-takers with a question (called a "stem") and then asks them to choose from among a series of alternative answers (a single correct answer and several distracters). Sometimes the question takes the form of an incomplete sentence followed by a series of alternatives from which the test-taker is to choose.

Advantages to multiple-choice items are that they can provide versatility in measuring topic areas. They can be scored quickly and accurately, provide objective measurement of student achievement or ability, and offer a wide sampling of content or objectives. Additionally, they have a reduced guessing factor when compared to true-false items. Finally, the different response alternatives provide diagnostic feedback, which is useful for formative evaluation of course content and methods.

One limitation to multiple-choice items is that developers find them difficult and time-consuming to construct. Also, untrained developers tend to write memory-level or simple-recall-of-fact items. Finally, the success of multiple-choice items is highly dependent on a student's reading ability and on a developer's writing ability.

Tips for Developing Multiple-Choice Test Items

1. When possible, state the stem as a direct question rather than as an incomplete statement. An undesirable phrasing would be, "Alloys are ordinarily produced by_____" A more desirable phrasing would be, "How are alloys ordinarily produced?"
2. Eliminate excessive verbiage or irrelevant information from the stem. The following statement contains extra information. "While ironing her formal, Jane burned her hand accidentally on the hot iron. This was due to a transfer of heat by _____" A more desirable test question would be, "Which of the following methods of heat transfer explain why Jane's hand was burned after she touched a hot iron?"
3. Include in the stem any word(s) that might otherwise be repeated in each alternative. This is an undesirable item: "In national elections in the United States, the President is officially: a. chosen by the people, b. chosen by members of Congress, c. chosen by the House of Representatives, d. chosen by the Electoral College." The stem would be more desirable restated, "How is the President officially chosen in national elections?"
4. Make all alternatives plausible and attractive to the less-knowledgeable or less-skillful student.
5. Make the alternatives mutually exclusive. An undesirable test item would be, "The daily minimum required amount of milk that a ten-year-old child should drink is: a. one to two glasses, b. two to three glasses, c. three to four glasses, d. at least four glasses." A more desirable selection of alternatives would be, "a. one glass, b. two glasses, c. three glasses, d. four glasses."
6. When possible, present alternatives in some logical order, e.g., chronological, most-to-least, alphabetical, and so on.
7. Be sure that there is only one correct or best response to the item.
8. Make alternatives approximately equal in length.
9. Use at least four alternatives for each item to lower the probability of getting the item correct by guessing.

10. Randomly distribute the correct response among the alternative positions throughout the test. Have approximately the same proportion of alternatives a, b, c, and d as the correct response.
11. Avoid using negatively stated items (*no, not, none*). When used, underline, highlight, and/or capitalize the negative word.
12. Avoid using *all, always,* and *never* in the distracters. Very few things in life are this definite and will cue the test-takers that this choice is probably not the correct one.
13. Check all test items to make sure that the options or answers to one item do not cue the test-takers to the correct answers of other items.
14. Avoid the use of "All of the above" as an alternative; test-takers who recognize two test answers as correct will then immediately assume that all the answers are correct and not even consider the other answers.
15. After the test items have been written, have them reviewed and edited by another knowledgeable person.

Test Length

The length of the test depends on the amount of the material being covered and the time limits for testing. A good rule for a true-false test is to allow one minute per two items, but time required for the other types of tests would be based on the material being tested. Since there must be at least one question to test each learning objective, the more learning objectives, the longer the test.

Arrangement of Items

Multiple-choice or true-false items are arranged so that the answers follow no set pattern. On multiple-choice tests, putting the alternatives in alphabetical order within items may accomplish this, but generally it is safer to randomize the order of alternatives. Placing short-answer items in groups of five or so reduces errors in taking and scoring the tests. On matching items, all the options appear on the same page. For short-answer items, sufficient space is provided. For behavioral checklists, items are rated in the sequence that the behaviors are typically performed. Concerning the layout of the test as a whole, the test-taker's task would be facilitated if all items of the same type (multiple-choice, true-false, and so on) and items dealing with the same topic are grouped together.

Number of Test Items

The number of items included on a test is determined by the criticality of the objectives. Objectives that pertain to less crucial course material require fewer test items than those objectives that are critical for the student to master. Both types of objectives are important, but criticality is an issue that should be considered when developing test items. You may use Table 3-2 as a guide when developing your tests.

If it is difficult to come up with many questions for an important objective, questions can be assigned different weights for scoring purposes. Frequency of performance may also be a consideration for the number of questions needed for each objective.

Test Directions

There are always test directions. They tell the students what they are supposed to do and may state how long they have in which to do it. An example would be, "Please circle the correct answer to the following questions. There will be only one correct answer for each question."

Test Scoring

Tests are constructed so that scoring can be done quickly, accurately, and with very little, if any, subjectivity. For example, an even number of questions allows for easier scoring than an odd number of questions, as there is a final percent-correct score for each test. If

Table 3-2
Decision Guide for Number of Test Items per Objective

Criticality of the Objective	Number of Test Items per Objective
High	10–20
Medium	3–9
Low	1–2

questions are weighted because some are more important than others, make that clear to the scorer to ensure scoring consistency and accuracy. Scoring normally needs to be done quickly for most organizations, so ease of scoring is taken into account in the test design.

PERFORMANCE-BASED TESTS

Performance-based tests can be measured by developing a simulated work task, project, or case study. Most common in the corporate environment is the simulated work task. Tests used in this situation include checklists, rating scales, or product-quality assessments. Performance-based tests are called *proficiencies* to distinguish them from knowledge-based pretests and posttests. Behavioral checklists that include "yes-no" check-off and rating scales are usually easiest to use and provide objective assessments.

Behavioral checklists are designed to assess the ability of a student to perform correctly in a simulated situation. In theory, a behavioral checklist can be constructed for any skill and real-life situation. In practice, most performance-based tests are developed for the assessment of vocational, managerial, administrative, leadership, communication, interpersonal, and physical-education skills in various simulated situations. Behavioral checklists work well for sales and customer service training programs or for physical proficiencies where discrete and sequential tasks are required, such as repair or installation work.

Behavioral checklists are composed of a list of *specific, observable behaviors* that the participants must demonstrate to convey competency in handling a given situation. Figure 3-1 shows an example of one type of customer service behavioral checklist.

Behavioral checklists have several important advantages. By measuring what they are designed to measure, behavioral checklists usually provide a degree of test validity not possible with standard paper-and-pencil test items. They are the best way to actually measure performance rather than predicting performance based on knowledge gained, and they can be used again as a tool by supervisors or consultants to measure job performance after the program event.

Behavioral checklists also have limitations. They are difficult and time-consuming to construct. They are primarily used for testing individuals rather than groups. They may not provide an objective measure of the participant's ability due to scorer bias or inconsistency

Performance Checklist

Simulation # _____   Manager _____
Date _____   Time _____
Listens and Responds with Empathy

	Yes	No	Missed opportunity
Maintains eye contact			
Nods head affirmatively			
Verbally acknowledges with "yes," "right," and so on			
Allows other person to finish speaking			
Paraphrases other person's dialogue			
States the other person's feelings or emotions			
Observer _____			

Figure 3-1. Sample behavioral checklist.

in grading performance. Behavioral checklists require training the user or observer.

Tips for Developing Behavioral Checklists

Preparation

1. Train the observer(s), so they are able to fairly and consistently score the behavior.
2. Practice using the checklist (via exercises) before it is used as an end-of-program learning-measure.
3. Clearly explain the simulated situation to the student before using the checklist.

Design

1. Clearly state the type of response needed from the participants.
2. Ensure the items elicit the type of behavior being measured.

3. Ensure the simulated situation matches the job requirements as closely as possible.

4. In exercise directions, clearly state the time, activity limitations, and the mastery standard.

5. Ensure that each item on the checklist measures only one behavior.

6. Ensure the selected behaviors are meaningful, significant, and representative of the behaviors that capture the learning objectives.

7. Begin each item with an action verb.

8. Be specific with the wording within items, so that they describe observable behaviors. Select the wording carefully to avoid ambiguity or subjective interpretations. For example, the following is a faulty checklist item: "Responds *with empathy* to the individual." The phrase "with empathy" may be interpreted in various ways by different raters.

9. Design the rating scale so it is simple and can be easily interpreted by the rater; make sure it is comprised of categories that do not overlap and are easily distinguished.

Scoring

1. Ensure the checklist is easy to score, with any weights assigned in multiples of two, five, ten, and so on.

2. Ensure the total points possible equal one hundred. This ensures that the score can easily be expressed as a percentage-correct score (ranging from 0–100 percent).

Using effective openings for the behavior to be observed is critical in describing the behaviors in measurable terminology. Table 3-3 provides some recommendations to replace ineffective openings, often seen on behavioral checklists.

Table 3-4 provides additional action verbs to use for a checklist design.

Alternative Approaches to Measure Learning

The guidelines offered thus far are for the more common types of assessments. But as Davis points out, the type used should be selected based on the type of learning that is taking place. Some other types of assessment are action planning and facilitator (or self) ratings.

Table 3-3
Ineffective and Recommended Alternatives for Behavioral Checklist Item Openings

Ineffective Openings	Recommended Alternatives
Understands. . .	Defines. . .
Shows appreciation for. . .	Gives examples of. . .
Thinks critically about. . .	Compares. . .
Is aware of. . .	Describes. . .
Feels the need for. . .	Classifies. . .
Is growing in ability to. . .	Summarizes. . .
Is familiar with. . .	Applies in a new situation. . .
Grasps the significance of. . .	Solves a problem in which. . .
Is interested in. . .	Expresses interest in. . .
Knows. . .	States what he would do if. . .
Enjoys. . .	Writes. . .
Believes. . .	Recites. . .

Table 3-4
Other Sample Verbs for Behavioral Checklist Item Openings

Adjusts	Diagnoses	Provides
Allots	Discriminates	Recalls
Apologizes	Discusses	Responds
Asks	Explains	Repairs
Assembles	Follows	Selects
Builds	Generates	Speaks
Calculates	Identifies	States
Categorizes	Lists	Updates
Chooses	Matches	Uses
Counts	Offers	
Creates	Operates	
Demonstrates	Performs	
Develops	Programs	

Action Planning

Action planning is typically used as a measure of job application, not learning. However, action planning is becoming a technique used in several large organizations as a method for measuring learning and performance because it is economical and effective. It is an excellent tool when the objectives of the program are to plan for areas of improved performance. A leadership program, for example, may provide sample behaviors that should be modeled. From the sample behaviors presented in the program, the participants must select (1) those behaviors on which they need to individually improve, and/or (2) those that they need in their particular environment. It is expected that the participants will learn the types of behaviors that are needed for different people in different situations. In this case, if the participant is able to accurately and clearly articulate those behaviors they are planning to apply on the job and document the expected results, it will be evident that they learned what was expected. The added advantage to using the action-planning process for measuring learning is that it can be used again to measure performance once on the job. In fact, if the participant knows that it will be used as a performance measure, it may reinforce the learning. Finally, action planning is an excellent method for ensuring transfer (Sherman and Stone 2001). In chapter 5, we will discuss action-planning construction. Examples of action plans can be found in Appendix A.

Facilitator- or Self-Ratings

Facilitator ratings are useful when no learning-measures existed for a program that has already taken place. They provide some level of assurance that learning has taken place. The facilitator is asked to give a rating on the extent to which each of the participants in their classes learned the material. Although normally used as a method most applicable to measuring job performance (Phillips 1997), it can be used successfully as a measure of learning if it has not been too long since the program event. If the facilitator or instructor understands that the measure of learning is to evaluate program effectiveness rather than their own particular instruction, they can offer good indications of the extent that learning took place. Obviously, these ratings are estimates, but in lieu of, or in combination with, other learning measures, they may be helpful.

Also helpful are *self-reports*, particularly when assessing attitude change. This can be done with a questionnaire or a focus group immediately following the program. Again, questionnaires and focus groups are typically used for measuring job performance, but there is no reason why this method cannot be adapted for measuring learning or attitude change. The participants are asked the extent to which they believed their knowledge, skills, or attitudes changed. If conducting a focus group, ensure the facilitator is skilled in the focus group process. Chapter 5 discusses in more detail the guidelines for creating good questionnaires and successfully employing focus groups.

CASE STUDIES IN PROGRESS

When choosing learning measures for a program, be creative. Try different techniques or combinations of techniques. Always measure against the objectives and you won't go wrong. Following are examples of learning measures designed for our three different case studies in progress.

Technical Training Program

The Technical Training Program is a multimedia program for warehouse employees. The program includes online assessment practicums. They serve as a knowledge-based posttest. Following are some sample test items, matched to the learning objectives in the objective map in chapter 2. This case study demonstrates the use of multiple-choice, true-false, completion, and a type of matching items.

To test objective 1f1: Identify how to avoid collisions with trains.

1. Directions: Circle the correct response.

What should the driver do to avoid collisions with trains?

    a. avoid going over railroad tracks
    b. look both ways before crossing railroad tracks
    c. follow railroad-crossing signals
    d. go over railroad tracks quickly

To test objective 3a1: Describe how a client is billed for the purchase of an item.

2. Directions: Using the blanks in the right-hand column, number the nine steps of the billing process in order.

The contact receives and fills the order. The technician
receives the widget.   Step ____
The system is billed through the 'Ship to' document.   Step ____
The contact replenishes its inventory of the widget
through the system.   Step ____
Using the scanning process, the technician orders widget #. Step ____
The order is shipped to the warehouse.   Step ____
The technician fills the order.   Step ____
The billing process starts after the order is filled.
A Replenishment Report is generated to show who
ordered the widget.   Step ____
The contact receives the order from the warehouse
through the system.   Step ____
The technician replenishes the widget into stock.   Step ____

To test objectives 3a3 and 3b2: Describe how a cycle count is conducted.

3. Directions: Circle the correct response.

A cycle count verifies the computer inventory balances compared to the on-hand balances.

   a. True
   b. False

4. Directions: Fill in the blank with a response that correctly completes the statement.

_____ is the company guideline that you may reference if you have questions about cycle counts.

Sales/Customer Service Training Program

The Sales/Customer Service Training Program includes a role-play using two typical types of customer calls. The facilitator will train someone to play the role of the caller in each scenario and use an observational checklist to score the participant during each call. Figure 3-2 is the observation checklist that the facilitator will use and is an example of a proficiency test. The learning objectives from the objective map in chapter 2 that are associated with each behavior on the checklist are enclosed in brackets.

Participant _____ Date _____

Rating		Task ↓
Yes	No	**Opening the Call**
		Rate whether the following tasks were performed within the first five minutes of the call. This portion of the call focuses on listening for reps' ability to establish a positive rapport and *guide the call*.
		1. Greets the caller (e.g., Hello, Good morning, Welcome to Company XXX) {*1a1*}
		2. Introduces self (e.g., My name is Jane Doe) {*1a2*}
		3. Uses enthusiastic tone of voice (friendly, positive, non-monotone voice—happy, upbeat, cheery, pleasant) {*1b1*}
		4. Listens to customer without interrupting {*1b2*}
		5. Conveys empathy through the use of at least one statement that acknowledges difficulty customer is having (e.g., that sounds like a pretty difficult situation you're in) {*1c1*}
		6. Establishes self as a resource by assuring customer that rep can help with problem {*2a4* and *2a5*}
		7. Avoids trying to diagnose or resolve problem before agreeing on a purpose for the call (e.g., asking diagnostic questions about specific problem, without setting up the purpose and priorities of the call first) {*2a3* and *2a4*}
		8. Defines purpose of call (e.g., so what we need to do is get x, y, and z working again for you) {*2a1*}
		9. Communicates what the initial plan will be (e.g., the first thing we'll need to do is....) {*2a2*}
		10. Probes for agreement (e.g., How does that plan sound? Or rep's verbal behavior does not indicate that customer is arguing about the initial plan) {*1b2, 1b4, 1c1,* and *2a3*}

Figure 3-2. Sales/customer service observation checklist.

Rating		Task ↓
Yes	No	**Opening the Call**
		Diagnosing Problems and Identifying Needs
		The goal of training was to teach the rep to actively learn what's been tried before, to understand timing issues, to check for changes, to communicate any observed patterns in the data, test any customer assumptions, consider any human factor issues, gain multiple perspectives by talking with more than one person about the problem, and discovering interrelationships. The more observable tasks are outlined below.
		11. Asks what has been tried before in resolving problem {2a5}
		12. Asks about timing issues (e.g., when was that tried, how long ago was that?) {2a6}
		13. Probes using both open- and closed-ended questions {1c1 and 1c4}
		14. Avoids using the word "but" when discussing issues with customer (e.g., but I thought that what you said was....) {1b1 and 1b2}
		15. Asks at least one question that clarifies the issue {1c2 and 2b1}
		16. Checks back with the customer to make sure rep understands issue/confirms to ensure understanding (e.g., so what you're saying is that...) {1c2 and 2b1}
		Assessing Progress and Updating the Plan
		Skills focus on assessing progress and updating the plan so that the customer knows where things stand and can keep others informed of status.
		17. Explains to customer progress made (e.g., OK, we've done X, Y, Z) {2b1}
		18. Reconfirms purpose/priorities (e.g., we're still working on X, and need to see if we can't get X completed) {1c2}
		19. Updates the plan (e.g., Let's keep on working on this, or let's try Y) {2b1}

Figure 3-2. Sales/customer service observation checklist (Continued).

		20. Probes for agreement (e.g., How does that plan sound? Or observation of rep indicates that customer is not arguing to change the plan) {2b3}
		Recommending Approaches for Results
		After rep explains his or her perspective, rep gains the customer's perspective, and then recommends an approach for solving or preventing the problem and meeting the need
		21. Explains to customer why rep is making the observation they are about to make (e.g., Given what you've told me about x, y, and z,. . .) {2a4}
		22. Explains observations (e.g., I've noticed that...) {2a4 and 2a3}
		23. Asks for customer's perspective {1c4 and 2b1}
		24. Makes recommendation after achieving shared perspective {2a4}
		25. Probes for agreement {1c1 and 2b3}
		Closes the Call
		Rep is focused on conveying the value of what has been accomplished and identifying follow-up actions
		26. Summarizes call (e.g., what was initial problem, steps taken, agreed upon action, current status, additional steps) {2b2}
		27. Uses "we"-language when summarizing call {2b2}
		28. Probes for agreement {2b1 and 2b3}
		29. Communicates any follow-up steps that need to be taken {2b1 and 2b3}
		30. Probe for agreement on any follow-up steps (e.g., Ok, I'll do X and you'll do Y) {2b3}
		Overall Listening Skills
		This section focuses on *active* and *empathic* listening skills
		31. Displays patience (does not interrupt customer, become upset, or alter positive/friendly/receptive tone of voice) {1b1 and 1b2}

Figure 3-2. Sales/customer service observation checklist (Continued).

Rating		Task
Yes	No	↓
		32. Concentrates intensely on conversation (e.g., avoiding visual distractions, looking around room when customer is talking, fiddling with papers, doodling, playing solitaire) {1*b*2}
		33. Listens empathetically by communicating at least one empathic statement (e.g., I'm sorry you're having trouble, I can imagine how frustrating that could be...) {1*c*1}
		34. Avoids internal or external finger-pointing (e.g., blaming others) {2*a*5}

Figure 3-2. Sales/customer service observation checklist (Continued).

Notice that all the behaviors are observable. Examples are provided to help the observer in the more general areas, such as showing empathy or finger-pointing. Every behavior measures at least one objective, and every objective is tested by at least one behavior. Also, the behavioral checklist provides several checks for a behavior that "could" be considered vague; objective 1b3 shows empathy is tested by three separate behaviors.

Leadership Development Program

Paper pretests and/or posttests are used as the learning measure for the Leadership Development Program. The pretest is given to the participant after they have arrived for the training and introductions are made, but before any part of the program is provided. When administering the pretest, the students are told that the purpose of the test is to determine what knowledge they have at this point and that they are not expected to know all the answers, and that after completion of the program, they will be given the exact same test. The pretest is labeled "pretest" and the posttest is labeled "posttest," and the participant's name or ID is on each, so that scores can be compared (chapter 5). This sample uses multiple-choice items only. Each option in each question is plausible, but only one is correct.

Following are some sample test questions for this case study as they relate to the learning objectives from the objective map in chapter 2.

To test objective 2a2: Open meetings with clearly stated goals

Directions: Circle the correct answer.

1. How should you open your team meetings?
    a. begin with an appropriate joke to ease tension
    b. define everyone's role in your organization
    c. go over the most recent corporate strategy and how it relates to your team
    d. state the goals for the meeting

2. Which of the following is a clearly stated goal?
At the end of this meeting we will . . .
    a. have developed an action plan for increasing our revenues
    b. understand how our behavior impacts our revenue generation
    c. agree on steps to be taken by each of us to generate new potential customers
    d. feel more comfortable in our role as account executives

To test objectives 1c3 and 2a1: Use active listening techniques.

3. Which is the most effective active listening technique?
    a. restating exactly what the subordinate has said
    b. using nonverbal communications signs, such as shaking your head or folding your arms
    c. using verbal communication signs such as "uh-huh" or "I see"
    d. staying completely quiet while the subordinate is talking

4. The most important goal in using active listening techniques is to make sure the subordinate
    a. feels that you care
    b. feels understood
    c. clearly states the problem
    d. respects you

SUMMARY

Tables 3-5 through 3-9 offer checklists to use for designing or developing learning measures. Use the appropriate checklist for the measure being designed.

Table 3-5

Checklist for Developing Multiple-choice Test Items		
Question	**YES (✓)**	**NO (✓)**
1. When possible, is the stem stated as a direct question rather than as an incomplete statement?		
2. Is irrelevant information or excessive verbiage eliminated from the stem?		
3. Are words that are otherwise repeated in all the responses included in the stem?		
4. Are all alternatives plausible and attractive to the less knowledgeable or skillful student?		
5. Are the alternatives mutually exclusive?		
6. Are alternatives presented in some logical order, for example, chronological, most-to-least, alphabetical, and so on?		
7. Is there only one correct or best response to the item?		
8. Are alternatives approximately equal in length?		
9. Are there at least four alternatives for each item to lower the probability of getting the item correct by guessing?		
10. Is the correct response randomly distributed among the alternative positions throughout the test, producing approximately the same proportion of alternatives a, b, c, and d as the correct response?		
11. Are negatively stated items (*no, not, none*) avoided or, if used, is the term underlined, highlighted, and/or capitalized?		
12. Are specific determiners (*all, always, never*) avoided in the distracters?		
13. Are options or answers to one item that may cue test-takers to the correct answer of other items avoided?		
14. Is the use of "All of the above" as an alternative avoided?		

Table 3-6

Checklist for Developing True-false Tests Items		
Question	YES (✓)	NO (✓)
1. Do the directions instruct students to *circle* the correct response?		
2. Is the use of the words "always," "all," "never," "only," and "none," avoided?		
3. Is the use of the words "sometimes," "usually," "maybe," "often," and "may" avoided?		
4. Are the statements unqualifiedly true or false?		
5. Are the statements relatively short?		
6. Is including two concepts in one item avoided?		
7. Are negatively stated items avoided?		
8. Is the source or authority on opinion questions cited?		
9. Are the true and false statements about the same length?		
10. Are the number of true and false statements approximately equal?		

Table 3-7

Checklist for Developing Matching Test Items		
Question	YES (✓)	NO (✓)
1. Do the directions clearly state the basis for matching the descriptors (left column) with the options (right column)?		
2. Do the directions indicate where to write the answer?		
3. Do the directions allow for options to be used more than once?		
4. Are only homogeneous (like) materials used in matching items?		

Table 3-7 (*continued*)

Checklist for Developing Matching Test Items

Question	YES (✓)	NO (✓)
5. Are matching items brief, limiting the list of options to less than ten?		
6. Are more options included than descriptors to help prevent answering through the process of elimination?		
7. When possible, is the amount of reading time reduced by including only short phrases or single words in the options list?		
8. Is the options list arranged in some logical order, for example, chronologically or alphabetically?		
9. Are the list of descriptors to be matched and the list of options on the same page?		

Table 3-8

Checklist for Developing Word Completion Test Items

Question	YES (✓)	NO (✓)
1. Are only significant words omitted from the statement?		
2. Are enough words included in the statement so that the intended meaning is clear?		
3. Is there only *one* correct response per blank?		
4. Are the blanks of equal length to avoid giving cues to the correct answer?		
5. When possible, are words deleted at the end of the statement after the student has been presented a clearly defined problem?		
6. Is the required response limited to a single word or phrase?		
7. Are lifting statements directly from the text, lecture, or other sources avoided?		

Table 3-9

Checklist for Developing Behavioral Checklists

Question	YES (✓) NO (✓)
1. Has the behavioral checklist been introduced and practiced appropriately (exercises) before being used as an end-of-course learning measure?	
2. Is the observer adequately trained to fairly and consistently score the behaviors?	
3. Are directions provided which clearly inform the student of the type of response called for?	
4. Do the items elicit the type of behavior you want to measure?	
5. Has the simulated situation been explained to the participant?	
6. Does the simulated situation match the job requirements as closely as possible?	
7. When appropriate, are the time, activity limitations, and the mastery standard clearly stated in the directions?	
8. Do the total points possible equal exactly 100 points?	
9. Is the checklist easy to score?	
10. Does each item on the checklist measure one behavior only?	
11. Have only behaviors that are meaningful, significant, and representative of the behaviors that capture the learning objectives been selected?	
12. Does each item begin with an action verb?	
13. Does the wording within each item describe specific, observable behaviors?	
14. Is the rating scale simple and easily interpreted by the rater?	

REFERENCES

1. Davis, J.R., and D.A. Cerqueira. 1999. "Assessing the Results of Training: The Case of Water Sanitation in Brazil." In *In Action: Measuring Learning and Performance*, ed. T.K. Hodges. Alexandria, Va.: American Society for Training and Development.

2. Dixon, N.M. 1990. *Evaluation: A Tool for Improving HRD Quality*. San Diego, Calif.: University Associates, Inc.

3. Ebel, R.L. 1961. "Improving the Competence of Teachers in Educational Measurement." *Clearing House* 36.

4. Phillips, J.J. 1991. *Handbook of Training Evaluation and Measurement Methods*, 3rd edition. Houston: Gulf Publishing Company.

5. Sherman, R., and R. Stone. *The Challenge of Finding the Right Data from the Right Source*, Presentation at the ASTD Conference, Orlando, Fla. June 2001.

CHAPTER 4

How to Test Learning Measures for Reliability and Validity

Once learning measures are designed, the next step is to test them for reliability and validity. It is easy for the evaluator to get discouraged or intimidated when thinking of the seemingly daunting task of testing learning measures for reliability and validity. After all, doing so takes time and expertise, so it is often a step many test designers avoid. In addition, time and resources are constraints the test designer faces in most organizations. It is rare that resources are available to meet expectations of academicians for testing for reliability and validity, but there are practical steps that can be taken to help ensure tests are measuring what they are meant to and that test results are used in the most appropriate way. The methods offered in this chapter are practical—give them a try.

TESTING MEASURES FOR RELIABILITY

If a learning measure is reliable, it is consistent over time. If learning has taken place, a reliable measure will yield the same student score on a second administration. The evaluator will want to do whatever possible to ensure testing measures are reliable, so that the scores for one test administration can be compared to those of subsequent administrations.

Reliability and Test Design

Sources of error due to the way in which the test is designed, which produce unreliable measures, include:

- Differences in the interpretation of the results of the instrument
- The length of the instrument

These errors can be reduced by designing tests that can be scored objectively and ensuring that the instrument is long enough, because short tests are usually not very reliable (Hopkins 1998).

Once a test is designed, the evaluator can use one of the methods discussed in Table 4-1 to determine its reliability.

Selecting the method to test for reliability may depend on the type and administration of the measure. For example, if the measure is one that requires an instructor assessment, the test designer or evaluator conducts a test for *inter-rater* reliability to make sure that the measure is not sensitive to the subjectivity of the rater. Ideally, if two different raters measure the same individ-

Table 4-1
Methods for Determining Reliability*

Test	Description
1. Test-retest	This method involves re-testing the individual with the same test on a separate occasion. This is done by administering a test at the end of the course and again one week later.
2. Parallel forms	This method requires that an equivalent form of a test be administered to the same individuals. It is done by administering two versions of the same test to ensure that both tests are equivalent.
3. Split-half	This method calls for dividing the test into two presumably equivalent halves. It is done by separating the odd and even items of a test and correlating them to ensure that the individual was consistent across the test.
4. Inter-item	This method requires calculating the correlation between each of the items on a test. It is done by comparing every item on the test to every other item to ensure internal consistency.
5. Inter-rater	This method requires calculating the degree to which two or more raters arrive at the same score for the same individual. It is done by having two or more raters compare their evaluations of a student to ensure that they are consistent in their ratings.

* Calculations for reliability require the statistical computations for correlations and may require the assistance of a statistician.

ual, they would arrive at identical, or acceptably close, results. If the measure is a written test, the *split-half* or *inter-item* methods for testing for reliability may be the most appropriate. The designer or evaluator can use the *test-retest* method successfully in corporate settings where subject matter experts are brought in at one point to take the test and again in two weeks to take the same test.

Reliability and Test Administration

Additional sources of error are due to the way in which the test is administered. These include:

- Fluctuations in the mental alertness of the participants
- Variations in the conditions under which the instrument is administered
- Random effects caused by the personal motivation of the participants

If the evaluator is part of a program planning task force, they may be able to take into account these potential sources of error prior to the program implementation. For example, they could plan for classroom-type program tests to be given at the same time of the day and under the same conditions. They could ensure that the instructor or test giver provides the same set of instructions to the participants for taking the test and explain to the participants how the results will be used. If not part of the planning task force, the evaluator can provide guidance to test administrators to help avoid these potential sources of error. Of course, such precautions cannot be taken for online programs.

Check at the end of this chapter to see how the three case studies in progress address reliability.

TESTING MEASURES FOR VALIDITY

Validity refers to the accuracy and precision of a measure. A valid measure is one that measures what it is supposed to measure. A measure or test can be reliable yet not be valid. For instance, a test may reliably measure "x" every time (high reliability), although it is supposed to measure "y" (low validity). But reliability is necessary for validity (Hopkins 1998). The validity of a test has direct implications for the appropriateness of drawing conclusions based on the results of the test. Many discuss test validation as the process of accumulating *evidence* to support inferences one can make about the measure. The American Psychological Association and others discuss three groups of validity evidence (American Educational Research Association 1996). Table 4-2 defines these categories of validity evidence.

Table 4-3 provides a more common way to distinguish validity types.

The type of validity selected will depend on the purpose for the measure, the objectives of the program, and the resources available.

Criterion-Related Validity

Criterion-related validity predicts performance (criteria) based on test results. Criterion-related evidence is a statistically significant positive correlation between test scores and actual job performance. There are two types of criterion-related validity: predictive and concurrent. A predictive study is used when the performance data will be obtained in the future. With a predictive study, a sample group of participants is tested. At a predetermined time following the test (usually about three months later), the same participants are evaluated on job performance to determine if there is a positive correlation between their test scores and their performance. The concurrent study is conducted when

Table 4-2
Validity Evidence Categories

Category	Definition
Construct-related evidence	This is when the evidence focuses primarily on the test score as a measure of the psychological characteristic of interest such as reasoning ability, spatial visualization, and reading comprehension.
Content-related evidence	This is when the evidence demonstrates the degree to which the sample of items, tasks, or questions on a test are representative of some defined universe or domain of content.
Criterion-related evidence	This is when the evidence demonstrates that test scores are systematically related to one or more outcome criteria.

Table 4-3
Types of Validity

Validity Type	Definition
Content validity	Content validity measures how well a test samples the universe of behavior, knowledge, or skill being tested. For a test to be valid, its design and delivery process must ensure that all knowledge, skill, or performance areas key to testing are adequately represented in the measurement device. Content validity is the most common validation approach for most testing.
Criterion-related validity–predictive	Predictive validity, the most common sub-class of *criterion-related validity* (Hopkins, 1998), refers to how well the test score predicts future performance in the area tested. It is less commonly measured than content validity because it requires more time and effort. However, predictive validity is desired for many job situations, such as when an individual will be fired based upon the test results.
Criterion-related validity–concurrent	Concurrent validity, a second sub-class of *criterion-related validity*, refers to the extent in which an instrument agrees with the results of other instruments or measures administered at approximately the same time to measure the same characteristics.
Construct validity	Construct validity refers to degree to which an instrument can accurately measure the concept that it is intended to measure. Examples of such concepts [constructs] are intelligence, efficiency, and sociability.

the performance data are obtained at the same time as the test is given. The test could be given to current performers, for example, to see if there is a positive correlation between their performance and the test scores they receive.

Some organizations use predictive validation to assist in selecting or de-selecting candidates for a job, allocate resources effectively, or provide coaching on the job more efficiently. It is, however, not always practical in large organizational settings to wait three or more months before using a learning measure. It may also be difficult for management to dedicate the evaluation resources for this effort. It is also difficult to keep everything the same during that three-or-more-months time frame. But if an employee is let go, based on his or her test score, conducting a predictive study may be the most prudent thing to do legally and the fairest to the individual being tested.

Concurrent validation is usually preferable for human resource professionals to use for predicting criteria such as job performance (American Educational Research Association 1996). It is also the most practical in organizations where these professionals need to make human resource decisions quickly. Evaluators or test-designers can use both predictive and concurrent validation to determine what score to use for passing or failing a participant (cut-off scores) if that is the purpose of the test.

Schulman (1997) provides examples of computer programs that conduct the type of testing required for criterion-related validation studies. However, this is an area that may require the help of an evaluation specialist with statistical expertise.

Criterion-Related Validation Testing and the Business

It makes good business sense to conduct tests to predict performance. An organization does not want to invest money in an individual who will not be able to perform. In addition, individuals are entitled to legal protection from actions taken against them based on invalid tests. The organization does not want to deal with lawsuits. If the test is valid, the business can make good strategic decisions. If the test is not valid, potentially successful employees may be lost, and the organization's reputation is potentially at risk.

Criterion-Related Validation Testing and the Test-Taker

Beside legal issues, the evaluator will want to ensure that every individual who takes a test or proficiency is treated fairly. It is important to consider predictive validation testing from an ethical perspective. It is unethical for test-givers to provide individual test scores, for example, to anyone who is in a position to take action on an employee's job based on the test score *unless* it has been tested positively for predictive or concurrent validity. It is not fair to predict someone's performance on a test score when we do not know if that score is indicative of how that person will perform on the job. How many times do poor test-performers prove to be high job-performers? It may seem to be appropriate that supervisors know the test scores for each of their employees so that they can help provide support for the lower testers. However, if supervisors "expect" lower performance from a particular performer, they may unintentionally put that employee in a position that will provide fewer opportunities to excel. Many organizations allow their supervisors to see only the average score for classes to avoid that situation. If the organization wishes supervisors to have access to individual test scores so they can provide customized coaching, and the test has not undergone the rigor of criterion-related validation testing, the individual should give their permission first.

Criterion-Related Validation Testing and the Evaluator

Unless a test has been tested positively for predictive or concurrent validity, its data should only be used by the program evaluator to determine how effective the training program is, not to predict performance. That being said, evaluators often find definite relationships between test scores and job performance. Alerting program designers and managers to low test scores from a sample group, reported without individual identification, can be a good use for testing data. The evaluator can investigate these courses or programs for problems before they are administered to a wider audience.

Construct Validity

Construct validity is used for testing attitude, skill, ability, and personality characteristics. Intelligence, anxiety, mechanical aptitude, musical ability, critical thinking, ego strength, dominance, and achievement motivation are examples of commonly used constructs (Hopkins 1998). Every aspect of the construct being measured must be defined. With construct validation, there is no single criterion, as there is with criterion-related validity. Many criteria are required to confirm what the test does and does not measure. This definition requires expert opinion, statistical correlations, logical deductions, or criterion group studies. Each method requires a different procedure. For this type of testing, an analyst experienced in this area is also recommended.

Content Validity

Content validation is a testing process that does not necessarily require an expert to conduct. This is the test the evaluator and the program designers could theoretically conduct for every learning measure. Content validity is not difficult to perform, and it requires few resources. Content validation ensures that the learning measure is measuring what the program planners want it to. The following is a three-part process for conducting a content validation. If the designer or evaluator only gets through steps one and two, or even only step one, due to organizational constraints, they should take heart in the fact that their learning measure has undergone more testing for validation than most. Once the evaluator and/or the program designers walk through this process once, they will be able to plan and conduct content validations for future programs more quickly.

Steps to Conduct a Content Validation

Step One: Review your learning measure for good construct.

Go over the guidance provided in chapters 1 and 2 to make sure that:

- The learning objectives are directly related to performance objectives.
- There is at least one test item for each learning objective.
- There is an appropriate number of test items for each objective, depending on its importance to the overall program.
- Test items follow the rules set forth in chapter 2.

At this point, the test is considered to have *face validity.* Face validity is the degree to which an instrument "looks" like it measures what it is supposed to measure. There is no rigorous way to test for face validity, except by reviewing the measure as listed in this step.

Step Two: Use subject matter experts (SMEs) as reviewers.

First, develop a survey template that has a table with two columns and fill in the left-hand column with the test items. List and number above the table each of the program objectives. Figure 4-1 provides a completed sample survey using such a template.

Instructions to reviewers: Please review the training objectives listed below. Indicate the objective being measured for each test item in the table below by writing the objective number in the column labeled "Training objective measured" next to each test item. Please read each test item and training objective carefully before responding.

Training objective 1: List the different components for evaluation.

Training objective 2: Define the three essential objectives used for program planning and evaluation.

Training objective 3: When provided with content, develop a good multiple-choice test item.

Training objective 4: Given various scenarios, select the most appropriate validation.

Test item	Training objective measured
1. Which of the validations listed below is the most common? a. Predictive validation b. Construct validation c. Content validation d. Concurrent validation	4
2. For multiple-choice test items, all alternatives should be mutually exclusive. a. True b. False	3
3. Which of the following is *not* one of the six components for program evaluation? a. Performance evaluation b. Vendor evaluation c. Learning evaluation d. Formative evaluation	1
4. Which of the following types of test items is the most difficult to develop? a. True-false items b. Word completion items c. Matching test items d. Multiple-choice items	3
5. The performance objective should be developed before the business and learning objectives. a. True b. False	2
6. Job selection should be based on which of the following types of validations? a. Predictive validation b. Content validation c. Face validation d. Construct validation	4

Figure 4-1. Sample survey template to use for content validation.

Next, gather field representatives or subject matter experts (SMEs) in a room to review the test. SMEs need to be individuals with extensive knowledge of the course content (individuals who know the job or those who have, or currently perform, the job). Three to five SMEs should be used for the validation process. The larger the number of SMEs, the more confidence you can have in the conclusions.

Estimate the time it will take for the review and inform the SMEs prior to the review how much of their time will be needed for the review. A review should not take more than one day, as fatigue will begin to compromise the results of the validation session. Inform the reviewers of the importance of their review. Explain that the test they are about to review will be used to determine the effectiveness of the program in meeting its intended objectives.

Provide the survey along with the program objectives and the test to each reviewer and have them record for each test item the objective it addresses. *There should be no discussion among the reviewers.* Using a tally sheet such as the sample in Figure 4-2, record the

Instructions: Use the table below to record SME ratings of objectives measured by individual test items.					
Test Item	**SME 1** Objective listed	**SME 2** Objective listed	**SME 3** Objective listed	**SME 4** Objective listed	**Is there agreement?** (2 out of 3) (3 out of 4) (3 out of 5)
1. Which of the validations listed below is the most common? a. Predictive validation b. Construct validation c. Content validation d. Concurrent validation	4	4	4	4	Yes
2. For multiple-choice test item, all alternatives should be mutually exclusive. a. True b. False	3	3	4	3	Yes

Figure 4-2. Sample tally sheet template.

3. Which of the following is *not* one of the six components for program evaluation? a. Performance evaluation b. Vendor evaluation c. Learning evaluation d. Formative evaluation	1	1	1	1	Yes
4. Which of the following types of test items is the most difficult to develop? a. True-false items b. Word completion items c. Matching test items d. Multiple-choice items	3	none	1	3	No
5. The performance objective should be developed before the business and learning objectives. a. True b. False	2	2	2	2	Yes
6. Job selection should be based on which of the following types of validations? a. Predictive validation b. Content validation c. Face validation d. Construct validation	4	3	4	4	Yes

Figure 4-2. Sample tally sheet template (Continued).

objectives listed by the SMEs as being measured by each test item and determine areas of agreement.

There should be agreement among the SMEs regarding the objective being measured by each test item. Use the following cutoffs to establish agreement:

- If there are 3 SMEs, 2 out of 3 agree.
- If there are 4 or 5 SMEs, 3 agree.

When there are more SMEs, there is slightly more latitude for some disagreement.

Remember, the SMEs will be experts on the content of the job and the content of the training. It is unlikely that they will be test design experts. Given this limitation, their ratings will *only* reflect whether the *content* of the test items reflects the *content* of the training objectives. They should not be asked to assess the construction of test items. This assessment should be left to the test-designers. However, during the review process, the SMEs may point out test or proficiency items that they believe can use revisions, such as the jargon used or the sequencing of events. These concerns or suggestions should, of course, be considered. These representatives may be able to provide valuable feedback on content criticality or frequency as well.

Step 3: Finally, analyze the results.

Items that do not achieve agreement in SME ratings on the objective(s) being measured should be reexamined. For items that SMEs indicate the objective being measured differs from the objective intended by the test-designer, the items should also be reassessed. In the example in Figure 4-2, question number 4 failed the content review.

Take this opportunity to discuss the individual ratings with the SMEs to gain insight into why they felt there was a disconnect or omission. This will help determine what revisions are necessary.

Once tested for content validity, the test will continue to measure what it is intended to measure. Analysts at Bell Atlantic conducted a content validation on test items for a Web-based safety program. The validation resulted in the test being revamped, so that all objectives were covered by at least one item. This was accomplished without altering test length, by removing redundant items (Masalonis 1999). The content validation process for this program proved valuable.

ADMINISTERING TESTS

The way in which a test is administered can have an impact on validity and reliability. Designers can build tests right into online courses. Scoring can also be done automatically, presenting the answers to the students and/or the program administrator or the evaluator. For programs given offline, in a classroom-type setting, the evaluator may want to consider the following tips.

BUSINESS REPLY MAIL
FIRST-CLASS MAIL PERMIT NO. 78 WOBURN MA

POSTAGE WILL BE PAID BY ADDRESSEE

DIRECT MAIL DEPARTMENT
Butterworth-Heinemann
225 WILDWOOD AVE
PO BOX 4500
WOBURN MA 01888-9930

NO POSTAGE
NECESSARY
IF MAILED
IN THE
UNITED STATES

t-takers that the pur-
ir subject knowledge
m that they are not
n them that they will
ly after the course is

t has been presented

s will help to deter-
hat their scores will
other management.
as part of the class

re the checklist with
. They should know
good idea to provide
m so that they can
event, linking each
iors. Avoid surprises
icipant is not a goal

ave to take the test
me to ask questions

distractions. Give
omplete the activity.

THE TEST ENVIRONMENT

In addition to the suggestions offered for test administration, be sensitive to the test-takers' potential reactions in a testing environment. Adult learners can find it demeaning in a non-degree situation to be taking tests. Make sure that the rules for validity are followed and that no one sees individual scores. Stress to the test-takers that the purpose for the test is to determine the effectiveness of the program rather than *their* performance. Some suggest using different words, such as *exercise*, rather than the word *test*. Review the test or proficiency with the participants after it is given. This will provide the participants the opportunity to reinforce their

learning by noting the correct answers to any questions they may
have gotten incorrect or behaviors that they may not have demonstrated correctly. The participants will feel the testing is part of
their learning experience.

CASE STUDIES IN PROGRESS

How a learning measure is tested for reliability and validity
depends upon the purpose for the measure, the type of measure,
and the constraints of the organization. Let's look at how
reliability and validity testing are done for our three case study
learning measures.

Technical Training Program

The technical training program is a multimedia program, with
an online knowledge-based practicum. To ensure the reliability of
the practicum, the test-retest, parallel forms, split-half, or inter-
items methods for testing could be used. The easiest method to
implement is a *test-retest* reliability test. A student is given the
same test they took upon course completion one week after completing the course to see how they score. Although there may be
some retention or job reinforcement problems, little should happen
in one week.

In the technical training program, no predictions will be made
based on test scores, so the online practicum is validated for *content
validity*. The steps provided in this chapter for content validation are
followed to ensure the practicum is measuring the learning objectives listed on the Technical Training Program objective map in
chapter 2.

Sales/Customer Service Training Program

The Sales/Customer Service Training Program includes a role-
play proficiency using a performance checklist. For the role-play
proficiency checklist, *inter-rater reliability* is verified. The
instructor(s) who uses the checklist to rate performance will get
the same or close to the same results as any other instructor.
Three or more people use the checklist with a sample set of (two
or three) people who closely resemble those who will complete
the training in the same setting as that planned for the training

event. They compare their results. For those behaviors that yield different results, wording of the behavior is revised and tested again until all observers rate the same for the same participant. This takes a few trials, but once this checklist has been tested for inter-rater reliability, it will be an excellent learning measure and could have an added advantage of being used as a performance measurement tool to measure job performance as well. It is imperative that those who will be using the checklist be trained in its use to ensure its reliability.

Because the Sales/Customer Service Program is part of initial training for these participants, the client organization wants to predict performance based on the proficiency test provided at the end of the program. They want to know that the participants are going to be able to perform the skills they were taught, that they are not wasting money on an expensive training program. But they do not have the waiting time required to conduct a predictive study. A *concurrent study*, therefore, is conducted to determine if the checklist designed for this program is a valid measure to predict performance. Individuals who are trained to use the checklist are sent to the field to observe current performers who have been identified by the supervisors as low-, medium-, and high-performers, in accordance with the identified performance objectives listed in the Sales/Customer Service objective map in chapter 2. The test scores are correlated with the performance ratings of those observed, to determine if there is a positive correlation.

Leadership Development Program

The Leadership Development Program is using pre- and post-knowledge-based tests. These tests can be tested for reliability using a test-retest, parallel-forms, split-half, or inter-item method. The parallel-form involves developing another test. Time constraints prevent using this method, so the test-retest method might be better. However, because the pretest and posttest are given under different conditions, each would have to be retested under the same condition. Testing the pretest for reliability would require giving the test to someone twice *prior* to their participating in the program and twice *after* their participating in the program. This approach, therefore, is not practical. The *split-half* or the *inter-item* methods avoid the extra work involved in the other methods and are the most practical. A statistician is brought in to assist in conducting the correlation analysis for these tests to determine reliability.

The pretest and posttest used in the Leadership Development Program are tested for *content validation*. The scores will be used only to provide the participants feedback on their knowledge gain and to determine the effectiveness of the program in meeting the learning objectives listed in the Leadership Development objective map in chapter 2.

SUMMARY

The test-designer or evaluator should take whatever steps are practical to ensure test reliability and validity. A reliable and valid test provides the organization with a sense of the value of its investments and the individual with a fair assessment of his or her knowledge and/or skill-gain. Following is a checklist to use when testing for reliability and validity.

Table 4-4
Checklist for Reliability and Validity Testing

Reliability-and-Validity Testing Checklist		
Question	YES (✓)	NO (✓)
1. Has the correct test for reliability been selected?		
2. Has the most practical test for reliability been selected?		
3. Has it been determined how the test scores will be used?		
4. Has the correct test for validity been selected?		
5. Have steps been taken to ensure test scores are kept confidential unless evidence shows a positive correlation between the test scores and job performance?		
6. Have steps been taken to ensure that the test is administered correctly?		
7. Have steps been taken to ensure the test takers are treated fairly and with respect?		

Table 4-5
Checklist for Content Validation–Testing

Content Validation Testing Checklist		
Question	YES (✓)	NO (✓)
1. Are the program objectives related to job performance, i.e., do the program objectives relate to knowledge, skills, and abilities needed for successful job performance?		
2. Does the program have clearly and behaviorally defined objectives?		
3. Is the program content directly related to the training objectives?		
4. Are the test questions directly related to the program content and program objectives?		
5. Do the test questions follow good test construction guidelines?		
6. Is information tested in the same manner that it will be used on the job?		
7. Are the technical terms used in test questions the same as the technical terms used in the program?		
8. Has the test been reviewed by at least two additional subject matter experts?		
9. Is there at least one test item for each program objective?		
10. Are the number of test items directly related to the importance of the objective to the overall program objective?		
11. Has the test been piloted with a sample of actual test-takers?		

Conducting a content validation is a process most test-designers or evaluators can accomplish in today's organizations. Following is a checklist to use when conducting a content validation.

REFERENCES

1. American Psychological Association and the National Council on Measurement in Education. 1996. *Standards for Educational and Psychological Testing*.

2. Hopkins, K.D. 1998. *Educational and Psychological Measurement and Evaluation,* 8th Edition. Boston: Allyn and Bacon.

3. Masalonis, A.J. 1999. "Application of Training Evaluation and Human Factors Principles to Piloting of a Web-based Training Program," In *InAction: Measuring Learning and Performance,* ed. T.K. Hodges. Alexandria, Va.: American Society for Training & Development.

4. Schulman, R.S. 1997. *Statistics in Plain English With Computer Applications,* London: Chapman & Hall.

CHAPTER 5

How to Analyze Learning Data

Whereas *measurement* is the development, administration, and scoring of assessment procedures, *evaluation* is a summing-up process in which value judgments play a large part (Hopkins 1998). Up to this point, the design and administration of learning measures have been discussed. These are measurement activities. Now it is time for evaluation. It is time to conduct analysis of the data collected from the learning measures and determine how effective the program is in meeting its learning objectives.

There are two users of learning data evaluation, the program designers who want to know the extent to which each of the learning objectives was met and the client organization that wants to know how effective the program is in meeting the program objectives overall. They want to know if "they got it," and if not, "why not?" To answer the designers' questions, an item-by-item analysis is done by grouping scores for each test item. Because the evaluator linked the test items to each learning objective, it is easy to determine the extent to which each objective was met. This chapter will focus on answering the questions the client typically asks because this requires using evaluation techniques that the evaluator needs to understand.

Whether looking at the results of a test administered once (as for a pilot program) or of a test that has been administered many times, the evaluator or analyst organizes the data in a way that makes sense and is easy to analyze. The evaluator then interprets the results, draws conclusions, and makes possible recommendations for test or program enhancements. During this process, the evaluator stays in close contact with members of the program task force. At different points, as the data is examined and analyzed, the test-designer or the client may have questions that trigger further analysis or investigations.

Before crunching numbers, evaluators want to anticipate the questions they will be expected to answer from the learning-data analysis.

1. How did everyone do overall?
2. Are the scores acceptable?
3. Did some do better than others? If so, why?
4. How different were the scores among the participants?
5. If there was a pretest and posttest, was there an acceptable increase or learning gain?
6. Did the individual scores vary with the different questions? Were there some questions that everyone had problems with?
7. What story is this telling us about the effectiveness of the program?

TABULATING THE DATA

If the learning event is online, the program may automatically score each test and provide a percent correct score for each participant who takes the test. But if the program is a classroom-type program, where paper tests are handed out and collected or proficiencies are used, someone must put on their teacher's hat and score the tests or proficiencies. After scoring each test, the analyst records the raw score (the total number of points achieved) and the percent-correct score (raw score divided by the total number of points possible). If part of the test strategy is to give some items partial or double credit due to their criticality in meeting the program objectives, the analyst accounts for this when calculating the raw score.

This process should go easily if the analyst uses the guidance provided in chapter 2. Having test items with only one correct answer, for example, will make scoring go quickly. If, when tallied, the scores come out to an even percent or can be converted to an even percent easily, the data can be summarized quickly and accurately. Depending upon the amount of data collected, entering the data into some kind of summary sheet may be helpful. Entering the percentages directly into Microsoft Excel or a statistical computer package will make large amounts of data easier to analyze. Or the data could be entered into a simple data summary

Table 5-1
Sample Data Summary Table for One Score Only

Name or ID Code	Score	Percent

table. If the program has posttest or proficiency scores, the data summary table will look similar to Table 5-1.

If the program has pretest and posttest scores, the data summary table will look similar to Table 5-2 (Mondschein 1991).

When entering the data into the tables, the analyst must be certain that the data is recorded accurately. It would be embarrassing to continue with additional analysis of the data and present the results to the client, only to realize that 80 percent was really 40 percent.

Table 5-2
Sample Data Summary Table for Pretest and Posttest Scores

Name or ID Code	Pretest Raw Score	Percent Pretest	Posttest Raw Score	Posttest Percent

EXAMINING THE DATA

If the program implemented does not have a large group of participants, the evaluator can quickly ascertain problem areas in the learning data if it is organized like Tables 5-1 or 5-2.

Let's look at an example by populating Table 5-2 with some fictional scores as depicted in Table 5-3. In this case there was a pretest and identical posttest with fifty questions, each question counting two points.

Before conducting any analysis, to what extent can any of the anticipated questions be answered for this example?

1. How did everyone do overall?
   Each participant's posttest score was higher than their pretest score, so there was a learning-gain.
2. Are the scores acceptable?
   There are 50 percent, 20 percent, and 64 percent scores for the posttest. In our school days, scores falling below 70 percent normally were not considered "good" scores. But that may not be the same standard set by the evaluator or the client for this program. The test should be designed with the profiles of those expected to go through the program in mind and with the simplicity or complexity of the questions considered. This will help determine what constitutes a "good" score.

Table 5-3
Example Test Score Summary Table

Name or ID Code	Pretest Raw Score	Percent Pretest	Posttest Raw Score	Posttest Percent
1	20	40	40	80
2	10	20	25	50
3	16	32	42	84
4	12	24	38	76
5	2	4	10	20
6	25	50	48	96
7	25	50	50	100
8	18	36	32	64
9	15	30	47	94
10	18	36	36	74

3. Did some do better than others? If so, why?

Clearly, in this example, some participants did better than others. Participant 5 in particular had both pretest and posttest scores that are much lower than the rest. The reasons for the variations in scores among the participants may warrant further investigation.

4. How different are the scores among the participants?

When comparing the raw data and mean scores, a difference is noticeable. Some participants definitely scored higher than others. The most important issue to notice, however, is that in every case, the participants scored higher on the posttest than the pretest.

5. If there are a pretest and a posttest, is there an acceptable increase?

Although there is an increase in each case, an acceptable learning gain cannot be determined unless someone has defined what is "acceptable." Acceptability may be based on a validity test conducted during the test design phase (chapter 4), knowledge of past results from the same program using the same test, or from past results from similar programs.

6. Did the individual scores vary with the different questions? Were there some questions that everyone had problems with?

The data summary table does not provide this information.

7. What story is this telling us about the effectiveness of the program?

Without further analysis, the data demonstrates only that there are varying scores and that there is an increase between the pretest and posttest scores, indicating that learning did take place.

DESCRIBING THE DATA

The client organization may be satisfied with what the data show thus far and the extent to which the questions posed can be answered. But if they are not satisfied with the scores or they have questions about some of the individual questions, the evaluator will need to conduct appropriate analyses.

Evaluating learning data does not typically require extensive statistical analyses. In fact, in many cases, just looking at the data set may immediately answer some of the questions the evaluator or the client has. Or a few simple calculations might answer others. Now is as good a time as any to bring up the dreaded word—*statistics*. Many authors have attempted to explain basic applied statistics, but everyone seems to have their own definition of "basic." Statistical analyses are done for one of only four reasons: to describe data, to determine if two or more groups differ on some variable, to determine if two or more variables are related, or to reduce data (Aamodt 1999). Jack Phillips does an excellent job in his "Data Analysis" chapter of describing the use of statistics (Phillips 1997). He cautions, however, that one part of the subject of statistics often leads to other possibilities and that many variables can influence the statistical techniques that should be used and the type of analysis to pursue. In a business environment, statistical rules are often broken because of practicality issues. However, when important decisions are being made as a result of the evaluation, the evaluator (if not skilled in statistics) will want to consult with a statistician.

The information provided in this chapter and the chapter on job performance analysis (chapter 8) is intended to provide a practical understanding of the type of calculations and analyses that are necessary for most program evaluations. Most analysts use computer applications to describe or evaluate data. This chapter and chapter 8 provide sample outputs using the statistical computer application, SPSS. Microsoft Excel can also be used for basic computations and charting. Other statistical computer programs to consider are SAS, STATPACK, DataDesk, Statview, and MINITAB. Schulman (1992) takes you through simple to advanced statistics using SAS, SPSS, and MINITAB. With these programs, computation can be done automatically, accurately, and quickly. But understanding what can be learned from the data will help the evaluator use these tools effectively.

Once the raw data have been recorded and percent correct scores calculated for each individual score, it is time to use the data to better answer the questions posed earlier.

How Data Relate

It is helpful to look at the data set as a whole to determine how the group performed on average. There are three measures of central tendency that describe where the middle (average) of the group is, the mean, median, and the mode (Aiken 1982). To calculate the arithmetic mean (referred to as the *mean*) for the raw scores, divide the total sum of the scores by the number of the scores. For the example data set in Table 5-3, the sum of the scores is 161 and the total number of scores is 10. Therefore, the mean is 161 divided by 10, or 16.1. The mean for the percent scores is calculated the same way. Table 5-4 provides the calculated means for the scores and percentages.

Table 5-4
Calculated Mean Scores and Percents

Name or ID Code	Pretest Raw Score	Percent Pretest	Posttest Raw Score	Posttest Percent
1	20	40	40	80
2	10	20	25	50
3	16	32	42	84
4	12	24	38	76
5	2	4	10	20
6	25	50	48	96
7	25	50	50	100
8	18	36	32	64
9	15	30	47	94
10	18	36	36	72
Mean Scores	16.1	32.2	36.8	74

The second measure of central tendency is the *median*, which is the middle value of all the scores. When calculating the median in a list of post-course scores, for example, the scores are listed in order of magnitude, such as the lowest score to the highest. There are an equal number of values above and below the median. Determining the median is useful as a shortcut to show an estimate of the whole group. By listing the pretest and posttest scores and their percentages from lowest to highest, in the example, the analyst creates Table 5-5.

Table 5-5
Determining the Median

Pretest Scores	Pretest Percent	Posttest Scores	Posttest Percent
2	4	10	20
10	20	25	50
12	24	32	64
15	30	36	72
16	32	38	76
18	36	40	80
18	36	42	84
20	40	47	94
25	50	48	96
25	50	50	100

When there is an odd number of items, there is a single value in the middle, and this value is the median. But when there is an even number, such as in the example, the average of the two middle values is determined. The pretest median is the average of 16 and 18, or 17. The pretest median percentage is the average of 32 percent and 36 percent, or 34 percent. The median for the posttest is the average of 38 and 40, or 39. The posttest median percentage is the average of 76 percent and 80 percent, or 78 percent. This can also be determined quickly using a computer. The medians in this case are fairly close to the calculated means.

The third measure of central tendency is the *mode*, which is the score that occurs most often. With small samples, using the mode to estimate the center of the population is not recommended. This is explained in the example; for the pretest, there are two scores and percentages that occur twice, 16 (32 percent) and 25 (50 percent), neither of which describes the center at all; the posttest scores do not even provide us with a score that appears twice. If the mean, median, and mode were the same or close to the same, it is a normally distributed data set, which, when graphically depicted, produces the famous bell-shaped curve. A thorough discussion of the nature, properties, and uses of the normal distribution can be found in Hinkle, Wiersma, and Jurs (1994).

When should the mean, median, or mode be used to describe data? Normally, data are described using the mean. The median is used if there is an outlier or a score that is atypical from the rest. In the example, there *is* an outlier (participant number 5). So the median pretest of 34 percent and posttest of 78 percent are the best descriptions of the central tendency for this data set. The medians in the example are still close to the calculated means, but there may be a time when the scores show a larger difference, where the median is the better measure of central tendency.

There is another way to deal with an outlier. Sometimes there is a score (or in the case of a large sample size, a few scores) that is very different from the rest. In the example, participant 5 had pretest and posttest scores that were atypical from the rest. Perhaps participant 5 should not have been in this course to start with—he or she did not have the prerequisite skills to take the course. Or perhaps there is a language or reading difficulty. If the analyst took participant 5 out of the sample, the results would look like those in Table 5-6.

When rounding the numbers and using only the percentages, means, medians, and adjusted means can be compared, as in Table 5-7.

If the analyst had calculated the means without accounting for the outlier, the percentages would be different. Finding out something

Table 5-6
Results of Adjusted Data

Name or ID Code	Pretest Raw Score	Percent Pretest	Posttest Raw Score	Posttest Percent
1	20	40	40	80
2	10	20	25	50
3	16	32	42	84
4	12	24	38	76
6	25	50	48	96
7	25	50	50	100
8	18	36	32	64
9	15	30	47	94
10	18	36	36	72
Mean Scores	17.6	35.3	39.7	79.6

Table 5-7
Adjusted Mean Scores

	Pretest Percent	Posttest Percent
Mean	32	74
Median	34	78
Adjusted Mean	35	80

about user 5 will help determine whether to include his or her data. If user 5 is representative at all of any of the types of users that will be taking this test, including their data will provide the most representative look at the test results.

How Data Vary

Now it is clear where most of the data is grouped. The degree to which the data vary from the mean is the *measure of dispersion*. There are three common measures of dispersion. The easiest to calculate is the *range* of the scores or the measure of spread, which would be the difference between the largest and smallest values. The sample range for the pretest percentages in our example is the difference between 4 percent and 50 percent, or 46 percent. The range for the posttest percentages is the difference between 20 percent and

100 percent, or 80 percent. Because the range is highly susceptible to erroneous or outlying values, it may not be the best way for the analyst to describe data. It could be misleading and, as in the example, in great part so because of participant 5.

A more useful measure of dispersion may be the square root of the variance, or the *standard deviation,* which will show how much the data deviate from the mean value of the group. (Variance is a mathematical computation of the amount of variability in the data.) Approximately 68 percent of all data fall between +1 and –1 standard deviation from the mean in a normally distributed sample. For example, if the mean of a group of test scores is 70 percent and the standard deviation for a group of those test scores is 10, it means that approximately 68 percent of all the scores are between 60 percent (70 percent –10) and 80 percent (70 percent +10). When the standard deviation is small, it means that most of the scores are grouped closely to the mean value. If the standard deviation is large, it means the scores are spread out—the larger the standard deviation, the more they are spread out. So determining the standard deviation can be helpful. It can tell if the mean closely represents the population or if it is an average that does not represent the population. As a sample size increases, the variability or variance around the average decreases. Remember to look at the relationship of the standard deviation to the number of scores. That will help demonstrate to the client how variable are the scores. The case studies in progress at the end of the chapter will illustrate this. There is a formula for calculating the standard deviation (Hildebrand 1991). But a computer will calculate it with the press of a button or two.

Generally, knowing the standard deviation is helpful when there are many scores. Typically, however, learning data sets in organizations do not include a large number of scores, because the class sizes are small. But the data set may be large or several data sets may be grouped together for analysis. In this case, it would be helpful for the analyst to get a sense of the dispersion by looking at, or reporting, the minimum and maximum scores and the range, in addition to the mean and the standard deviation. Table 5-8 provides descriptors for the example.

How Data Differ

One way to determine if the difference between the pretest and posttest is "different enough" is to determine if the difference is *statistically significant.* For small samples, statisticians have developed

Table 5-8
Example Pretest and Posttest Descriptors

	N	Minimum	Maximum	Range	Median	Mean	Standard Deviation
Pretest	10	4%	50%	46%	34%	35%	6.9514
Posttest	10	20%	100%	80%	78%	73%	12.1271

this procedure to assist in determining whether the difference can be attributed to chance (sampling error) or whether a genuine relationship exists (Hopkins 1998).

The level of significance defines the amount of risk assumed when saying the differences between two groups indicate that learning occurred. Convention accepts a .05 level of significance, meaning that we may be incorrect in our assumption of learning gain 5 percent of the time. The lower the significance level, the less the risk. The significance level is often referred to as the *p-value* (*p*). So, if the difference between the pretest and posttest scores is significant at .05 or less, it would be written as $p \leq .05$. If the level is higher than .05 ($p > .05$), it means that the difference is too small to be statistically significant—that, more than 5 out of 100 times, the difference does NOT represent a learning gain. There are different types of significance testing that can be used. The analyst, if not skilled in statistics, may want to consult a statistician when selecting the test.

When testing for significance with the example pretest and posttest scores, the analyst finds that the difference between the sets of scores is significant at a .001 level of significance ($p < .05$). When reporting this finding to the client, it may be better to say that the difference is significant ($p < .01$), which is a higher level of significance—only 1 out of 100 times will the difference NOT represent a learning gain.

Now that some evaluation of the example learning-data has been done, let's go back to the questions we asked in the beginning of this chapter to see if we can provide more insight into the effectiveness of the example program.

1. How did everyone do overall?

    The difference between the median pretest and posttest percentages is 44 percent, so learning did take place. Remember that the median does account for the outlier (participant 5). When the mean was adjusted by taking out participant 5's scores (Table 5-7), a difference of 45 percent was found, so the analyst can feel comfortable that learning did take place.

2. Are the scores acceptable?

There are two areas for acceptability that may need to be addressed, the posttest and pretest scores and the learning gain. The median posttest score is 78 percent. Is this high enough? Looking at how 78 percent compares relative to other similar courses may provide the analyst with some insight. But another consideration is the pretest median of 34 percent. Is this an acceptable level of knowledge for someone entering this program? Do they have adequate prerequisite skills? Are they the right people in this program? The learning gain of 44 percent may be acceptable to the client. Again, note how this gain compares to other, similar programs in the organization. There is no fast rule for acceptability; it is one that the evaluator and the client will ideally want to decide before the program design or implementation. But it is okay as well to look at the scores afterward and compare them to other programs.

3. Did some do better than others? If so, why?

This question was answered just by looking at the data. Some did do better than others. It is not clear from the learning data why this is so. Perhaps reaction data collected might provide some clues.

4. How different were the scores among the participants?

The more astute client and evaluator will ask this question as the follow-up to question number 3. There is variability among the scores, but a higher variability for the posttest scores (range = 80 percent and standard deviation = 12.13) than the pretest scores (range = 46 percent and the standard deviation = 6.95). Although learning did take place, it may be helpful for the client to see the minimum and maximum numbers or even the individual (anonymous) scores, so they can see the variability among the scores. Or, if there are many scores, explaining the range and/or standard deviation may be helpful enough. It is probably important that everyone understands that the participants left the course with varying degrees of knowledge or skill.

5. If there was a pretest and posttest, was there an acceptable increase?

When a test for significance is run, it is found that the difference between the pretest scores and posttest scores is well under the .05 level that convention accepts as significant. It is a good idea, when reporting results such as these to the client, for the evaluator to present them as objectively and accurately as possible. It is tempting, for example, to tell the client that "there is an incredible difference" between the scores. It is preferable to report it more objectively as, "there is a significant difference $(p < .01)$," explaining what this means. Remember that the client will be the one taking action on these results and is, therefore, the one assuming the risk, no matter how small.

6. Did the individual scores vary with the different questions? Were there some questions that everyone had problems with?

   Looking at the data item by item may be required if there is a suspected problem in a particular area that certain questions cover. The client may not find a 73 percent mean score acceptable, for example, and may want to investigate the test scores, question by question. However this is done, be sure to protect the anonymity of the participants, unless a test for criterion-related validity has been conducted on the test.

7. What story is this telling us about the effectiveness of the program?

   Here is the "bottom line" for the evaluation of the learning-measure. Much of the story will depend on the answers to some of the previous questions. How do these results compare, for example, to other programs in the organization that are the same or similar? Learning did take place. But since the sample size for the example was so small, the evaluator may want to encourage the client to look at the same data for two or three more classes before drawing any conclusions about program acceptance or revisions. Also, someone may want to investigate why participant 5 had such different scores from the rest of the participants. Prerequisite skills may need to be part of the program description because having someone attend a program from which they cannot learn is a waste of company dollars.

Displaying the Data

There are several ways that learning data can be presented. The data summary table with the calculated means is one way. Another

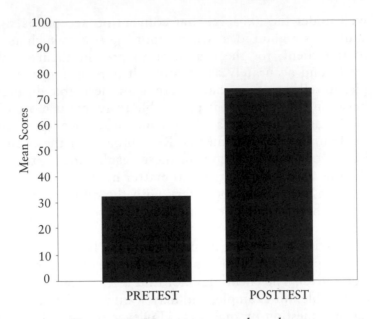

Figure 5-1. Mean test score bar chart.

might be a graphic depiction, such as Figure 5-1, which provides a quick depiction of the difference between the pretest and posttest results.

Another way to display the data would be to provide the individual participant scores as they relate to one another, as depicted in Figure 5-2.

This chart provides an "at a glance" indication of the difference between the pretest and posttest scores as well as the variability of the posttest scores. This type of chart is also useful when displaying only posttest data, as it provides a quick assessment of how well the group did as a whole. The client will be able to quickly see the variability among the participant scores in this chart.

However the data are displayed, the analyst must remember to protect the confidentiality of the participants. Also, making sure that any graph or chart used does not distort the true comparisons of the data is important. For example, if comparing scores from two classes and presenting two charts, one for each class, make sure the X- and Y-axis values are the same for each chart.

REPORTING GROUPS OF LEARNING DATA

The evaluator may find the need to provide reports on all of the department's tests or proficiencies. At Bell Atlantic, test scores were

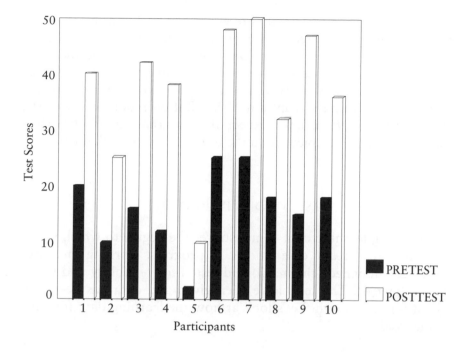

Figure 5-2. Individual test score bar chart.

presented monthly and quarterly (Hodges 1998). In addition, the Measurement and Evaluation (M&E) group analyzed the data quarterly and provided conclusions and recommendations from their analysis. Scores were sent via a roster for instructor-led courses, and software programs were developed to send electronic scores to the M&E database. The clients were able to compare data between lines of business and different media types. After about six months of data collection and reporting, the M&E group looked at the data and determined where most of the data fell and what scores should be pointed out for investigation. Pretest scores that were above 70 percent, posttest scores below 85 percent, and proficiency scores below 90 percent triggered the database to issue "alerts" to the responsible design or delivery managers via company email. These alerts were then aggregated for the monthly and quarterly reports to provide the opportunity to compare the number of alerts received by line of business and media type. The alert process enabled course designers and implementers to "fix" problems as they occurred, so their test data were used for both continuous improvement and to monitor training effectiveness of the company as a whole.

However the group data are presented, the evaluator must ensure that it is being presented in a way that is useful for the audience. Summary data may be fine for one group, but more specific data, such as the "alert" process described above, may be more useful for another. Periodically, survey the audience to determine if the method of reporting is helpful to them. But do report it if it exists. Remember that we cannot expect the programs to meet performance and business objectives if the tests demonstrate that no learning occurred.

CASE STUDIES IN PROGRESS

Analyzing learning data demonstrates the degree to which learning occurred. In our case studies in progress, learning measures have been designed (chapter 3) and tested for reliability and validity (chapter 4). The tests have been given and data has been collected for one month. Let's look at how the learning data for each is analyzed.

Technical Training Program

The technical training program is a multimedia course with an online, knowledge-based practicum. There are 100 posttest questions, each receiving 1 point of credit. Table 5-9 is the data summary table for learning data for this course. Because each question receives 1 point and is therefore worth 1 percent, raw scores are not provided. The one month of data collection resulted in twenty test-takers.

There are no real outliers in this data, so it is appropriate to calculate the mean. The analyst uses a computer to calculate the mean and the standard deviation. The range can be easily calculated. Table 5-10 provides the descriptors for the program.

A near 80 percent average test score may or may not be acceptable to the organization. The test probably is not too difficult for this audience, as many received scores in the 90th percentile, one even receiving a 100 percent. With such high scores, an evaluation of the different items is not warranted. The range of 45 and standard deviation of 10.89 shows some variability. A comparison of these scores with those from other sessions may be interesting. Or the client may want a closer evaluation to determine why those who had low scores did not do as well as the others. Questions the evaluator

Table 5-9
Technical Training Program and Calculated Percent Scores

Participant ID	Score (in percent)
1	65
2	82
3	92
4	55
5	82
6	88
7	75
8	72
9	71
10	80
11	90
12	91
13	100
14	86
15	78
16	87
17	72
18	75
19	65
20	78

Table 5-10
Technical Training Program Descriptors

	N	Minimum	Maximum	Range	Mean	Standard Deviation
Posttest	20	55	100	45	79.2%	10.8850

may anticipate would include:

1. Are the right people taking this class?
2. Could it be that there is some type of reading difficulty with some of this population, such as English as a second language?
3. Could it be that some of the test-takers are already experienced in this area and knew much of the information already?
4. Should data be collected for another month, for further evaluation, to see if there is a trend?

If another month of data demonstrates a trend, the client will want to determine if these are acceptable scores going forward or if they want to make adjustments to the test. The client may also want to consider validating the test to determine if the posttest scores are good indicators of job performance. That type of validation will put the "acceptability" issue to rest.

Sales/Customer Service Training Program

The Sales/Customer Service Training Program includes a role-play proficiency, using a performance checklist. Scores for thirty-six participants (six classes with six participants in each class) were collected, utilizing a checklist. The checklist has thirty-four items, each with a possible rating of "yes" or "no." The percent-correct score for each participant is determined by dividing the number of "yes" blocks checked by the total items on the checklist (thirty-four). The role-play calls are contrived so that it is possible for each behavior to be rated. Table 5-11 is the data summary table for this training program, showing the percentages each participant received.

Table 5-11
Sales/Customer Service Training Program
Calculated Percent Scores

Participant ID	Score (in percent)
1	90
2	86
3	88
4	92
5	100
6	85
7	82
8	80
9	65
10	82
11	72
12	80
13	96
14	100
15	98

Table 5-11
Sales/Customer Service Training Program
Calculated Percent Scores (*continued*)

Participant ID	Score (in percent)
16	100
17	92
18	100
19	68
20	75
21	80
22	82
23	78
24	85
25	98
26	95
27	100
28	100
29	90
30	100
31	72
32	75
33	80
34	78
35	74
36	82

There are no real outliers for this data set, so calculating the mean is appropriate. Table 5-12 provides the descriptors for this program.

A mean of 86 percent is good by most standards. It looks as if this course is achieving its objectives. There is some variability with the

Table 5-12
Sales/Customer Service Training Program Descriptors

	N	Minimum	Maximum	Range	Mean	Standard Deviation
Posttest	36	65	100	35	86.11%	10.4602

range of 35 and a standard deviation of 10.46. But looking at the data summary table a little more closely reveals a pattern. Doesn't it appear that there are some groupings of the scores? Let's separate the groups into their classes and compare their scores (Tables 5-13 through 5-18).

Table 5-13
Sales/Customer Service Training Program—Class 1

ID	Score (in percent)
1	90
2	86
3	88
4	92
5	100
6	85

Table 5-14
Sales/Customer Service Training Program—Class 2

ID	Score (in percent)
7	82
8	80
9	65
10	82
11	72
12	80

Table 5-15
Sales/Customer Service Training Program—Class 3

ID	Score (in percent)
13	96
14	100
15	98
16	100
17	92
18	100

Table 5-16
Sales/Customer Service Training Program—Class 4

ID	Score (in percent)
19	68
20	75
21	75
22	82
23	78
24	85

Table 5-17
Sales/Customer Service Training Program—Class 5

ID	Score (in percent)
25	98
26	95
27	100
28	100
29	90
30	100

Table 5-18
Sales/Customer Service Training Program—Class 6

ID	Score (in percent)
31	72
32	75
33	80
34	78
35	74
36	82

Table 5-19
Sales/Customer Service Training Program Class-Grouping Comparison

				Average
Class group A	Class 1—90.17%	Class 3—97.67%	Class 5—97.17%	95%
Class group B	Class 2—76.83%	Class 4—77.17%	Class 6—76.83%	77%

Classes 1, 3, and 5 appear to have done better than classes 2, 4, and 6. To do some comparisons, let's group the data for classes 1, 3, and 5 under "class group A" and those for classes 2, 4, and 6 under "class group B." Table 5-19 provides the mean scores for class groups A and B.

Well, isn't that interesting? The mean score for class group A (95 percent) is definitely higher than the mean score for class group B (77 percent).

Before going any further with analysis, some investigation is warranted at this time to see if it makes sense to continue doing further comparisons. Sure enough, some checking discovers that one instructor taught and scored the students' proficiency for classes 1, 3, and 5 (class group A) and a different instructor for classes 2, 4, and 6 (class group B). What is happening here? Could one instructor be better than the other? Perhaps the facilities were different for each class and some were more conducive to learning. Perhaps the different regions in which the classes were taught offered different incentives.

It's time, perhaps, to go to the statistician and ask some specific questions, such as:

1. Is there a true difference between class group A and class group B?
2. Is there a true difference between the individual classes?
3. Is there some interaction between the instructor and the individual classes; for example, that instructor A is significantly different from instructor B, but only in certain classes?

When running the appropriate statistical tests, it is determined that there is a significant difference between instructor A classes and instructor B classes. There is no significant difference, however, between the individual classes and no significant differences indicating particular interactions between the instructors and the classes.

To determine if the instruction was better for the classes with higher scores (instructor A classes), the evaluator uses the existing reaction data from these classes. The reaction data shows that there was no difference in the post-course questionnaire scores from each instructor group; the participants in the groups did not perceive one instructor to be better than the other in any of the rated categories.

Since there were no apparent environmental differences and no perceived instruction problem, perhaps the way in which the learning data was collected could be an issue. Remember that a proficiency checklist is used for this program. The instructors in each class used the same scenarios to test each participant and observed their performance using the same checklist to rate their performance in accordance with the program objectives. That being the case, perhaps there is an inter-rater reliability problem using the proficiency checklist. That is, each instructor possibly placed different criteria or levels of acceptance on their scoring procedure. In chapter 4, it was recommended that all instructors who use a checklist be trained in its use to increase inter-rater reliability. Further investigation shows that instructor B was *not* trained to use the checklist. *The evaluator at this point recommends that instructor B be trained and that both instructors be shown these evaluation results, so they can determine the areas where they differ in their assessments.* It is not fair to the course participants that one participant gets a higher score on their role-play just because he or she had instructor A. And the learning data need to be consistent before a meaningful impact is conducted on this program. The client may want to monitor this situation to see if it continues. It is fortunate that the learning data for this program were analyzed before company-wide implementation.

Leadership Development Program

The Leadership Program provides a pretest and a posttest, in written form, with fifty questions on each test. The tests are identical. Each question receives 2 points. Two classes were taught during the month, one with 8 participants and one with 11 participants. Tables 5-20 and 5-21 provide the data summary tables for each class.

Table 5-20
Leadership Program—Class 1

Participant ID	Pretest Raw Score	Pretest Percent Score	Posttest Raw Score	Posttest Percent Score
1	30	60	45	90
2	25	50	50	100
3	18	36	40	80
4	36	72	50	100
5	22	44	42	84
6	31	62	48	96
7	10	20	35	70
8	28	56	46	92

Table 5-21
Leadership Program—Class 2

Participant ID	Pretest Raw Score	Pretest Percent Score	Posttest Raw Score	Posttest Percent Score
1	25	50	50	100
2	22	44	48	95
3	20	40	35	70
4	33	66	45	90
5	23	46	44	88
6	15	30	36	72
7	18	36	35	70
8	20	40	38	76
9	38	76	50	100
10	25	50	42	84
11	34	68	48	96

Let's just take a quick look at the data in the summary tables. It looks like there was a learning gain in both classes. Table 5-22 provides the descriptors when combining both class scores.

When class data are combined, there is a learning gain of 37.68 percent. The difference between the pretest and posttest is significant at a .000 level ($p < .01$).

There doesn't seem to be a large difference between the classes. Table 5-23 provides the descriptors for Class 1.

There is a learning gain for Class 1 of 40.13 percent, which is significant at a .006 level ($p < .01$). There is more variability among the pretest scores than the posttest scores. Table 5-24 provides the descriptors for Class 2.

Table 5-22
Leadership Program Descriptors

	N	Minimum	Maximum	Range	Mean	Standard Deviation
Pretest	19	20	76	56	49.79%	14.9056
Posttest	19	70	100	30	87.47%	10.9968

Table 5-23
Leadership Program Descriptors—Class 1

	N	Minimum	Maximum	Range	Mean	Standard Deviation
Pretest	8	20	72	52	50%	16.4577
Posttest	8	70	100	30	90.13%	9.8443

Table 5-24
Leadership Program Descriptors—Class 2

	N	Minimum	Maximum	Range	Mean	Standard Deviation
Pretest	11	30	76	56	49.64%	14.5002
Posttest	11	70	100	30	85.55%	11.8437

There is a learning gain of 35.91 percent for Class 2, which is significant at a .006 level ($p < .01$). The variability is fairly consistent with Class 1. So there is little difference between the two classes. The evaluator can probably feel comfortable telling the client the following about their leadership program:

- Learning did take place.
- There was little variability among participants' test scores.
- There was little difference between two separate classes given.

From these results, the client may conclude that the program is consistent from one implementation to another and that the subject matter is having the same effect on learning from one participant to another. Whether they are able to *apply* what they learned to their work environment is another matter and one that will be tackled in the next chapter.

SUMMARY

Evaluation of learning data is the process of summing up and analyzing data collected from learning measures. The evaluator uses different techniques to determine the story that the data tell. Table 5-25 offers a checklist to use for analyzing learning data.

Table 5-25

Checklist for Analyzing Learning Data

Question	YES (✓)	NO (✓)
1. Have the raw scores and percentages been recorded accurately in the data summary table?		
2. Was a meaningful measure of *central tendency* (mean, median or mode) calculated?		
3. Were outlying scores accounted for in the calculations?		
4. Was the *range* of the percentages determined to demonstrate the variability of the scores?		
5. Was the simplest and most useful statistical method used for analyzing the data?		
6. If there is a large data set, was the *standard deviation* calculated to determine the variability of the scores?		
7. If comparing pretest and posttest scores, was it determined if the scores were *significantly different*?		
8. Were questions regarding the learning data anticipated and used to guide the evaluation?		
9. Has anonymity of the participants' scores been ensured?		
10. If data are depicted graphically, is it done so that there are no distortions?		
11. If providing groups of learning data, are they provided in a way that is useful for the audience?		

REFERENCES

1. Aamodt, M. 1999. "Why Are There Five Million Types of Statistics?" *Public Personnel Management,* 28, 1 (Spring).

2. Aiken, L. R. 1982. *Psychological Testing and Assessment,* 4th edition. Boston: Allyn and Bacon, Inc.

3. Hildebrand, D. K., and L. Ott. 1991. *Statistical Thinking for Managers,* 3rd edition. Boston: PWS-Kent Publishing Co.

4. Hinkle, D. E., W. Wiersma, and S. G. Jurs. 1994. *Applied Statistics,* 3rd edition. Houghton Mifflin Co.

5. Hodges, T. 1998. "Measuring Training Throughout the Bell Atlantic Organization," In *In Action: Implementing Evaluation Systems and Processes,* series ed. Jack J. Phillips. Alexandria, Va.: ASTD.

6. Hopkins, K. D. 1998. *Educational and Psychological Measurement and Evaluation,* 8th edition. Boston: Allyn and Bacon.

7. Mondschein, M. 1991. *Tracking Training Impact Manual,* Shawnee Mission, Kans.: Measurit.

8. Phillips, J. J. 1997. *Handbook of Training Evaluation,* 3rd edition. Boston, Mass.: Butterworth-Heinemann.

9. Schulman, R. S. 1997. "Statistics in Plain English with Computer Applications." London: Chapman & Hall.

CHAPTER 6

How to Ensure Learning Transfers to Job Performance

The Program Task Force has been convened. It has developed the program business, performance, and learning objectives. The stakeholders and the evaluator have determined the methods for measuring the extent to which the business objectives are met. Meanwhile, the program developers have designed ways to determine the extent to which the learning objectives have been met, and they have tested those measures for reliability and validity. The delivery folks have administered the learning measures and they have been scored. The evaluator has analyzed the scores and determined the extent to which knowledge or skills have been acquired. But have we taken steps to ensure the newly gained knowledge or skills make their way to the participant's job successfully? What can we do to clear away any distracters that may impede successful transfer? If we anticipate the enemy, we can plan the attack.

THE TRANSFER PROBLEM

It is estimated that, although American industries spend up to $100 billion annually on training and development, not more than 10 percent of these expenditures actually result in transfer to the job (Baldwin and Ford 1998). What a shame to invest time, resources, really good brainpower, talented delivery personnel, or sophisticated technology, only to find that the knowledge and skills that we know were *successfully* taught are not applied on the job. We know they learned it—we measured that. But there are evidently demons out there that are keeping all the new knowledge and skills at bay. Soon, without any application, they will be lost forever. What are those demons?

Identifying the Barriers to Transfer

What factors influence transfer of learning? It is widely agreed that transfer of learning involves the application, generalizability, and maintenance of new knowledge and skills (Ford and Weissbein 1997). Researchers have generally viewed transfer as being affected by a system of influences. Baldwin and Ford (1988) see transfer as a function of three sets of factors: trainee characteristics, including ability, personality, and motivation; training design, including a strong transfer design and appropriate content; and the work environment, including support and opportunity to use. Rigorous studies are being conducted to closely examine the transfer system. Holton, Bates, and Ruona (2000) developed a Learning Transfer System Inventory (LTSI) that they administered to 1,616 training participants from a wide range of organizations. The study revealed sixteen transfer system constructs. Table 6-1 provides the list of these and the definitions for the constructs.

Table 6-1
Learning-Transfer System Inventory Factor Definitions

Transfer Factor	Definition
Learner readiness	The extent to which individuals are prepared to enter and participate in training
Motivation to transfer	The direction, intensity, and persistence of effort toward utilizing in a work-setting skills and knowledge learned
Positive personal outcomes	The degree to which applying training on the job leads to outcomes that are positive for the individual
Negative personal outcomes	The extent to which individuals believe that not applying skills and knowledge learned in training will lead to outcomes that are negative
Personal capacity for transfer	The extent to which individuals have the time, energy, and mental space in their work lives to make changes required to transfer learning to the job

Table 6-1
Learning-Transfer System Inventory Factor Definitions (*continued*)

Transfer Factor	Definition
Peer support	The extent to which peers reinforce and support use of learning on the job
Supervisor support	The extent to which supervisors-managers support and reinforce use of training on the job
Supervisor sanctions	The extent to which individuals perceive negative responses from supervisors-managers when applying skills learned in training
Perceived content validity	The extent to which trainees judge training content to reflect job requirements accurately
Transfer design	The degree to which (1) training has been designed and delivered to give trainees the ability to transfer learning to the job, and (2) training instructions match job requirements
Opportunity to use	The extent to which trainees are provided with or obtain resources and tasks on the job enabling them to use training on the job
Transfer effort—performance expectations	The expectation that effort devoted to transferring learning will lead to changes in job performance
Performance—outcomes expectations	The expectation that changes in job performance will lead to valued outcomes
Resistance—openness to change	The extent to which prevailing group norms are perceived by the individual to resist or discourage the use of skills and knowledge acquired in training
Performance self-efficacy	An individual's general belief that he is able to change his performance when he wants
Performance coaching	Formal and informal indicators from an organization about an individual's job performance

Of these barriers, organizations can usually determine those that happen most frequently for them. Newstrom (1986) asked a group of organizational trainers to identify the major barrier categories to successful transfer based on their experience. From that list a group of thirty-one trainers, from a diverse set of organizations, ranked the list from highest to lowest in inhibiting transfer. Table 6-2 provides the result of the ranking.

The top three barriers deal with the employees' work environment, suggesting that management support is critical to transfer. The evaluator should gather barrier data for each program evaluated within the organization to see whether trends can be found and develop a list of those that most frequently cause the problems for transfer.

THE EVALUATOR'S TRANSFER ROLE

When do these barriers rear their ugly heads? Broad and Newstrom (1992) analyzed the timing of the major impediments to transfer of training and classified them along two dimensions: timing of the barrier and the source of the barrier. Table 6-3 provides the results of the analysis.

Regardless of *when* these barriers have an impact, if the evaluator can facilitate the planning for them in advance, actions can be taken to prevent them from becoming barriers before the program is implemented.

Rutledge (1997), from the Central Intelligence Agency, found that transfer strategies are most effectively accomplished if built into the design, development, and delivery of the program. The biggest impact that can be made to overcoming potential barriers to transfer

Table 6-2
Trainers' Perceptions of the Most Important Barriers to
Transfer of Training (Table adapted by Broad 1997)

Rank: Highest to Lowest	Organizational Barrier
1	Lack of reinforcement on the job
2	Interference in the work environment
3	Nonsupportive organizational structure
4	Trainees' view of the training as impractical
5	Trainees' view of the training as irrelevant
6	Trainees' discomfort with change
7	Trainees' separation from trainer after training
8	Poor training design and/or delivery
9	Peer pressure against change

Table 6-3
Timing of Barriers to Transfer

Before	During	After	Barrier
Dominant Timing*			
		1	Lack of reinforcement of the job.
	2	1	Interference from immediate (work) environment
1	2	2	Nonsupportive organizational structure
	1		Trainees' perception of impractical training programs
	1		Trainees' perception of irrelevant training content
2	2	1	Trainees' discomfort with change and associated effort
		1	Separation from inspiration or support of the transfer
	1		Trainees' perception of poorly designed/delivered training
2		1	Pressure from peers to resist changes

* Key: 1 = primary time of impact; 2 = secondary time of impact

is to plan for them to ensure they are addressed during program planning.

One problem in overcoming barriers to performance is that often no one person takes on the assignment. The program developers design to meet learning objectives and may do a great job doing so (as evidenced by the learning analysis). The program implementers focus on ensuring that the program is delivered without a hitch. Most often, neither believes they have much influence on what happens in the field once the participant leaves the classroom or the online site. This is where the evaluator can step in. The evaluator can be the *gatekeeper* for transfer by ensuring the program task force (stakeholders, managers, designers, implementers, and sometimes trainers and participants) addresses the issue in the planning phases of the program. They can use the objective mapping process to facilitate the effort by having the members complete the "barriers/ enablers" column that is mapped to objectives. The task force can then select or develop specific strategies to put into place to avoid the barriers identified. And finally, the evaluator can ensure constant and ongoing communication among task force members throughout the program life cycle to ensure each member is accountable for doing their part to ensure transfer.

STRATEGIES FOR ENSURING TRANSFER

Fortunately, work has been done to determine ways to overcome barriers. There are strategies that can be employed to ensure transfer occurs based on the particular anticipated barrier. Broad and Newstrom (1992) identified seventy-nine strategies. Seventeen organizations from varying industries have identified and documented specific strategies that they have used successfully in their own programs (Broad 1997). These lists are available for program planners. One method for selecting effective strategies would be for the evaluator to take the lead and help the task force focus on five general areas that provide the opportunities to ensure transfer.

1. Market the program. If the entire organization does not truly appreciate the importance of transfer, few commitments will be made by those most necessary to make it happen. And if the potential participants and their management do not see the benefits of transfer, entire programs or portions of them will be a waste of time and money.
2. Design transfer strategies into the program. Anticipating barriers before the program is designed provides the best opportunity for the field to work hand in hand with program designers.
3. Ensure involvement by all players before, during, and after the program. Program task force members determine their roles as enablers by planning for overcoming barriers and determining the best enablers to put in place for the newly skilled employee. They ensure the training design addresses potential barriers during the program so ways in which the participant can overcome them are addressed. They follow up to see how effectively the impact of the barriers has been reduced or eliminated.
4. Demonstrate the extent to which transfer takes place by summative evaluations. These evaluations will provide detailed data to assist future programs.

5. Communicate program successes (and failures) to the organization, so that the lessons learned can be used for future programs.

Tips for Marketing the Program

1. Ensure the program objectives are aligned with the organizational mission. Every program, no matter how large or small, can be linked to the organization's goals. If it cannot, throw it out. The linkage is discovered when the business objectives are determined. Improving sales, for example, is a business objective that can be directly linked to nearly every organization's goals if they design, develop, or represent any type of product. Other objectives may seem a little more obscure, such as increasing employee motivation. If a strong case exists that increasing motivation will help reduce the employee turnover rate by 30 percent, the link is that the company will save unnecessary expenses, such as those incurred in hiring and training new employees. It is easier to "sell" the necessity of a program to a field supervisor when someone shows how it is directly linked to company performance. The supervisor will then be more apt to participate in transfer activities.
2. Take steps to get the future participants excited about the program. Advertise it using posters and email announcements. Show tapes of the company CEO or president talking about the importance of being current in skills during competitive times. Use 360-degree feedback, so the participants see areas of weakness they can address in the program (Waldman and Atwater 1998). The Virginia Sunshine Healthcare Network (ASTD Conference 2001) used 360-degree feedback successfully for a leadership development program. By understanding how their peers assessed their leadership abilities, the participants became very motivated to improve their leadership skills. There was no way they could believe they had nothing to learn from the program. All of these strategies will develop a commitment on the participant's part to get everything they can out of the program.
3. Build transfer of training into supervisory performance standards. Supervisors should be praised for the actions they have taken to ensure appropriate training for their employees and to support the transfer of training by the employees to their job.

4. Set specific program expectations. By understanding what gap their performance needs to fill, the participants and their management will know what to expect from the program. And by knowing exactly what is expected for their performance after the program, the participants will become more active learners and the managers will become more active enablers.

5. Brief participants on the importance of the training and on course objectives, content, process, and application to the job. Someone of influence, such as the employees' supervisor or manager, tells participants in advance that they will be receiving training that is relevant, useful, and likely to improve their job skills or advancement potential (a powerful incentive to learn), which is expected to produce a measurable organizational payoff. This will create a much more active learner and someone who will be much more willing to transfer their knowledge or skills to their job.

6. Select program participants carefully. A successful program includes having the "right" employee attending the program at the "right" time. The evaluator investigates learning data to look for outlier test scores to see who the "wrong" person is for the program. These individuals are identified to management as a group not appropriate for the program. They are either too far behind or too far advanced. They may not need the skills yet, or they needed them a long time ago.

7. Offer rewards and promotional preference to participants who demonstrate new behaviors. An example would be a bonus for improved sales after a sales training program. The prospect of future advancement is another example. This type of incentive is important to consider when the program provides skills that are going to be difficult to learn or use, such as new technology training. If this strategy is to be successful, however, the offers must be clearly stated and consistently carried out.

8. Arrange conferences with prior trainees. Have potential participants meet with those who have completed the program successfully and been able to apply their learning successfully on the job. QUALCOMM, a wireless communications company in California, invites past program participants to a company-paid function to talk informally about how they have used the knowledge or skills on the job. These functions are videotaped and used to demonstrate to management the success of the program.

Tapes like these could also be sent to participants prior to the training to demonstrate the value of the program in which they will be investing their time.

9. Review instructional content and materials. The different members of the task force will have different roles to play in a detailed review of the course content, materials, structure, style, and approach. The stakeholder looks at the course design to ensure it is congruent with the organization's culture. The delivery managers ensure it is consistent with the diverse cultural values of the participant group. The program designers make sure that the audience will easily understand the language used in the material. And of course the evaluator is making sure the learning measures are appropriate for the program and the audience and designed well.

Tips for Designing Transfer Strategies into the Program

1. Ensure that the program designers or developers develop realistic exercises. The participant will go back to the job feeling more confident in his or her ability to handle actual job assignments and better able to do so because of the practice.

2. Provide a positive training environment. If the program is to be held off-site, ensure the physical facilities are effective in establishing a good learning environment. Instructional designers learn a lot about how to make the training room conducive to learning. The task force may have determined as part of the needs assessment that the program skills can best be taught on-the-job or embedded in the job itself. That being the case, the manager or supervisor is integrally involved in the process. If the program is online, supervisors ensure that their employees have the computer time and equipment they need to access and use the program.

3. Design a peer-coaching component for the program. Peer-coaching is a deliberate and structured method for establishing a partnership prior to, during, and after the program. Before the program, participants agree to be partners and to keep their mutual feedback confidential. During the program, the partners discuss how they are going to apply the skills they are learning. After the program, they observe one another in the work situation, record the behaviors observed and offer feedback on the observation.

4. Anticipate barriers and be prepared to assist participants in developing methods for overcoming those barriers. This is done during the program, as part of the training design.
5. Use action planning. It is one of the most effective tools to ensure transfer. Chapter 7 provides a detailed explanation of action planning and how important it can be for ensuring job performance. And chapter 3 discusses how it can be used as a learning measure as well. Appendix A provides examples of different action plans that organizations have used successfully. The program task force should consider using this method during the planning phase of the design. It can have a powerful impact on transfer.
6. Tell the participants they will be tested not only at the end of training but on the job as well. This will alert them to the fact that job performance is an important expected outcome (Zemke and Gunkler 1985). If the test is performance-based, make it the same as or similar to the performance measure that will be used on the job. And tell the participants this is the case. They will become active learners and testers, knowing this is the way it really will be regarded on their job.
7. Conduct follow-up sessions. The follow-up visits could be conducted with the program facilitator, where they consult with the participant (or groups of participants) to solve problems, conduct refresher training, or use other activities to encourage transfer (Sullivan 1998).
8. Encourage support groups. Plan as part of the program design the opportunity for the participants to form support groups after they leave the program. Provide names and contact information or get the groups established prior to program completion.
9. Develop job aids and use them during as well as after the program. The more the participants use the material they were trained to use after they are on the job, the more useful these aids will be to them for transfer.

Tips for Ensuring Involvement

1. Involve supervisors and potential participants in the needs-analysis. The future participants in the program may be members of the task force or be brought in periodically. The program participants ensure the performance and learning objectives are realistic for both learning and job performance. And the planners feel sure they have captured any

additional needs the participants identify. An evaluation of a program at Bell Atlantic (Keuler 2001) demonstrated little transfer. The evaluator wasn't brought in until the program was completed. They conducted follow-up evaluations where they discovered that the participants believed the program taught them skills that were not relevant to their job situation. This seems like a simple thing to have been avoided.

2. Develop a supervisor/trainee contract. Have supervisors and participants develop a contract in advance of their program attendance, specifying each party's commitment to maximizing the results of the program. The participant may agree to:

- Attend all sessions
- Complete all pre-work, reading, and other assignments
- Actively participate in all training modules, keeping an open mind
- Create specific action plans detailing their expected application of the training content, and discuss these with their supervisor
- Share highlights of the training with relevant co-workers or perhaps provide a "mini session" for their co-workers (anticipating having to present material learned creates a very active learner)

In return, the supervisor may commit to:

- Release the employee from work assignments to allow for sufficient program participation
- Attend and participate in all advance briefing sessions for supervisors
- Meet with the participant following the program to determine highlights of the session and mutually explore opportunities for application
- Minimize all interruptions to the program
- Model desired behaviors for the participant
- Provide encouragement, support, and reinforcement for the new behaviors
- Provide specific opportunities for the participant to practice the new behaviors and skills

The participant and the supervisor sign and date the contract.

3. Provide supervisory coaching skills. Because lack of reinforcement on the job is one of the biggest barriers to transfer, it is critical that supervisors are encouraged and trained to provide coaching that reinforces the skills and/or knowledge taught in the program. If lack of reinforcement has been noted frequently as a problem in past programs, particularly if it has been noted fairly consistently for one group within the organization, part of the program planning may include a one-day supervisor workshop for programs developed for that group. The workshop reviews the course content with the managers or supervisors and provides coaching skills specific to the program performance objectives.

4. Provide time to complete pre-course assignments. Have supervisors monitor the distribution of pre-course material, invite the participants to complete assignments by a certain (pre-program) date, provide job release time for their completion, and then discuss the assignments with the participants prior to the training. This can be very powerful in two ways: it saves training time (an increasingly precious commodity) and it reinforces to the participants the importance management is placing on the program.

5. Send co-workers to training together. Two heads are better than one. What one participant may have forgotten another will remember. The co-workers can coach one another and keep each other motivated.

6. Have the supervisor plan to participate in training sessions. The key word here is *plan*. Supervisors and managers are busy and need to schedule their participation in advance to ensure this enabler happens.

7. Encourage trainees to attend all sessions. If participants see their program participation is important to their work assignments, they will be encouraged to be diligent about their attendance.

8. Ensure uninterrupted delivery. Sales or marketing professionals must take time off from their sales activities in order to attend training. They are, therefore, looking for ways to not jeopardize their active sales opportunities and may slip out during the program to make customer calls or come back late from breaks or lunch because they need to address pressing problems to keep their customers happy. This is a

conflict because the organization needs sales. But if the sales management is in support of the program and believes it is a good investment, they can establish a policy that no interruptions are allowed during the program. In this example, if the program objectives are to teach product knowledge and the task force anticipates nonparticipation as a potential barrier for learning and transfer for this particular participant group, they will want to consider alternative delivery types. The product knowledge could be provided, for example, as an online program from which the participant can quickly get the product knowledge they need when they need it and get "back on the street" right away. They will learn just what they need, and it will be reinforced on the job immediately.

9. Transfer work assignments to others. Don't inhibit learning by having the participant worry the entire time about their increasing workload while they are attending the program. And having to manage a backed-up workload when they return to the job will not allow the time for them to use the new knowledge or skills. They need to use them right away if transfer is to take place. Getting the supervisors involved is necessary.

10. Monitor attendance and attention to training. In a classroom situation, the trainer has little influence on attendance. Organizations are not schools—we rely on individual accountability. If many of the strategies described are used, this should not be an issue, unless other pressing problems such as family or health occur. These problems can interfere with total involvement as well. Plan for the supervisor to drop in on occasion just to show how much the participants' involvement is supported by management.

Tips for Demonstrating and Communicating Success

1. Throughout the planning, development, and implementation phases of the program, communicate program progress via email or conference calls. Indicate outstanding action items and those responsible for ensuring their completion. Time marches on, priorities shift, and faces change. To ensure transfer, this ongoing communication is critical. The evaluator can be the facilitator for this activity.

2. Ensure a good learning-analysis (chapter 5) was conducted and communicate the results to:

   • The program participants
   • The participants' management
   • The program facilitator(s) and other implementers
   • The program designers
   • The stakeholder

3. Ensure a good job performance analysis (chapter 8) is conducted and communicated to the same groups as above.
4. Ensure successes are advertised company-wide. Put articles in company newsletters. Ask the CEO and/or leaders within different lines of the organization to send out emails of congratulations. What an encouragement this will be for continued transfer and for future program transfer success!

Take Extreme Measures to Ensure Transfer

If it is discovered during the program-planning phases or from previous program data that there are too many obstacles to overcome in order that transfer takes place, the evaluator can take the lead to consider creative methods to ensure learning does get linked to performance. If it is anticipated, for example, that the systems will not be in place at the end of the program to support the new skills the participants will learn, strongly suggest that the program be held off until the systems are in place. Understand that this is a difficult stance for the design and delivery groups to take because it often means the money for the program gets withheld from their budget. But if it is not attended to, money will be lost. There may be historical data to show that the targeted audience does not have the prerequisite knowledge or skills for the program, and no amount of pre-training work will give it to them. The entire intervention strategy may need to be revised or the company's selection group may need direction in hiring policy. The evaluator ensures that the focus group uncovers this evidence during the objective mapping process and addresses it before further development. There should be no surprises in program design. Everyone should know what they are up against and should plan for it or change the requirements. Again, the evaluator can be the honest broker by helping to uncover potential barriers that must be addressed.

CASE STUDIES IN PROGRESS

Look at the seventeen case studies offered in the *In Action* series to see how different organizations have anticipated and dealt with barriers to transfer in a variety of different scenarios (Broad 1997). Meanwhile, let's see how the different case studies in progress look at ensuring transfer.

Technical Training Program

The technical training program is a multimedia program designed to provide warehouse employees with the operational and safety skills needed to receive and fill customer orders. The performance objectives center around driving and warehouse operations safety behaviors. An online training program focuses on driving safety skills and warehouse operations skills.

One potential barrier to job performance is *motivation to transfer.* Although improved performance in both the driving and warehouse operations areas will be of benefit to the company, this participant group may not see what is in it for them. To overcome this potential barrier, the program task force plans to offer the participants incentives to reduce their individual motor and warehouse accidents. They will be given individual cash bonuses for each month without individual accidents. It is hoped that by using a positive incentive program rather than a negative one (docked pay, etc.), safety will be seen as a win-win situation for the employee and the company. In addition to the incentives, colorful, humorous posters are placed throughout the warehouse to remind the employees of both the rules and the results of not following the rules.

One potential barrier to business and learning performance is *learner readiness.* There is a lot of memorization required for both the driving and warehouse safety components. The online method of delivery was selected to overcome this barrier because it is self-paced, and the participant can go over the material as often as he or she needs to in order to pass the online practicum.

The potential barriers and enablers are documented on the Technical Training Program objective map.

Sales/Customer Service Training Program

The Sales/Customer Service Training Program case study is targeted for sales/customer service representatives. The job performance goals stress following the established protocol for customer calls. The classroom training program is designed to teach the participants how to follow set procedures for different customer calls. The participants practice customer calls and are tested using a performance checklist.

An anticipated barrier to both performance and learning is *perceived content validity*. The participants expressed concern that the content may not be relevant to their jobs. It is possible that the customer call scenarios are not realistic to the type of calls the participants receive on the job. To overcome this potential barrier, developers work closely with subject matter experts (SMEs) to develop scenarios that are the most typical and frequent type of customer calls the representatives receive. They developed a checklist and tested it for relevance by using it in the field to score actual calls. The checklist was modified as necessary. To assist in ensuring transfer, the participants are told during the training that they may be part of a group that will be measured for performance on the job. And they are told that the checklist being used in the classroom to test their proficiency is the same checklist that will be used to measure their job performance. The potential barriers and enablers are documented on the sales/customer service objective map.

Leadership Program

The Leadership Program is designed for supervisors. It is a classroom program that focuses on group and individual communication and management skills.

One learning objective is for the participant to recognize different learning styles and personality types in others so that he or she can conduct more effective individual and group meetings. They are taught to administer personality indicator tests to the people who report to them. A potential barrier to performance is *transfer design*. The participants expressed the concern during the planning meetings that there wasn't enough time during the workday to conduct these types of individual test situations. A potential barrier to learning is also *transfer design*. The program facilitators expressed the concern that the learning event did not allow enough time to teach this procedure well enough for effective transfer. The task force decided to leave it in and measure for learning and job performance. The learning analysis (chapter 5) did not find this to be a learning difficulty. We will have to wait for the job performance analysis (chapter 8) to see if there is a transfer problem.

The potential barriers and enablers are documented on the leadership development objective map.

SUMMARY

The evaluator has the opportunity to play an active part to ensure what is learned transfers to the job. They can be the *broker* for transfer by applying evaluation techniques and facilitating strategies for transfer with stakeholders, program designers, and implementers.

Table 6-4 offers a checklist for the evaluator to use for ensuring learning transfers to the job.

Table 6-4
Ensuring Learning Transfer Checklist

Question	YES (✓)	NO (✓)
1. Have potential performance and learning barriers been identified (and recorded on the objective map)?		
2. Have all the members of the task force been consulted in the identification exercise?		
3. Is historical data used for the identification?		
4. Are strategies for overcoming each identified barrier considered?		
5. Are all the members of the task force consulted (to include potential participants and facilitators) in strategy considerations?		
6. Is management committed to ensuring transfer?		
7. Are action items assigned to task force members to ensure transfer?		
8. Are the members of the task force informed about the status of the action items?		
9. Are exceptional measures taken to ensure transfer when successful transfer strategies cannot be found?		

References

1. Baldwin, T.T., and J.K. Ford. 1998. "Transfer of Training: A Review and Directions for Future Research." *Personnel Psychology 41*.

2. Broad, M.L., and J.W. Newstrom. 1992. *Transfer of Training: Action-Packed Strategies to Ensure High Payoff from Training Investments*. Reading, Mass.: Addison-Wesley Publishing Company.

3. Broad, M.L, editor. 1997. *In Action: Transferring Learning to the Workplace*. Alexandria, Va.: American Society for Training and Development.

4. Ford, J.K., and D.A. Weissbein. 1997. "Transfer of Training: An Update Review and Analysis." *Performance Improvement Quarterly 10*.

5. Holton, E.F., A.B. Reid, and W.E.A. Ruona. 2000. "Development of a Generalized Learning Transfer System Inventory." *Human Resource Development Quarterly 11: 4*.

6. Keuler, D., 2001. "Measuring ROI for Telephonic Customer Service Skills." *In Action: Return on Investment*, Volume 3, Alexandria, Va.: American Society for Training and Development.

7. Newstrom, J.W., 1986. "Leveraging Management Development Through the Management of Transfer." *Journal of Management Development 5*.

8. Rutledge, L.S., 1997. "Building Transfer of Training into the Course Design Process," *In Action: Transferring Learning to the Workplace*. ed. M.L. Broad, Alexandria, Va.: American Society for Training and Development.

9. Sherman, R., and R. Stone. 2001. "The Challenge of Finding the Right Data from the Right Sources." Presentation for the American Society for Training and Development International Conference Orlando, FL.

10. Sullivan, R.L., 1998. *The Transfer of Skills Training*. Alexandria, Va.: American Society for Training and Development, Info-line Issue 9804.

11. Waldman, D.A., and L.E. Atwater. 1998. *The Power of 360 Degree Feedback*. Boston, Mass.: Butterworth-Heinemann.

12. Zemke, R., and J. Gunkler. 1985. "28 Techniques for Transforming Training into Performance." *Training Magazine*.

CHAPTER 7

How to Design Job Performance Measures

At this point in the program evaluation, the business, performance, and learning objectives have been established. Learning measures have been designed and tested for reliability and validity. The extent to which the program learning objectives have been met has been determined, using these measures. And steps have been taken to ensure that successful learning will transfer to successful job performance. It is feasible that most programs can be evaluated to this extent, either for a pilot to enhance a program design or implementation or to assess ongoing success. Now it is time to see the extent to which the learning did transfer to those special programs that the organization has designated for further examination. Let's determine the extent to which the performance objectives have been met.

PLANNING FOR JOB PERFORMANCE DATA COLLECTION

Even if a plan for an overall program evaluation has not been established, a tactical plan for measuring job performance is critical. Robinson and Robinson (1989) suggest that the evaluator considers the following issues when designing a job performance data collection strategy:

- The purpose of the assessment
- Who will be reviewing the data and making related decisions
- The sources of information that will be needed
- How the data will be compared
- How many people should be included in the assessment
- The preferred data collection method
- Skill and resource limitations

The evaluator who understands the importance of each of these considerations and how each is to be included in the evaluation strategy will be armed with the knowledge necessary to develop a foolproof yet practical approach for evaluating job performance.

Understand *the purpose of the assessment* because it serves as the guiding force for the evaluation effort. Just as the client has expectations for the program, they may have specific expectations for the performance evaluation. This will make a difference in planning for the evaluation. If, for example, the client is going to use the evaluation program as an example to demonstrate to the company the value of the program, the evaluation is comprehensive, covering the entire program from design to transference, or it uses several experimental design techniques. If, however, the evaluation is to check the impact of teaching particular skills, the evaluation is short and very focused.

Determine *who will be reviewing the data and making related decisions,* so that reports or briefings are written in language that can be understood by the audience (see chapter 10). A high-level briefing of the evaluation purpose, results, and recommendations is most appropriate for executives who do not have the time or inclination to understand a comprehensive report. There may be others who will review the program results, however, who are representing or advising the client or stakeholder. It may be a subject matter expert or even another analyst. For this audience, the evaluator prepares a full report with all the details to accompany the briefing, so that, if any part of the study is challenged, the results can be supported.

Identify *what sources of information will be needed* to complete the objective map and design the evaluation effort. Remember that the performance data needed and the sources for that data depend on the identified performance objectives. The sources and the type of data they are able to provide may even guide the evaluation design.

Consider *how the data will be compared* in the planning phases to ensure that the appropriate variables are defined. Look for differences between regions or user groups or the media-type used because comparisons may be needed. One way to anticipate comparisons is by talking with the client while completing the objective map. If a task force has been convened for the program, consult them. Explain the type of data needed and ask them if they believe there could be differences among different groups.

Determine the *number of people used for evaluation.* One of the questions often asked by the client and discussed frequently among evaluators is what constitutes a good sample size. This can be a complex question. Generally, it is recommended that a sample as large as possible be used (Phillips 1991). But in large organizations particularly, testing the entire target population is not feasible because of the expense or the intrusiveness to the field. So a sample group that represents the population is selected. Selecting this sample requires random (selecting every "nth" name on a list) or stratified (selecting based on specified variables such as region, years with the company, etc.) sampling. The sample sizes in Table 7-1 can be used as general guidance for determining what sample size to use for general target audiences. Although the table is designed for proportions, it can be used to approximate samples (Dixon 1990).

Most analysts will tell you that it does not take a statistically valid sample size to see distinct patterns in the data, and unless trying to prove or disprove hypotheses (Phillips 1997), seeing distinct patterns or trends is the general goal.

When selecting a sample group, it is important for the evaluator to consider the characteristics that may impact the participants' performance in addition to the program. These characteristics could include participant performance level prior to the program event, age, geographical location, or systems they use. In this case, the evaluator strives to get a sample from each group, so that the population is adequately represented. But again, organizational constraints may limit the evaluator to using a convenient sample. There may also be cases where the evaluator is simply given the group to use for the performance assessment. In this case, the evaluator ensures that all the task force members, particularly the client or stakeholder, understand that the data do not necessarily represent the total population and should be used cautiously. If detailed statistical verification is needed to support a sample size selection, the evaluator will want to consult a statistician if he or she does not have the necessary skills for the verification.

Finally, consider *the preferred data collection method*. Some data collection methods may be too intrusive to field organizations. If the evaluation design is to use observations, for example, and the participants resent being observed and their supervisors see the observations as interfering with office operations, the data will surely be compromised. Or, if a low return rate for questionnaires in a particular group is a continual problem, try a different method for data collection.

Table 7-1
Sample Size Table for Proportions

Population	Sample	Population	Sample	Population	Sample
10	9	230	144	1,400	301
15	14	240	147	1,500	305
20	19	250	151	1,600	309
25	23	260	155	1,700	313
30	27	270	158	1,800	316
35	32	280	162	1,900	319
40	36	290	165	2,000	322
45,	40	300	168	2,200	327
50	44	320	174	2,400	331
55	48	340	180	2,600	334
60	52	360	186	2,800	337
65	55	380	191	3,000	340
70	59	400	196	3,500	346
75	62	420	200	4,000	350
80	66	440	205	4,500	354
85	69	460	209	5,000	356
90	73	480	213	6,000	361
95	76	500	217	7,000	364
100	79	550	226	8,000	366
110	85	600	234	9,000	368
120	91	650	241	10,000	369
130	97	700	248	15,000	374
140	102	750	254	20,000	376
150	108	800	259	30,000	379
160	113	850	264	40,000	380
170	118	900	269	50,000	381
180	122	950	273	60,000	381
190	127	1,000	277	70,000	382
200	131	1,100	284	120,000	382
210	136	1,200	291	160,000	383
220	140	1,300	296	1,000,000	383

An additional planning consideration that the evaluator should address is to determine what *will be done with the results*. If the evaluation is aimed at determining if a program is to continue, for example, increasing the sample size or using several types of methods for data collection may be needed to ensure that the findings are based on good information. If the program is very expensive, the evaluation may need to be expanded to include a ROI analysis, to determine whether the expense of the program is warranted.

Also consider the *timing of the evaluation*. If an organization is trying a new media type or changing a learning philosophy, for example, performance evaluations can be very useful to determine which type of media or philosophy is the best with which to go forward.

Once the evaluator has planned the job performance evaluation, it is a good idea to develop a measurement plan or a data collection strategy to which the program task force (to include the client or stakeholder) agrees. Figure 7-1 offers a sample format for a plan.

In addition to these sections, the plan also provides a table that plots the objectives, evaluation method, timing, and responsibilities for each type of data collection and analysis. Phillips (1997) calls it an "Evaluation Plan: Data Collection Table."

It is important to take the time to do this tactical data collection-planning and prepare this document for several reasons:

1. It forces the evaluator to clearly and distinctly think out how the evaluation will be conducted.
2. Even though the plan may be negotiated in general terms with the client, the document provides them the opportunity to review the plan in detail and prepare the field for the evaluation.
3. It ensures everyone's schedules are coordinated.
4. Usually, several months pass before the field assessment is actually conducted, and it's amazing how, with shifting priorities, specific plans are forgotten.
5. It serves as a good source of accountability.

The plan becomes part of the overall program plan the task force developed for the program. It is recommended that the development of this plan begin before the program begins, when there is time to design the evaluation. It is only then that control groups, for example, can be set aside for evaluation purposes.

WHEN TO MEASURE JOB PERFORMANCE

There are three general types of experimental designs for measuring job performance.

1.0 Introduction or Background

This paragraph or two provides a brief program description along with the business objectives for the program. It describes who the program participants are and how their job functions relate to the business objectives. It also discusses the purpose for the evaluation.

2.0 Evaluation Objectives

This section describes the business, performance, and learning objectives. If an objective map has been completed, it is provided here. If not, the objectives are listed.

3.0 Methodology

This section describes the methodology that will be used to collect the data. It can be divided into the following subparagraphs:

    3.1 Reaction Data. *If reaction data are collected for this program, this section describes what tool was used and how the data will be used for the evaluation.*

    3.2 Learning Data. *If learning data are collected, this section describes the measurement tool used and how the data will be used in the evaluation.*

    3.3 Job Performance Data. *This paragraph describes in detail how job performance data will be collected and the tools that will be used for data collection. If a questionnaire or observation checklist is being described and has been developed at this point, it would be a good idea to include it in the appendix to the plan.*

Note: If the evaluation includes a business impact assessment, such as an ROI, an additional paragraph prior to 3.5 would include the following:

    3.4 Business Impact Data. *This describes the business metrics that will be collected and how they will be collected. If the plan is to conduct an ROI analysis or cost-benefit analysis, the formula and the cost data that will be used are provided.*

    3.5 Analysis. *This paragraph briefly discusses the type of analysis that will be conducted using the data. It is not necessary to discuss the statistical tests that will be run unless it is important to understand the rationale for the analysis.*

4.0 Schedule

This section provides the schedule for the data collection. If different sites are to be used, the dates as they relate to the collection times for each site are provided.

5.0 Documentation of Results

This section provides a description of how the data will be presented. For example, it might say a Final Report and an Executive Briefing.

Figure 7-1. Sample measurement plan format and paragraph descriptions.

1. The *one-shot program evaluation* is one in which the measurement is made at some point after the intervention. The one-shot program evaluation is appropriate when it is assumed little or no skills or knowledge existed prior to the program, such as initial training.

2. The *before-and-after program evaluation* is one in which the same measurement is made before the event and then at some point after the event. The before-and-after program evaluation

is used when seeking to measure a change in behavior as a result of the program. This is useful when the client organization knows that little is happening to the participants between the measurements, other than the program.

3. The *control versus experimental group program evaluation* is one in which measurement is made in either of the two cases listed but the data are gathered from a group that went through the program and a group that is identical in every way, except that they did not go through the program. The control-versus-experimental-group is the method to strive for, because it is the most effective way to isolate the impact of the program from anything else that is happening in the environment that may also be impacting behavior or performance. When using control groups, the evaluator takes care to ensure that the control group is not demoralized during the assessment because they believe they are being deprived of something (Gordon 1994). Using the control versus experimental group design requires that the evaluator be involved early in program planning, so that a group is set aside to serve as the control group.

When selecting the post-program evaluation design, there is no hard and fast rule for when to measure performance on the job following an intervention program. In the planning phases, when completing the objective map, for example, seek guidance from the group that is designing the training. Ask them when they would expect to see performance impacted. Consider the enablers or barriers to transfer. Consider the performance objectives. If measuring motor skills, for example, expected transference may be expected almost immediately after the program, particularly if all the enablers (such as systems, coaching, and so on) are in place and enough practice was given during the program itself. Research shows, as a matter of fact, that, if these types of skills are not used quickly, the likelihood of them being used is reduced significantly (Broad and Newstrom 1992). But there may be situations when the participant may need more time to practice the new skill and adjust to the support systems available on the job. If measuring knowledge application or the difference in behaviors due to attitude change, determine how long it is expected to take to transfer the knowledge or attitude change to specific behaviors. Normally, after three months, things have settled down to a point at which the behavior they are demonstrating can be expected to continue.

Central Electric Corporation developed an employee development program as one way to improve market share and shift from the old profile of command and control to an organization of people knowledgeable about business (Whalen 1999). The company believed that they needed to do this to reduce costs and to improve profit contribution. This would allow them to adjust to a very stiff competition and tight government regulations where there is little room to maneuver pricing. One method they used to measure the effectiveness of the program was to administer a follow-up questionnaire one month after the training course because they felt that would be an appropriate timeframe in which to determine the application of skills. Further investigation revealed that they chose this time frame because the skills they were learning in the training were to teach them how to more efficiently conduct the functions that were already part of their job. So, because they were not learning "new" tasks, they believed one month was more than sufficient to see a difference. In this case they also used a before-and-after measure.

HOW TO MEASURE JOB PERFORMANCE

Phillips (1997) offers the following list as appropriate post-program data collection methods for measuring job performance:

- Follow-up surveys
- Follow-up questionnaires
- Observation on the job
- Interviews with participants
- Follow-up focus groups
- Program assignments
- Action planning
- Performance contracting
- Program follow-up sessions

Selecting which method to use will depend on the type of data needed and the organizational situation with which the evaluator is faced.

Follow-up Surveys

Follow-up surveys are useful for measuring the extent to which attitudes, beliefs, and opinions have "stuck" following a program. Although it is recommended that program planners state program objectives in behavioral language based on the performance desired, there are times when management feels "comfortable" that if the attitudes or opinions are changed or developed, good things will follow. They may base this feeling on historical data or on their own business intuition.

Follow-up Questionnaires

Follow-up questionnaires (sometimes called *surveys*) gather the participant, peer, or supervisor perceptions of the effectiveness of the program. This is the most widely used method of data collection, probably because it is the most convenient to use. Most evaluations aim to gather "hard" data, such as output, time, costs, and quality (Phillips 1996) because it is indisputable. But alas, hard data can be elusive. Often company databases do not exist, and if they do, they may not tie results to individuals. So many have found that they need to rely on perception data.

Because the perception measures are not based in fact, they should be considered as indicator measures, rather than actual measures (Swanson and Holton 1999). Recently, however, many evaluators have experimented with perception data-gathering techniques and have found that they can use follow-up questionnaires effectively and feel comfortable with the results. Consider using them in addition to any other type of method used for data collection, as questionnaires can provide useful information. For example, when examining the performance data for the individuals participating in the program, the program evaluator discovers groups of data that vary by region; the questionnaires can provide clues for the reason(s) for that difference. Did the participants in that region feel that their supervisors did, or did not, reinforce their learning? Were there different expectations from the supervisors in that region? Did the participants in that region perceive their training provided them with fewer or more skills than the other regions? These are all questions that the evaluator can anticipate by working with the field personnel or other knowledgeable sources and develop questions that pertain to them. Careful planning allows the evaluator the opportunity to gain rich insights from follow-up questionnaires.

Tips for Planning a Follow-up Questionnaire

1. Determine the type of data needed. These data are linked to the business and performance objectives.

2. Involve management in the process. Develop a draft survey for the client to review.
3. Select the type(s) of questions appropriate for the required information. Objective, closed-ended questions are best, because they "force" the participant to consider the question content and make for easier data analysis.
4. Check the reading level of those surveyed. Many questionnaires fall down on this one.
5. Test the questions. This is a good way to determine if the reading level is right, the terminology is appropriate, and whether the questions can be understood. Select two people from the audience that will be surveyed to test the questionnaire.

Once planned, design the questionnaire to ensure that the participants can provide their most accurate perceptions. Also make sure that the questionnaire is designed so that it can be scored easily and recorded for easy analysis. Avoid duplicate effort, for example, by recording the data in a spreadsheet such as Microsoft Excel or SPSS, that can be used for computer calculations. Use open-ended questions very selectively but always offer an "other" category for questions where all the possible choices are not known. If there is little or no data from the "other" category, it means the questionnaire has adequately anticipated what the participant might select.

Tips for Designing a Follow-up Questionnaire

1. Always keep the questionnaires as brief as possible to ensure participants will complete them. Make sure that every question is necessary and that you can do something with the data from each question.
2. Develop the appropriate questions. Many of the rules that we discussed in test construction apply here. Make the questions clear and concise, make sure each question addresses only one issue, and be sure that the terminology used is understandable to the respondents.
3. Make the questionnaires attractive and professional looking. Use multiple colors (Phillips 2003). If using colors is too expensive, consider shading, bolding, or strategic grouping of questions.
4. Develop the questionnaire to be appropriate for the audience. Some audiences can respond to more sophisticated surveys than others.

5. Design questions so that the participant can give the "degree" or "extent" to which they agree or disagree with the statement or the "degree" or "extent" to which they believe the behavior has taken place. Make sure that the scale for this is laid out very clearly on the page so that the respondent can quickly and accurately provide his or her estimates.
6. Make sure the questions are tied directly to the performance objectives.
7. Provide clear directions for the completion of the questionnaire.
8. Stress to the respondents the importance of their response in the cover letter or advance communication and explain how the data will be used. Consider having a person sign the cover letter or advance communication who the respondents know to be important to their organization.

Look carefully at the results from your questionnaires. How people are responding will demonstrate whether they understand the questions and the scale. For example, if all or most of the checks made are the same on the scale used, the questions or the design of the questionnaire are not helping the respondent distinguish their answers from one another. But if the checks vary from one question to the next, it indicates that the respondents are considering each question. Experiment until a format is found that works well. Appendix B has several different examples of surveys that practitioners have used successfully.

Achieving an adequate *response rate* is often an area of difficulty in collecting job performance data using questionnaires at most organizations. The goal is to get as many of those questionnaires back as possible to increase the sample size. Following are some suggestions for increasing your response rate.

Tips for Increasing Questionnaire Response Rate

1. Have the client prepare the participants in advance for receiving the questionnaire. Have them tell the participants the reason for, and importance of, their response. An electronic mail (email) message sent to each participant a few days prior to their receiving the questionnaire may work well.
2. Prepare a cover letter for the questionnaire that clearly describes the purpose for the study and the importance of their participant's response. Have an executive sign the letter.

3. Provide an addressed return envelope for paper questionnaires.
4. Use an email process if you know that your participants all review their email daily. If you use this process, make sure the process for completing the online questionnaire is very simple (Shneiderman 1992).
5. Make sure that, regardless of the method used, anonymity is ensured. Although it would be helpful to have the managers distribute the questionnaire to indicate its importance, do not have them collect the questionnaires. Make it clear in the cover letter or email message that an unbiased evaluation specialist is the only one who will see the individual questionnaires and that the results will be aggregated.
6. Keep the questionnaire as brief and simple as possible.
7. If you can, ensure that the participants will see the final results. Let them know they can expect to see a report of the results when completed.
8. Send follow-up reminders or call the supervisors or managers and ask them to remind the participants to complete the questionnaire. Be prepared to send additional questionnaires for those who have "lost" their original one.
9. If possible, visit the site, distribute the questionnaire, explain the purpose for, and importance of, it and collect them when completed. This is a good way to get a 100-percent return-rate (a great day in the life of an evaluator!).
10. There is no historical data to show that incentives really increase response rates. And it may not be feasible for you to use incentives in your organization, but you may want to experiment with different types of incentives such as a small gift or a guilt dollar.

Experiment with different ideas to see what will work best within your own organization.

Observations on the Job

Observations on the job are an excellent method for determining the extent to which behaviors are taking place and the extent to which they are manifested correctly. This method is used when the *performance objectives* are those that can be clearly observed and can be separated from other aspects of the job.

Many of the rules outlined in the "Performance-Based Tests" section in chapter 3 apply here. The same issues of *inter-rater reliability*, for example, apply if more than one observer is used. But, unlike measuring learning using observation, when measuring performance on the job using observation, the participant and the observer are in the real work environment. Unlike measuring learning in a contrived situation, it is impossible to control the real work environment, so many factors may be contributing to the observed performance—factors that may have nothing to do with the observed skill level. Select a sample group to observe based on criteria that may impact their performance. For example, ensure that the group selected for observation contains an equal number of low-, medium-, and high-performers according to that job function's existing performance evaluation criteria. Or ensure the group contains an equal number of people from different offices or regions or an equal number of people with different years on the job. Be careful not to include any unnecessary criteria, as it will be difficult enough for the field to get these groups together for observation.

Many times, the trainers or facilitators of the interventions are selected to be the observers because they understand the tasks to be observed so well. The risk in doing this is that it is often difficult for the trainers or facilitators to be objective in their observation because they will want so badly for the people to do well and may score too leniently. On the other hand, someone who is unbiased may not understand the skills to be observed as well and will need to be trained. It's a trade-off. It is often easier to train an unbiased observer in the skills than to train a subject matter expert to be unbiased. Know the risks and plan for them. Develop an observation tool that is clear and concise and follows the rules of the behavioral checklist in chapter 3. Practice using the tool and prepare the field.

Pay particular attention to the line managers or field team leaders—prepare them for the observation. Be sure to explain to them the benefits of the study and assure them that the observers will take precautions to be nonintrusive. Consider bringing gifts to those being observed and the supervisors on the day of observation, if it does not compromise the professionalism of the observations. A show of appreciation almost always ensures cooperation.

Preparation for this type of measurement is critical. Some guidelines to use when preparing for observation are offered.

Tips for Observation Preparation

1. Make sure the behaviors measured are linked directly to the performance objectives and that all of the objectives are included.
2. Test the observation tool for reliability.
3. Train those who will conduct the observation and pilot the tool.
4. Brief the site(s) selected for observation completely as to the purpose, schedule, and method for observation. Ensure there is an on-site supervisor to support the observation event.
5. Select the sample group that will be observed so they represent the population.
6. Ask the participants selected for observation their permission to be observed and make sure they understand completely the purpose of the observation. Ensure them that their data will be reported as a group and not individually.
7. Set up the schedule for observation, so that the times do not coincide with other company initiatives, which may influence behavior unusually, for example, incentive programs, lay-offs, and so on.
8. Set up the schedule to account for vacation and holiday schedules.
9. Consider telling participants at the end of the actual intervention program that observations will be conducted on the job in X number of months to see how the skills they have learned actually transfer to the job.
10. Tell the participants and the supervisors that the results of the evaluation will be shared with them. And make sure that happens.

When conducting the observation, take all the precautions possible to reduce anything that would change the employee's behavior or performance from what would normally occur on the job. It is not necessarily fun to be observed, and although the participants are told that it is the program that is being rated, not their performance, it will be difficult for them to shed the feeling of being judged. The goal is to have the person perform as he or she normally would. It may be helpful to spend some time with the participants to establish a level of rapport prior to the observations, but that will depend on the style of the observer.

Hartford Life Insurance Company used observation as part of an evaluation study to assess a professional development project (Kehrhahn, Pedersen, and Kite 1999). New roles were being taught to participants in the project. The participant-observer strategy was to have the professor and the evaluators participate with teams and record copious observational notes on pilot project work, phone conversations, and email exchanges to see the extent to which they tackled follow-up assignments. In some cases, they used the delayed-report method in which they participated in the meeting and wrote down observations and interpretations afterward. This method is somewhat risky, because there is room for subjectivity and data-recording inaccuracy. But they used this observational data successfully *along with* actual workplace documents that demonstrated the team's work.

Remember, when selecting observation as the strategy for gathering job performance data, that there may be some unobservable benefits of the program that are tied to the performance objectives, such as an increase in understanding or change in attitude. So using a follow-up questionnaire in addition to the observations may be helpful. In addition to careful observation planning, consider the following tips for conducting observations.

Tips for Conducting Observations on the Job

1. Show up for the observations on the exact day and time arranged.
2. Be as inobtrusive as possible—try to disappear into the woodwork.
3. Reassure the participants at the beginning of the observation if they express concern.
4. Maintain a pleasant demeanor. Make sure facial and body movements do not convey anything except neutrality. Make sure verbal comments or "noises" are kept to a minimum so as to avoid distraction. Remember, the goal is to capture what *normally* happens.
5. Under no circumstances (except in a situation involving personnel safety) interfere with the employee's activities.
6. Always thank the employee after the observation if it does not interfere with their functions.

Follow-up Focus Groups

Follow-up focus groups can be particularly valuable when attempting to gather constructive data, such as ways to improve a program. The participants motivate one another and "feed off" each other's suggestions. But focus groups can be limiting when trying to gather actual performance data. And it can be difficult to identify and get a homogeneous sample that the supervisors are willing to pull off the job at the same time.

Tips for Conducting Focus Groups

1. Make sure that the focus group facilitator is trained as a facilitator.
2. Carefully plan leading and follow-up questions, so that all necessary data are collected.
3. Make sure the participants are there voluntarily.
4. Record all comments accurately.
5. If using a tape recorder, make sure to get the participants' permission before using it.
6. If notes are taken, make sure someone other than the facilitator takes notes and make sure that the recorder is someone who will not inhibit discussion by his or her presence (such as the participants' supervisor).
7. If notes are taken, make sure the recorder is unbiased and non-intrusive during the session.
8. Keep the group small, but make sure it is a representative sample of the program's participants.

Kehrhahn, Pederson, and Kite (1999) used focus groups successfully, in addition to observation, for evaluating the Hartford Life Insurance training project. The participants were asked about the learning experience and how they were using what they were learning. Themes and comments were recorded. Focus groups were used in addition to action planning to evaluate executive education programs at AT&T (Fawson 1999). The goal was to determine cause-and-effect relationships. Appendix C offers a focus group checklist and a template for recording focus group comments.

Interviews

Interviews are a versatile method for collecting post-program data. They can be conducted with different participants, supervisors, peers, or the program's stakeholders. They can be conducted in person or over the phone, although in-person interviews are recommended whenever possible. In-person interviews allow the evaluator to obtain large amounts of data, perform in-depth probing, and ask more complicated or sensitive questions (O'Sullivan and Rassel 1999). People tend to consider questions more carefully when they are face to face with the interviewer, knowing that the interviewer is taking the time (and using resources) to visit their site to conduct the interview. In addition, it is easier to ask better follow-up questions when the interviewer can see the interviewee's facial expressions or other nonverbal language. Sometimes interviewees provide more information than they would over the phone, information that is perhaps confidential or negative. However, there are times when cost or time constraints prohibit in-person interviews, and phone interviews have to suffice.

Try a combination of structured and unstructured interview processes (O'Sullivan and Rassel 1999). Prepare standard questions, but have follow-up questions prepared, depending on the answers given. If using this approach, ensure the interviewer is trained in active listening skills and able to accurately collect the information. The following tips for conducting interviews are offered.

Tips for Conducting Interviews

1. Keep the interview situation as private as possible.
2. Put the respondent at ease, using a relaxed and natural conversational style.
3. Assure the respondent that all information will be kept confidential. One way to do this is to assume the policy that general results will be available to management and other relevant personnel, but no data will be associated with any one particular person.
4. Treat the respondent with respect, and be courteous, tactful, and nonjudgmental. Your job is to elicit the interviewee's ideas, not change them.
5. Dress and act professionally but in a way that is appropriate for the interview situation. For example, a formal interview style and attire may be appropriate for an executive interview, but a more casual interview style and attire may be best when interviewing someone working in the field. Ensuring that those being interviewed are at ease with the interviewer's presence is important, so they are forthcoming in their responses.

6. Ask the questions in their proper sequence, in the order written. Although flexibility is required, make sure that the conversation follows the predetermined content sequence as much as possible to ensure everything is covered and the respondent does not lose relevant thoughts.
7. Do not assume the answer to any question or answer questions for the respondent.
8. Use good active listening skills. For example, use positive words such as "yes," "I see," and so on, to encourage responses. Use nonverbal encouragement, such as nodding of the head, to indicate that their response is understood.
9. Do not allow respondents to fall into a mode of complaining or use this as an opportunity to air all of their unrelated problems. Stay on track and remain focused.

An example of a structured interview is a Return on Expectation (ROE) interview (Hodges 1998), where program stakeholders are interviewed as part of an evaluation. This process was used successfully at Bell Atlantic for many evaluations. They were used regardless of other methods of data collection. The stakeholders are normally executives, but the process can be useful with supervisors as well. The process is outlined below.

Step 1: Call the interviewee to explain the purpose for the interview and to ask permission to conduct it. Explain that the interview will not last longer than twenty minutes.

Step 2: Set up a date and time convenient for the interviewee.

Step 3: Fax or email the person a copy of the questions that will be asked in the interview.

Step 4: Ask if you can tape record the interview. This allows the interviewer the freedom to pay attention to the discussion and not have to take notes. Also, the data will be more accurate.

Step 5: Conduct the interview using the structured questions and appropriate follow-up questions.

Step 6: Thank the interviewee for his or her time and assure the person that the data provided is very valuable (and it always is).

This method of data collection is successful when used for interviewing executives, partly because the people selected for the interviews are used to talking about bottom-line results and appreciate being asked about them. In fact, it can have the added benefit of demonstrating to stakeholders the importance the HRD group places on measurement and that HRD programs are supposed to be linked to bottom-line results. This process can also provide data to support the additional data collected from the field and serve as the basis for an ROI calculation. Table 7-2 provides the questions that were used for ROE interviews at Bell Atlantic.

Again, ensure that the person conducting the interview has facilitation skills and treats the situation very professionally.

Performance Monitoring

Performance Monitoring is the preferable method of data collection because real or "hard" outcomes, rather than perceived or predicted outcomes, are measured. Examples of hard data are output, time, quality, costs, and customer satisfaction (Phillips 1997). Many organizations have this data in existing company databases. For an evaluation effort with Central Electric Corporation (Whalen 1999), the evaluator reviewed payments made on customer claims for faulty services three months before and three months after the training. This tracking was considered the crucial business measure and management's biggest concern for the project. It was felt that, if the performance objectives for the training were met, a reduction in faulty services would be seen.

Determine in the evaluation planning if such databases exist and if they track the data to individuals, because in most cases a sample group of participants will be used, not the entire population. At Bell Atlantic (Hodges 1997), central office technicians were trained to better diagnose the problem calls that they receive. One of the business expectations for the training was to reduce the number of unnecessary field technicians sent out to repair calls due to misdiagnosed problems. The field had a dollar amount that they associated with each field call. The data collection plan was to measure the number of misdiagnosed calls that resulted in sending out field technicians incorrectly, requiring a repeat visit by the technician (a repeat call), resulting in additional cost to the company. Although the company database tracked which Central Office Technician sent the field technician out the second time (the repeat call), it did not track it back to the Central Office Technician who misdiagnosed the call originally. So there was no way to find out how often the calls were misdiagnosed by the people who had gone through the training. In this case, the data collection plan had to be changed to rely on a follow-up

Table 7-2
Sample Questions for an ROE Interview

Question	Guidance
1. What were your expectations for this training or intervention?	You may need to assist in adjusting these to be concrete goals. For example, they may provide two expectations in one statement so you may need to rephrase to divide them. Make sure to get their concurrence with your rephrasing.
2. Have any of your expectations changed since you first came to the training department (or performance consultant or whomever)? If so, how?	Ask them this for each expectation you noted.
3. Are you aware of any behavior changes that have occurred as a result of the training or intervention?	Try to tie these to each expectation listed.
4. Are you aware of any financial benefits that have been derived as a result of the training or intervention? If so, would you explain what they are and an estimate of the dollar amount?	Here is where your probing may help. You may offer some suggestions to trigger their thinking, but never put words into their mouth. Be prepared with examples.
5. To what degree (0–100 percent) were your expectations met?	Remind them of each expectation they listed for question 1.
6. Of those rated below 80 percent in question 5, do you know what the problems were?	Just ask them this for those estimates that are under 80 percent. If none, then proceed to the next question.
7. Would you come to our organization for similar program needs?	If they say no, and the reason is not obvious from their answers to the questions above, follow-up with questions asking for the reason, but do not push if they seem reluctant to provide a reason.

questionnaire to get the trainees' perceptions of the reduction in the number of repeat calls due to training.

Blocks of data may exist, so sample group performance can be tracked. For example, if the program was implemented in only one region, the data for the performers in that region as a whole (average percent performance) can be used to compare with data for performers in a different region as a whole (average percent performance.)

Sometimes, a temporary performance monitoring system can be created just for the evaluation. For example, "spot checking" sales data on individuals may be feasible. Or the evaluator could request that the supervisors look at or record other individual performances, such as the time individuals are spending on activities. But use existing databases wherever feasible. Do not hesitate to seek out those database people. It is a mistake to assume that these folks will resent being asked for data or for the time to put some reports together for the evaluation. Usually, they will be happy to share "their" data. This is their world, and they are normally pleased someone is going to find good use for their data.

Action Planning

Action planning can be a powerful evaluation method for collecting job performance data. Practitioners are using this method very successfully. The goal for an action plan is to involve the program participant in setting specific and measurable goals for themselves (and perhaps others they associate with) to complete once they leave the training. As explained in chapter 3, the ability for the participants to set the goals and complete the plan may indeed be an indication that they have met the learning objectives. The focus here is on how to set up and carry out an action plan for collecting performance data.

There are three general components of an action plan:

- The goals to be completed
- The dates in which each needs to be completed
- The person responsible for the completion

Apple Computer implemented an action plan process when evaluating a train-the-trainer initiative to promote structured on-the-job training (Burkett 1997). The training consultant and the managers monitored and measured on-the-job behavior change. In the action plan, each participant targeted behavioral objectives and improvement measures that were linked to the training objectives, which were linked to the training program. They also estimated the potential cost-benefits to their unit by applying select skills over a 30-day period after the training. A 30-day follow-up questionnaire was also used to determine the extent to which participants utilized their action plan or experienced barriers in their planned application of skills or knowledge. The action plan used in this case can be found in Appendix A. The follow-up questionnaire used can be found in Appendix B.

Central Electric Corporation used the action-planning process successfully while evaluating the effectiveness of a technical training program for marketing and customer service consultants (Whalen 1997.) The action-planning document asked participants to identify the action steps they would apply when they returned to the work environment. The plans were to facilitate post-training discussion for the managers and marketing consultant to establish performance expectations and necessary improvements. And then with a follow-up questionnaire the participants were asked the extent to which their plans were complete. Appendix A provides the action plan template used for this program. Appendix B provides the follow-up questionnaire used.

Another example of the successful use of action planning is an evaluation conducted for a worldwide pharmaceutical company where a training program was initiated to improve the sales force in essential selling skills as part of a promotional program (Stone 1999.) The action plan used both enhanced the transfer of learning and enabled collection of evaluation data. It required participants to track progress and collect performance data for a six-month period following the training. Like the previous two examples, a follow-up questionnaire was used to determine the extent to which participants used the training and achieved on-the-job success. Appendix A provides the action plan document, and Appendix B provides the follow-up questionnaire used in this case.

Bell Atlantic used action planning for a mentoring program wherein mentors and their proteges needed to sit down and determine what the goals for their mentoring relationship were going to be and what actions each needed to take to meet those goals. Deadlines were established and the results were tracked. The evaluation strategy was to collect copies of the action plans at periodic points during the year. Appendix A provides the action plan used for this evaluation.

These four examples demonstrate the various ways action plans can be used for evaluation. It is important, when using action planning, that the evaluator is involved at the design phase of the intervention program, so that its design is linked to the performance objectives and incorporated into the program as part of the program or course offering. The program facilitator may need to be trained to guide participants to use the action plans. An added benefit of the action-planning process is that it gets participants actively involved in their learning. They leave the learning event with the *understanding* of the performance that is expected of them on the job and with a *sense of confidence* that they will apply what they learned. The may even know the kind of support they need and the time in which they will be expected to perform. Action planning can be powerful in helping the learner become an integral part of the learning and performance experience. It is an excellent tool to ensure transfer.

Tips for Using Action Planning

1. Educate your program design group and the facilitators on the value of action planning. Provide examples of cases that have successfully used the action-planning process, such as those provided above.
2. Volunteer to help them design the action plan document.
3. Educate the facilitators on how to implement the action plan within their sessions. Phillips (1997) recommends that the facilitators approve the plans before they are put into the design.
4. If measuring for business impact as well as performance transfer, make that measurement part of the action plan. If not measuring for business impact, leave those elements off the action plan.
5. If the action plan requires cooperation from the participants' field environment, provide some type of communication to them and explain their role.
6. If possible, review the action plan with the participants at the time indicated for action completion.

Follow-up Assignments

A cousin to the action-planning process is follow-up assignments. If tasks were assigned during or at the end of the program, the evaluator simply needs to follow up to see if the assignments were completed and the extent to which they were completed successfully. Again, important here is to link the assignments directly to the program objectives.

Performance Contracts

Performance contracts are particularly useful in that they not only provide performance data but also imply by their nature an active supervisor involvement in assisting the participant to successfully apply the knowledge/skills taught during the program. They are an excellent tool for transfer. An example performance contract is provided in chapter 6.

CASE STUDIES IN PROGRESS

Different tools are available for the evaluator to measure job performance. Finding the appropriate tool and applying it correctly is a critical component for measuring job performance. Let's look at some job performance measurement techniques that are selected for the three case studies in progress.

Technical Training Program

The Technical Training Program is a multimedia online program that teaches warehouse employees driving and operational warehouse safety skills. The performance behaviors that are being measured for this program are those performance objectives listed in the technical training objective map in chapter 2.

To determine the extent to which the participants in the training program met the performance objectives, the supervisors in the warehouses will observe the warehouse employees. Fortunately, the evaluation team was able to work with the client prior to the training program implementation, which afforded the opportunity to establish a control group. The warehouse supervisors designate one-half of their employees to be given the online training program before the other half. The half given the training serves as the *experimental group*, and the half not given the training serves as the *control group*. The supervisor assigns the same number of low-, medium-, and high-performers to each group. The experimental group is sent to a nearby performance lab that has computers for the participants to access the online training program. Everything else except the training remains the same for both groups. As mentioned in the beginning of this chapter, the experimental versus control group is the best method to isolate the effects of the program versus anything else that may be impacting performance. There are two risks encountered in the design of this evaluation method for this program. One is that there is no way to hide the fact that one group is receiving training and one group is not, because the employees converse on a daily basis. This knowledge might engender hard feelings among those in the control group because they may feel that they are being deprived. This could impact their job performance. To mitigate this risk, the control group is told that they will be receiving the training shortly—that only a certain number of computers are available in the performance lab. And although there is some amount of "attitude adjustment" to the training, particularly for the driving objective, most of the training is geared to skill development. So, although the control group may try to be on their best behavior, they won't have (or even know) the skills taught in the training. The second risk that may compromise the evaluation is that the supervisor who is conducting the observations may be either biased in favor of the experimental group, expecting to see changed behavior, or biased for or against certain of his employees. To help mitigate this risk, a performance log is developed for the supervisor to use to gather the performance data. This will help the supervisor maintain objectivity. In addition, the purpose for the evaluation is explained to the supervisor and the importance of their maintaining objectivity is emphasized. The performance log is developed with the supervisor's input, which also gains buy-in. This input also ensures the log is realistic to the job and that the supervisor is able to complete the log. Inter-rater reliability is not an issue because the same person will be observing for everyone. Take a look at the log developed for measuring the performance objectives in Figure 7-2.

The ride rating noted on the log is based on the score received using an established checklist currently used for weekly rides that the supervisor takes with each employee. The checklist lists those behaviors on the objective map that are linked to the driving business objective.

The log is completed for each employee for each week during the observation period. The observation period begins one month after the experimental group has completed training because the subject matter experts believe that this is enough time for the new behaviors to "settle in." The observations continue for six weeks. After the evaluation period, the control group is sent to the performance lab to receive their training. If it were not too intrusive to the field, data could also be collected for the control group to provide a before-and-after evaluation effort. This would provide additional data to support the evaluation effort. But it probably would be asking too much of the supervisor to do this.

The logs are turned in to the evaluation group at the end of the observation period. When completing the objective map, it was determined that the driving objective, "Reduce motor vehicle accidents," costs the

Warehouse Employee Performance Log

Employee _____

Week _____

Rating received on weekly ride evaluation _____

Performance	Rating	
	Yes	No
1. Lifts objects properly		
2. Maintains correct posture when using the computer		
3. Wears goggles and gloves when handling hazardous materials		
4. Wears gloves when handling boxes over approximately 20 lbs.		
5. Wears steel-toe shoes		
6. Drives forklift slowly (less than 1 mile/hour)		
7. Inspects forklift prior to operation each day		
8. Does not exceed height and weight restrictions while using forklift		
9. Places loads evenly while using forklift		
10. Completes customer invoices with correct product type, quantity, and prices		
11. Competes customer orders correctly		
12. Load trucks for transport with correct shipment		

Figure 7-2. Technical training program warehouse log.

company a great deal of money. Because of that and because employee and other car inhabitants' safety is critical to the company, those performance objectives mapped to this objective were worth approximately one-half the value of the entire program. Therefore the following scoring procedure is established.

Riding Observation:
0% = 0 points
1–10% = 1 point
11–20% = 2 points
21–30% = 3 points
31–40% = 4 points
41–50% = 5 points
51–60% = 6 points
61–70% = 7 points
71–80% = 8 points
81–90% = 9 points
91–100% = 10 points

Behaviors 1 through 12 = 1 point each.

Just as when the learning-data was scored, more points are given to those tasks that are more critical or required more frequently. All parties agree upon the scoring strategy prior to the observations.

The planning for the performance evaluation of the technical training program is now complete. The method to evaluate learning has been determined (chapter 3) and the enablers and barriers for meeting the performance and learning objectives have been predicted (chapter 6), so the objective map is now completed (see Figure 7-3).

Sales/Customer Service Training Program

The Sales/Customer Service Training Program case study is targeted for sales/customer service representatives. The program is intended to teach the representatives to conduct effective customer service calls by following established protocol for customer calls. The job performance behaviors measured are those listed on the Sales/Customer Service Training Program objective map (chapter 2).

A *before-and-after* experimental design is used for measuring job performance for this program. The observation checklist used for the learning evaluation is slightly modified to use as the job performance measurement tool. Figure 7-4 is the checklist that will be used.

The difference between this checklist and the one used for measuring learning is that an "NA" category has been added. In the training program, simulated scenarios were created where the checklist was used. But in the real environment, not every call affords the participant the opportunity to display each behavior.

Two evaluation specialists are trained by the trainers to use this tool. The trainers share the criteria they used when using the tool, and the evaluation specialists practice with the simulated scenarios used in the class. They practice by both observing the same person and scoring the calls. They compare their scores and discuss differences each has. They continue to do this until they have the same scores on five consecutive calls. This ensures inter-rater reliability.

The field supervisors and those being observed are told what to expect from the observations and the importance of the evaluation. It is emphasized to those being observed that the purpose for the evaluation is not to evaluate their performance, but rather

Business Objectives	Metrics	Enablers/ Barriers	Performance Objectives	Measurement Methodology	Enablers/ Barriers	Learning Objectives	Measurement Methodology	Enablers/ Barriers
1. Save 80 percent of cost due to reduction in motor vehicle accidents.	Reduced motor vehicle accident reports. Associated cost savings.	Barrier: learner readiness. Enabler: promised rewards.	1a. Use safety belt consistently. 1b. Locate blind spots. 1c. Follow defined defensive driving procedures. 1d. Maintain safe following distance. 1e. Use headlights and wipers as defined. 1f. Follow railroad-crossing rules. 1g. Follow correct rules for adverse driving conditions. 1h. Follow safe passing procedures.	Control-versus-experimental program evaluation design. Weekly ride observations.	Barrier: motivation to transfer. Enabler: rewards and incentives offered.	1a1. and 1c.1. Identify the safety devices that can protect you and your passengers in collisions. 1a2. Describe why you should wear your safety belt. 1b1. Locate blind spots. 1d1. Estimate average stopping distance. 1d2. State the rules for following distances. 1e1. and 1g1. Identify the conditions of driving and spot the hazards for each condition. 1e2. and 1g2. Identify a defensive strategy for each adverse condition. 1f1. Identify how to avoid collisions with trains. 1h1. Identify the conditions upon which a pass is safe, legal, and necessary. 1h2. Identify the three maneuvers for a safe pass.	Online practicums.	Barrier: learner readiness. Enabler: online delivery.

Figure 7-3. Completed technical training objective map.

Business Objectives	Metrics	Enablers/ Barriers	Performance Objectives	Measurement Methodology	Enablers/ Barriers	Learning Objectives	Measurement Methodology	Enablers/ Barriers
2. Reduce on-the-job accidents by 90 percent.	Cost savings due to medical treatment savings. Cost savings due to retained employees. Cost savings due to reduction in employee time off the job.	Barrier: learner readiness. Enabler: promised rewards.	2a. Lift objects properly. 2b. Maintain correct posture when using the computer. 2c. Wear goggles and gloves when handling hazardous materials. 2d. Wear gloves when handling boxes over 15 lbs. 2e. Wear steel-toe shoes. 2f. Drive forklift at proper defined speed. 2g. Inspect forklift prior to operation each day. 2h. Do not exceed defined height and weight restrictions while using forklift. 2i. Place load as directed properly while using forklift.	Warehouse performance observations using observation logs.	Barrier: resistance. openness to change. Enabler: job aids.	2a1. Identify some basic principles of ergonomics. 2a2. Identify correct movement and postures that will minimize stress while lifting and moving objects. 2a3. Identify the parts of the back. 2a4. Recognize the stress that lifting can put on the back. 2b1. Identify correct ergonomic postures and work practices. 2c1. Describe elements of the OSHA program for controlling exposure to asbestos. 2c2. Identify the two primary means of controlling lead exposure when working on a lead-sheathed cable. 2c3. Identify methods of controlling exposure and preventing creation of hazardous waste. 2c4. Identify the basic types of hazardous materials.		

Figure 7-3. Completed technical training objective map (Continued).

3. Improve customer satisfaction by 90 percent.	Reduction in customer complaints.		3a. Customer receives correct product type. 3b. Customer receives correct quantity of items. 3c. Customer receives order on time. 3d. Re-visits reduced.	Warehouse performance observations using observation logs.	2c5. Identify hazardous materials you are most likely to encounter. 2c6. Identify job tasks in which hazardous material exposure is likely. 2d1. & 2e1. List required safety gear. 2f1. Explain the operations of the forklift. 2g1. Define the pre-operation inspection of the forklift. 2h1. Define operator physical requirements for using forklift. 2i1. Describe load-handling techniques. 3a1. Describe how a client is billed for the purchase of an item. 3a2. & 3b1. & 3c1. Use each menu option (XXX system) in support of the normal functions of the storekeeper. 3a3. &3b2. Describe how a cycle count is conducted. 3b3. Describe how to conduct a system order entry. 3.b.4. Describe how to conduct a phone order entry. 3d. Prepare load for transport.

Figure 7-3. Completed technical training objective map (Continued).

Rating			Task ↓
Yes	No	N/A	**Opening the Call**
			Rate whether the following tasks were performed within the first five minutes of the call: This portion of the call focuses on listening for rep's ability to establish a positive rapport and *guide the call*.
			1. Greets the caller (e.g., Hello, Good morning, Welcome to company…)
			2. Introduces self (e.g., My name is Jane Doe)
			3. Uses enthusiastic tone of voice (friendly, positive, non-monotone voice—happy, upbeat, cheery, pleasant)
			4. Listens to customer without interrupting
			5. Conveys empathy through the use of at least one statement that acknowledges the difficulty the customer is having (e.g., that sounds like a pretty difficult situation you're in)
			6. Establishes self as a resource by assuring customer that rep can help with problem
			7. Avoids trying to diagnose or resolve problem before agreeing on a purpose for the call (e.g., asking diagnostic questions about specific problem, without setting up the purpose and priorities of the call first)
			8. Defines purpose of call (e.g., so what we need to do is get X, Y, and Z working again for you)
			9. Communicates what the initial plan will be (e.g., the first thing we'll need to do is…)
			10. Probes for agreement (e.g., How does that plan sound? Or rep's verbal behavior does not indicate that customer is arguing about the initial plan)
			Diagnosing Problems and Identifying Needs
			The goal of training was to teach the rep to actively learn what's been tried before, to understand timing issues, to check for changes, to communicate any observed patterns in the data, test any customer assumptions, consider any human factors issues, gain multiple perspectives by talking with more than one person about the problem, and discovering interrelationships. The more observable tasks are outlined below.

Figure 7-4. Sales/customer service observation checklist.

			11. Asks what has been tried before in resolving problem
			12. Asks about timing issues (e.g., when was that tried, how long ago was that?)
			13. Probes using both open and closed-ended questions
			14. Avoids using the word "but" when discussing issues with customer (e.g., but I thought that what you said was...)
			15. Asks at least one question that clarifies the issue
			16. Checks back with the customer to make sure rep understands issue/confirms to ensure understanding (e.g., so what you're saying is that...)
			Assessing Progress and Updating the Plan Skills focus on assessing progress and updating the plan, so that the customer knows where things stand and can keep others informed of status
			17. Explains to customer progress made (e.g., OK, we've done X, Y, Z)
			18. Reconfirms purpose/priorities (e.g., we're still working on X, and need to see if we can't get X completed)
			19. Updates the plan (e.g., Let's keep on working on this, or let's try Y)
			20. Probes for agreement (e.g., How does that plan sound? Or observation of rep indicates that customer is not arguing to change the plan)
			Recommending Approaches for Results After rep explains his/her perspective, rep gains the customer's perspective, and then recommends an approach for solving or preventing the problem and meeting the need
			21. Explains to customer why rep is making the observation they are about to make (e.g., Given what you've told me about X,Y, and Z...)
			22. Explains observations (e.g., I've noticed that...)
			23. Asks for customer's perspective
			24. Makes recommendation after achieving shared perspective
			25. Probes for agreement

Figure 7-4. Sales/customer service observation checklist (Continued).

			Closes the Call
			Rep is focused on conveying the value of what has been accomplished and identifying follow-up actions
			26. Summarizes call (e.g., what was initial problem, steps taken, agreed upon action, current status, additional steps)
			27. Uses "we"-language when summarizing call
			28. Probes for agreement
			29. Communicates any follow-up steps that need to be taken
			30. Probe for agreement on any follow-up steps (e.g., Ok, I'll do X and you'll do Y.)
			Overall Listening Skills
			This section focuses on active and empathic listening skills
			31. Displays patience (does not interrupt customer, become upset, or alter positive/friendly/receptive tone of voice)
			32. Concentrates intensely on conversation (e.g., avoiding visual distractions, looking around room when customer is talking, fiddling with papers, doodling, playing solitaire)
			33. Listens empathetically by communicating at least one empathic statement (e.g., I'm sorry you're having trouble, I can imagine how frustrating that could be...)
			34. Avoids internal or external finger pointing (e.g., blaming others)

Figure 7-4. Sales/customer service observation checklist (Continued).

the effectiveness of the training program. Permission is acquired from each participant before they are observed. The participants are also assured that independent evaluators who are in no way connected with their job performance ratings are doing the observations. It is necessary that the observers identify each participant being observed on the checklist because they each need to be compared with the observations done after the training. But the participants are assured that their anonymity will be protected. Three months after the training, the same evaluation specialists observe the same participants again. Observations are conducted for as many of the class participants as possible. When not too intrusive to the field, each is observed twice so that as many call scenarios as possible are caught and, therefore, more behaviors rated.

After the observations, the checklists are scored by taking the total number of items (34) minus the number of NAs received, thus equalizing the items that are scored with a "yes" or "no." Remember that the "NAs" are used only for those calls that do not have the opportunity to use the skill listed. The total number of yes's received is then divided by this new number. For example, if participant 1 received 4 NAs and 25 yes's, the 4 are subtracted from the 34, leaving 30 items to be addressed. The 25 yes's divided by the 30 provides a score of 83 percent for participant 1. The scores for the observations made before the training are then compared to those made after the training.

The planning for the performance evaluation of the sales/customer service training program is completed so the objective map can be completed (Figure 7-5).

Leadership Program

The Leadership Program provides supervisors skills to effectively manage. The performance behaviors that are measured are based on the performance objectives listed in the Leadership Program objective map in chapter 2. The technique selected to measure on-the-job performance for the Leadership Program is a *one-shot evaluation*. A follow-up questionnaire is designed.

A company email message is sent to each participant by their director informing them of the evaluation and instructing them to expect a questionnaire. The importance of the evaluation is explained and a point of contact from the evaluation group is provided in case they have questions. Figure 7-6 is the questionnaire that is sent to each participant via email.

The evaluation plan also includes using completed action plans that the participants set up as part of the program. Asking this executive audience to "turn in" their action plans might be insulting, so at the end of the questionnaire a separate section focuses on their action plans (Figure 7-7).

The planning for the performance evaluation of the leadership development program is done so the objective map is completed (Figure 7-8).

Business Objective	Metric	Enablers/Barriers	Performance Objective	Measurement Methodology	Enablers/Barriers	Learning Objective	Measurement Methodology	Enablers/Barriers
1. Improve customer satisfaction by 90 percent.	Reduction in customer complaints.		1a. Opens call with IAW-established procedures 1b. Demonstrates interest in caller's needs. 1c. Closes call with correct understanding of actions to be taken.	Before after program evaluation design. On-the-job observations using observation checklist.	Barrier: perceived content validity. Enabler: realistic observations.	1a1. Greets caller with standard company opening. 1a2. Introduces self. 1b1. Uses enthusiastic tone of voice(friendly, positive, non-monotone voice—happy, upbeat, cheery, pleasant). 1b2. Listens to customer without interrupting. 1c1. Conveys empathy. 1c2. Asks for customer's perspective. 1c3. Probes for agreement. 1c4. Restates agreed upon follow-up actions to be taken.	Simulation using observation checklist.	Barrier: perceived content validity. Enabler: realistic simulation.
2. Reduce escalations by 80 percent.	Cost savings due to reduction in time required of team leader and processing clerk.		2a. Diagnosis customer's problem or need correctly. 2b. Gains customer agreement of follow-up actions that need to be taken.	On-the-job observations using observation checklist		2a1. Defines purpose of call. 2a2. Communicates what the initial plan will be. 2a3. Asks customer probing questions. 2a4. Uses Company Problem Questions Checklist. 2a5. Asks what has been tried before in resolving problem. 2a6. Asks about timing issues. 2b1. Checks back with the customer to make sure rep understands issue/confirms to ensure understanding. 2b2.Summarizes call. 2b3. Probe for agreement on any follow-up steps.		

Figure 7-5. Completed sales/customer service training program objective map.

DIRECTIONS: Please begin with column A and place an "X" along the line at the point that most accurately reflects your opinion. Please note any comments with the question number on the back of this page.

A. How effective are you in performing each skill listed?

B. How much of this effectiveness do you attribute to the Leadership Development Program?

Not at all		Moderately		Very Effective	Demonstrated ↓ Skill ↓	None		Some		All
0% 20%	40%	60%	80%	100%	1. Communicate using positive language	0% 20%	40%	60%	80%	100%
		—X—								
0% 20%	40%	60%	80%	100%	2. Determine when subordinates need assistance	0 20%	40%	60%	80%	100%
		—X—								
0% 20%	40%	60%	80%	100%	3. Conduct individual meetings so that subordinates' concerns and ideas are accounted for	0 20%	40%	60%	80%	100%
0% 20%	40%	60%	80%	100%	4. Open team meetings with clearly stated goals.	0 20%	40%	60%	80%	100%
0% 20%	40%	60%	80%	100%	5. Encourage group participation using active listening techniques.	0 20%	40%	60%	80%	100%

Figure 7-6. Leadership program follow-up questionnaire.

A. How effective are you in performing each skill listed?				Demonstrated ↓ Skill ↓	B. How much of this effectiveness do you attribute to the Leadership Development Program?				
Not at all	Moderately	Very Effective			None	Some	All		
0% 20% 40% —X— 60% 80% 100%				6. Keep discussion on track during team meetings.	0% 20% 40% 60% 80% 100%				
0% 20% 40% —X— 60% 80% 100%				7. Accomplish stated meeting goals	0% 20% 40% 60% 80% 100%				
0% 20% 40% —X— 60% 80% 100%				8. Close meetings with clearly stated follow-up actions	0 20% 40% 60% 80% 100%				
0% 20% 40% 60% 80% 100%				9. Task team members based on their individual personality types.	0 20% 40% 60% 80% 100%				

Overall, how confident are you in the estimates you provided above?

Not at All	Somewhat	Extremely
0% 20% 40% 60% 80% 100%		

Figure 7-6. Leadership program follow-up questionnaire (Continued).

A. How effective are you in performing each skill listed?	Demonstrated ↓ Skill ↓	B. How much of this effectiveness do you attribute to the Leadership Development Program?
Not at all Moderately Very Effective 0% 20% 40% 60%—X— 80% 100%	10. Explain to team members how to use	None Some All 0% 20% 40% 60% 80% 100%
0% 20% 40%—X— 60% 80% 100%	11. Prioritize goals and activities in accordance with Action Plan	0 20% 40% 60% 80% 100%
0% 20% 40% 60% 80% 100%	12. Complete goals and activities in order of priority	0 20% 40% 60% 80% 100%
0% 20% 40% 60% 80% 100%	13. Conduct only necessary meeting	0 20% 40% 60% 80% 100%

Figure 7-6. Leadership program follow-up questionnaire (Continued).

Listed below are some factors that may help you exhibit the skills you learned in the *Leadership Development Program*. For each one, estimate the percent you feel that factor enables you to effectively manage labor relations. For example, if you think that your ability is half the result of coaching from peers and half from job aids, you would enter 50 percent in the *Coaching or Feedback from peers* category and 50 percent in *Management style reference material or job aids* category. You can assign any percentage from 1–100 to a factor, and you can give a percentage to any one, two, or more factors, **but the sum of the percentages you enter must equal 100 percent.**

Factor	Percent
Knowledge, skills or experience you had before the Leadership Program	
Knowledge, skills or experience you gained from the Leadership Program	
Knowledge, skills or experience you acquired on your own, after the Leadership Program	
Management style reference material or job aids unrelated to the Leadership Program, e.g., bulletins, methods & procedure documentation	
Coaching or feedback from peers	
Coaching or feedback from your Executive Director	
Coaching or feedback from your subordinates	
Observing others	
Organizational changes–Please specify:	
Market changes–Please specify:	
Other internal factors or resources–Please specify:	
Other external resources (vendors, course, conferences, etc.)–Please specify:	
Other–Please specify:	
Total	100%

TOTAL MUST BE 100%

Figure 7-6. Leadership program follow-up questionnaire (Continued).

How many actions did you establish on your action plan for you to complete?

How many of those actions that were to be completed by now, have you completed?

For each action completed, please rate the level of satisfaction you feel with the results.

Action #1

Completely Dissatisfied   Somewhat Satisfied   Completely Satisfied

|---------|---------|---------|---------|---------|---------|---------|---------|---------|---------|
0%   20%   40%   60%   80%   100%

Action #2

Completely Dissatisfied   Somewhat Satisfied   Completely Satisfied

|---------|---------|---------|---------|---------|---------|---------|---------|---------|---------|
0%   20%   40%   60%   80%   100%

Action #3

Completely Dissatisfied   Somewhat Satisfied   Completely Satisfied

|---------|---------|---------|---------|---------|---------|---------|---------|---------|---------|
0%   20%   40%   60%   80%   100%

Action #4

Completely Dissatisfied   Somewhat Satisfied   Completely Satisfied

|---------|---------|---------|---------|---------|---------|---------|---------|---------|---------|
0%   20%   40%   60%   80%   100%

Figure 7-7. Leadership program action plan questions.

Business Objective	Metric	Enablers/ Barriers	Performance Objective	Measurement Methodology	Enablers/ Barriers	Learning Objective	Measurement Methodology	Enablers/ Barriers
1. Reduce turnover rate by 25 percent.	Cost savings due to reduction in turnover of subordinates.		1a. Communicate using positive language. 1b. Determine when subordinates need assistance. 1c. Conduct effective individual meetings.	One-shot program evaluation design. Follow-up questionnaire and action plan.		1a1. and 1c1. Distinguish between negative and positive phrases. 1a2. and 1c2. Provide examples of positive responses to different real-life scenarios. 1a3. and 1b1. Recognize different learning styles and personality types in others. 1a4. and 1b2. Learn your own learning style and personality type. 1b3. Recognize verbal cues indicating assistance is required. 1b4. Recognize non-verbal cues indicating assistance is required. 1c3. and 2a1. Use active listening techniques.	Pre/post tests.	
2. Increase individual efficiency and increase productivity.	Cost savings due to reduction in time spent in meetings. Productivity increase (percent set by each individual unit).		2a. Conduct productive team meetings. 2b. Provide personality type tests to team members effectively. 2c. Complete action plan.	Follow-up questionnaire and action plan.	Barrier: transfer design. Enabler: not planned.	2a2. Open meetings with clearly stated goals. 2a3. Encourage group participation. 2a4 . Keep discussion on track. 2b5. Close meetings with clearly stated follow-up actions. 2b1. Administer personality indicator tests. 2b2. Explain the meaning of the results. 2b3. Explain the importance of the result.s for team effectiveness. 2c1. Determine areas for improvement. 2c2. List specific goals to ensure. improvement of determined areas. 2c3. List resources required for goal completion. 2c4. List deadlines for meeting goals listed. 2c5. Communicate action plan to supervisor.		Barrier: transfer design. Enabler: not planned.

Figure 7-8. Completed leadership development objective map.

3. Increase team efficiency.	Cost savings due to value of each team member's time.	3a. Prioritize goals and activities. 3b. Complete goals and activities in order of priority. 3c. Conduct only necessary meetings.	Follow-up questionnaire and action plan.	3a1. and 3b1. Complete weekly and daily priority lists. 3c1. Using weekly and daily priority lists, develop areas where team input is required.		

Figure 7-8. Completed leadership development objective map (Continued).

Table 7-3
Checklist for Measuring Job Performance

Question	YES (✓) NO (✓)
1. Have the program task force members been consulted in the development of the data collection strategy?	
2. Does the data collection strategy take into consideration the constraints of the field situation?	
3. Have sources of information and their access been determined?	
4. Is the experimental plan selected feasible to implement?	
5. Has the sample group for evaluation been identified?	
6. Will the measurement tool(s) selected, provide the data needed?	
7. Are the data collection measurement tools feasible to implement?	
8. Has a descriptive, tactical measurement plan been developed?	
9. Has the client and the rest of the program task force agreed to the plan?	
10. Have steps been taken to ensure field cooperation for the data collection?	

SUMMARY

Designing the method for evaluating job performance takes careful planning and collaboration with all program task force members. The plan includes the timing for job performance measurement and the measurement tools that are to be used. Table 7-3 is a checklist to use when designing job performance measures.

REFERENCES

1.   Broad, J.L., and J.W. Newstrom. 1992. *Transfer of Training*. Reading, Mass.: Addison-Wesley Publishing Company.

2.   Burkett, H. 1999. "Measuring a Train-the-Trainer Approach to Support Build-to-Order Capabilities." In *In Action: Measuring Learning and Performance*. ed. T.K. Hodges, Alexandria, Va.: American Society for Training and Development.

3.   Dixon, N.M. 1990. *Evaluation: A Tool for Improving HRD Quality*. San Diego, Calif.: University Associates, Inc., in association with American Society for Training and Development.

4. Fawson, T.J. 1999. "A Study of Executive Education Programs at AT&T." In *In Action: Measuring Learning and Performance*. ed. T.K. Hodges, Alexandria, Va.: American Society for Training and Development.

5. Gordon, S.E. 1994. *Systematic Training Program Design*. Englewood Cliffs, N.J.: PTR Prentice Hall.

6. Hodges, T. 1998. *Measuring Training Throughout the Bell Atlantic Organization*. In *In Action: Implementing Evaluation Systems and Processes, ed.* JJ. Phillips, Alexandria, Va.: American Society for Training and Development.

7. Hodges, T.K. 1997. "Computer-Based Training for Maintenance Employees." In *In Action: Measuring Return on Investment*, Vol. 2, ed. J.J. Phillips, Alexandria, Va.: American Society for Training and Development.

8. Kehrhahn, M., J. Pederson, and A. Kite. 1999. "Learning to Evaluate Training Effectiveness: Measuring the Performance of HRD Specialists." In *In Action: Measuring Learning and Performance*, ed. T.K. Hodges, Alexandria, Va.: American Society for Training and Development.

9. O'Sullivan, E., and G.R. Rassel. 1999. *Research Methods for Public Administrators*, 3rd edition. New York: Longman.

10. Phillips, J.J. 1997. *Handbook of Training Evaluation and Measurement Methods*. Houston, Tex.: Gulf Publishing Company.

11. ———. 1996. *Accountability in Human Resource Management*. Houston, Tex.: Gulf Publishing Company.

12. Phillips, P., and H. Burkett. In press. *ROI Field Book*, Boston, Mass.: Butterworth-Heinemann.

13. Robinson, D.G., and J.C. Robinson. 1989. *Training for Impact*. San Francisco, Calif.: Jossey-Bass Publishers.

14. Shneiderman, B. 1992. *Designing the User Interface*, 2nd edition. Reading, Mass.: Addison Wesley Publishing Company.

15. Stone, R.D. 1999. "Successful Use of Action Planning to Measure the Impact of Training." In *In Action: Measuring Learning and Performance*, ed. T.K. Hodges, Alexandria, Va.: American Society for Training and Development.

16. Swanson, R.A., and E.F. Holton III. 1999. *Results: How to Assess Performance, Learning, and Perceptions in Organizations*. San Francisco, Calif.: Berrett-Koehler Publishers, Inc.

17. Whalen, J.P. 1999. "Enhancing Job Performance Through Technical Training and Education." In *In Action: Measuring Learning and Performance*. ed. T.K. Hodges, Alexandria, Va.: American Society for Training and Development.

CHAPTER 8

How to Analyze Job Performance Data

Analyzing job performance data is an exciting part of evaluation. It is the opportunity to determine how effective a program is in meeting its goals. People have invested time and money planning for, designing, and implementing the program, and now it is time to determine the *extent* to which the program participants are able to apply what they have learned. This part of the evaluation can be fun because there are many ways performance data can be looked at, and the evaluator can play with the data and the analysis. Just as in analyzing learning data, the evaluator needs to ask basic questions of the performance data.

1. Were the business objectives of the program met?
2. Were the performance objectives met and if so, to what extent?
3. Did the performance vary among the participants, locations, or other identified variables?
4. What is helping or inhibiting them as they perform in their job environment?

TABULATING AND ORGANIZING THE DATA

The job performance data collection tools discussed in chapter 7 are designed so that the data, when collected, can be easily tabulated. How the data are organized for summary or analysis will depend on the evaluation design and the purpose of analysis. For example, if the evaluation is a control versus experimental group design, the data need to be organized for group comparisons. If it is a one-shot evaluation design, data do not need to be organized. Different computer applications will require the data to be organized differently. If relying on a statistician to do the analysis, consult this person to determine the way in which the data need to be recorded. Make sure the statistician understands the business and performance objectives. If the data are being collected electronically, set up the program for data transfer to an appropriate data summary table.

Analyzing the Data

How performance data are analyzed is dependent upon the design of the measurement program. If a one-shot post-program evaluation design is used, the performance data set is evaluated against standards that were set by the performance objectives. If a control group versus experimental group program evaluation design is used, comparisons between the two groups' data sets are conducted. If a before-and-after program evaluation design is used, the performance data set collected before the program is compared to the performance data set collected after the program. Additional analyses may then be required dependent upon the results.

Sales Program Example

Let's use an example to walk through the steps for analyzing job performance data. Notice that many of the analytical methods used for analysis here are the same used for analyzing learning data discussed in chapter 5, so refer to that chapter as needed. Following is a relatively simple yet typical example of a job performance evaluation:

The business objectives for a sales course are to:

- Increase sales by 200 percent
- Save time by increasing the sales associates' efficiency

The associated performance objectives are to improve the sales associates':

- Communication skills
- Ability to manage their accounts
- Ability to uncover business problems
- Ability to effectively delegate
- Leadership skills

Tabulating and Organizing the Sales Data

A before-and-after program evaluation design is used. It is expected to take about six months for the new skills to be practiced and used effectively in the business environment. Fortunately, sales for each sales professional are already recorded in a company database, so actual data can be retrieved. Table 8-1 provides a sales performance table populated with fictional sales data. Data is tracked for each of the twenty-three professionals scheduled to go through a two-week class for each month. It is collected six months before, and six months after, the training.

If there is not much data, as is often the case with learning data, just looking at the raw data can be instructive, as discussed in chapter 5. When there is a large quantity of data such as those in Table 8-1, it is difficult to see trends or areas where the data vary without summarizing it.

As the data are entered, take a quick look to see if there are data that are very different from the rest. In this case, a quick comparison can be made between the beginning sales and the ending sales. In nearly every case, the sales improved after the training. For two participants, 6 and 18, however, the sales remained stable throughout the entire twelve-month period. Remember that these data are from a database that stores data for every sales professional in the organization. The client may be able to help determine what may be making these two individuals' data so different from the rest, before further analysis is conducted. The client, in this case, informed the evaluator that these two individuals did not participate in the training program after all. So their data are pulled out of the table because their performance is irrelevant or "erroneous" to the study. Accounting for erroneous or obviously incorrect data and adjusting for them is often called "cleaning up the data."

Once that is complete, chart the data in a bar chart to give a visual picture of differences. A quick look at the data as graphed from an SPSS file in Figure 8-1 shows the differences.

The training program occurred during month 6 (M6). Prior to month 6, the data are pretty stable. The fact that the sales staff was in training for two weeks in month 6 and not selling could account for the drop in sales for that month. Month 7 (M7) is also lower than months 1 through 5. For months 8 through 12, sales increase incrementally.

Table 8-1
Sales Performance Data

Participant ID	Monthly Sales before Training (Dollars)						Monthly Sales after Training (Dollars)					
	M1	M2	M3	M4	M5	M6	M1	M2	M3	M4	M5	M6
1	12,255	10,900	9,400	8,450	11,200	4,400	6,350	12,500	20,500	32,300	51,300	52,400
2	15,400	16,850	13,300	10,500	12,000	5,300	7,500	14,400	25,500	55,500	62,000	64,300
3	5,500	6,200	5,700	6,800	6,400	2,300	3,200	7,200	8,300	10,000	13,400	13,900
4	13,300	12,200	14,600	12,300	11,250	6,200	7,350	13,300	15,400	25,100	32,200	33,300
5	16,550	15,240	17,350	14,200	15,600	8,300	8,750	20,300	28,200	40,300	52,200	55,400
6	12,320	14,350	16,220	15,300	14,200	10,100	11,000	13,300	12,880	14,200	15,200	13,400
7	12,900	13,550	11,400	12,790	14,560	6,490	8,890	15,350	18,400	22,890	34,500	36,900
8	16,480	17,470	15,330	15,000	14,200	8,500	9,400	17,600	30,900	49,800	67,700	65,880
9	6,890	7,560	7,000	6,890	8,100	3,590	4,880	10,890	14,500	22,200	46,900	45,880
10	13,300	14,200	13,990	12,400	13,500	7,500	8,700	24,500	35,400	46,400	55,500	54,300
11	16,700	18,500	17,560	21,400	25,100	10,500	11,500	26,100	35,700	51,900	66,890	67,400
12	12,200	13,500	11,600	13,500	12,900	6,500	5,600	12,300	23,900	45,900	60,200	61,000
13	15,760	14,500	14,900	16,300	15,390	10,000	9,890	18,600	27,400	48,000	62,000	63,270
14	14,760	15,680	14,560	16,780	15,970	6,990	7,890	19,230	30,440	49,550	65,040	59,670
15	12,220	12,500	14,570	13,560	12,900	5,990	6,890	15,890	29,990	42,880	63,020	64,550
16	20,780	22,880	25,670	26,550	30,990	13,890	15,880	30,880	46,990	67,500	82,660	85,990
17	13,660	14,000	12,440	13,670	14,100	6,500	7,100	16,440	25,990	36,760	59,450	58,750
18	12,900	12,780	13,550	11,500	12,880	12,880	13,990	12,600	12,890	14,670	15,100	13,500
19	14,550	16,450	17,450	15,300	14,200	5,900	7,450	16,890	23,400	39,670	51,880	52,000
20	21,650	20,550	18,670	22,000	21,500	10,220	11,300	25,990	36,890	47,700	60,200	61,400
21	18,500	17,650	19,670	20,100	19,990	7,660	8,230	20,660	32,000	46,700	59,500	60,200
22	15,400	16,800	14,900	15,560	17,200	7,000	66,800	18,690	27,000	38,600	52,000	49,360
23	22,300	23,140	19,440	20,990	22,660	9,900	9,300	26,789	30,450	42,990	48,880	50,300

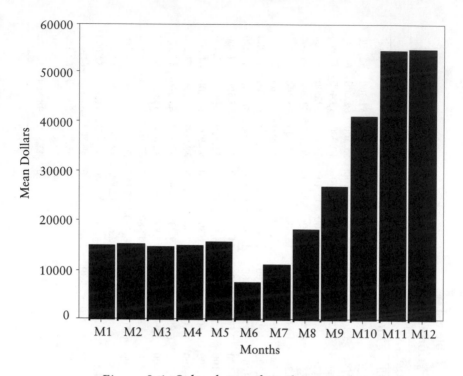

Figure 8-1. Sales data in bar chart graph.

Analyzing the Sales Data

The next step is to summarize the data by finding a measure of central tendency. As discussed in chapter 5, this will describe how the group performed on average. Calculating the mean is acceptable and is the most common method. Then comparing the mean scores for months 1 through 6, and months 7 through 12, will demonstrate the extent to which sales have changed. Table 8-2 provides a sum-

Table 8-2
Summary Statistics for Sales Data Comparisons

Months	Mean Dollars	Standard Deviation
1 through 6	13803.61	915.5202
7 through 12	34530.23	9447.7254

mary of the sales data, which will assist in a comparison between the two time periods.

There is a 250 percent increase after the sales training program. Running the correct statistical test shows that the difference between the two time periods is statistically significant ($p < .01$).

Can any of the evaluation questions be answered at this point?

1. Were the business objectives met?

    Sales were increased overall by 250 percent. That business objective was met. But these figures do not tell us anything about improved efficiency.

2. Were the performance objectives met, and if so, to what extent?

    The sales figures alone cannot determine if the participants used the skills taught in the program. This and the remaining questions cannot be answered, so analysis must continue.

Fortunately, this study included using a follow-up questionnaire that was distributed to the participants six months after the training. Also fortunate for the study, the evaluators were able to attend a monthly sales meeting to distribute and collect the questionnaires so there is a 100 percent response rate—music to an evaluator's ears. The questionnaire asked a series of questions pertaining to the performance objectives. Figure 8-2 is the follow-up questionnaire that was given to the course participants.

Note that question 1 (Q1) could be used for learning data if there were no learning measure in the course. Questions 2 through 6 (Q2–Q6) pertain to the participants' work environment. Questions 7 through 11 (Q7–Q11) address the skills taught in the course. Question 12 (Q12) addresses productivity and questions 13 through 16 (Q13–Q16) pertain to efficiency. Question 17 (Q17) is an "overall perceived effectiveness" assessment question.

Table 8-3 provides the results of the questionnaire. Each participant's percent rating is provided for each question. Notice that the total number of participants has been reduced by two. The two professionals who did not attend the course were not given a questionnaire to complete.

Again, this is a large data set, so it needs to be summarized. To help in analysis, it might be useful to graph it as done with the sales

Instructions: Please check (√) the appropriate box for each question.

To what extent . . .

	Not at all		Moderately			Very Effective
1. have you increased your confidence in using the knowledge and /or skills taught in this course?	0%	20%	40%	60%	80%	100%
2. does the content of this course accurately reflect what happens on the job?	0%	20%	40%	60%	80%	100%
3. have you had the opportunity to apply the knowledge and /or skills covered in this course?	0%	20%	40%	60%	80%	100%
4. are you expected to apply the knowledge and/ or skills covered in this course?	0%	20%	40%	60%	80%	100%
5. do you have the necessary resources, e.g. epuipment and information, required to apply the knowledge and /or skills taught in this course?	0%	20%	40%	60%	80%	100%
6. do you receive coaching or feedback on how you are doing?	0%	20%	40%	60%	80%	100%
7. has this course improved your communication skills?	0%	20%	40%	60%	80%	100%
8. has this course improved your ability to manage your accounts?	0%	20%	40%	60%	80%	100%
9. has this course improved your ability to uncover business problems?	0%	20%	40%	60%	80%	100%
10. has this course improved your ability to effectively delegate?	0%	20%	40%	60%	80%	100%
11. has this course improved your team leadership skills?	0%	20%	40%	60%	80%	100%
12. has this course improved your productivity, e.g. number of sales calls, number of dales solution, more installations.	0%	20%	40%	60%	80%	100%
13. has this course reduced the time required to complete your work?	0%	20%	40%	60%	80%	100%
14. has this course reduced the amount of time you require of your Supervisor for sales leadership topics?	0%	20%	40%	60%	80%	100%
15. has this course reduced amount of time you require of your co-worker(s) for sales leadership topics?	0%	20%	40%	60%	80%	100%
16. has this course reduced the amount of time you require of your customer ?	0%	20%	40%	60%	80%	100%
17. would you recommend this course to those who have similar jobs?	0%	20%	40%	60%	80%	100%

Thank you for your assistance in helping [Company] measure the results of the Sales Program.

*Figure 8-2. Follow-up questionnaire
for Sales Training Program.*

Table 8-3
Sales Course Questionnaire Results Recorded as Percentages

Participant ID								Percent Ratings for Questions									
	Q1	Q2	Q3	Q4	Q5	Q6	Q7	Q8	Q9	Q10	Q11	Q12	Q13	Q14	Q15	Q16	Q17
1	80	85	90	80	50	85	60	55	30	40	45	75	25	20	25	40	90
2	90	80	100	80	60	80	55	65	35	40	50	70	30	25	25	45	100
3	85	70	95	90	45	85	70	70	40	50	45	80	35	30	35	35	90
4	75	60	80	80	65	90	65	55	45	50	50	70	0	25	35	30	85
5	90	80	90	90	50	100	75	65	50	50	45	75	10	30	25	35	90
6	85	80	90	85	45	90	45	50	35	50	45	80	25	25	20	35	90
7	90	75	95	90	60	95	40	50	35	45	60	70	20	10	15	40	90
8	65	70	90	85	50	85	50	45	25	45	55	85	10	20	10	25	85
9	70	65	95	90	65	85	55	50	30	45	55	80	0	10	25	30	90
10	80	70	85	85	45	90	60	50	40	45	45	80	25	25	35	25	85
11	85	70	90	90	30	100	70	60	55	50	45	75	30	25	40	30	80
12	90	75	85	90	40	95	60	55	40	45	50	75	25	25	45	25	85
13	90	80	85	85	50	90	50	55	45	50	45	70	20	30	35	20	90
14	75	65	75	85	40	95	45	50	35	45	50	75	10	25	35	10	95
15	85	75	85	85	50	95	60	50	45	50	45	80	15	20	25	25	75
16	80	65	80	90	60	90	55	60	50	45	50	75	20	10	20	35	85
17	95	70	95	90	45	100	70	65	50	35	45	70	35	20	25	10	90
18	75	80	95	90	70	100	35	40	45	35	45	85	20	30	30	25	95
19	85	80	90	80	65	95	50	40	50	35	45	70	35	25	30	30	80
20	75	80	95	85	35	90	45	45	50	45	50	75	30	20	25	25	85
21	80	70	85	85	40	95	50	45	40	45	50	80	25	30	25	25	90

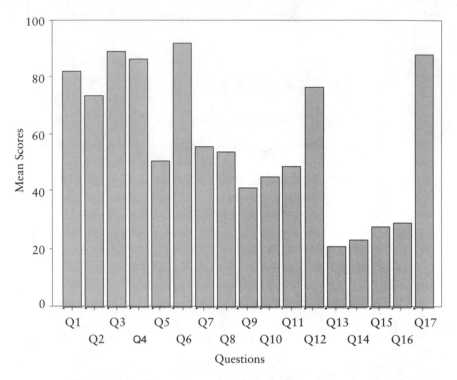

Figure 8-3. Questionnaire data in bar chart graph.

data. Figure 8-3 is a bar chart of the mean scores for each question on the follow-up questionnaire.

The graph shows some grouping of the mean scores but also some variability among the questions. Table 8-4 provides summary data for the questionnaire to show actual mean scores and measures of central tendency for each question (range and standard deviation). "N" refers to the number of participants of which the data is reflective.

The shading in the graph is done to help visualize the grouping of the questions according to the categories defined above. That is:

- Question 1 pertains to *confidence using the skills taught.*
- Questions 2 through 6 center around *work environment support.*
- Questions 7 through 11 address the specific *skills* taught in the course.
- Question 12 is a *productivity* question.
- Questions 13 through 16 discuss *efficiency.*
- Question 17 is an *overall* effectiveness question.

Table 8-4
Summary Statistics for Questionnaire Ratings

Question	N	Minimum (percent)	Maximum (percent)	Range	Mean (percent)	Standard Deviation
1	21	65.00	95.00	30	82.14	7.6765
2	21	60.00	85.00	25	73.57	6.7348
3	21	75.00	100.00	25	89.05	6.2488
4	21	80.00	90.00	20	86.19	3.8421
5	21	30.00	70.00	40	50.48	10.9436
6	21	80.00	100.00	20	91.90	5.8043
7	21	35.00	75.00	40	55.48	10.7127
8	21	40.00	70.00	30	53.33	8.4163
9	21	25.00	55.00	30	41.43	8.0844
10	21	35.00	50.00	15	45.00	4.7434
11	21	45.00	60.00	15	48.33	4.2817
12	21	70.00	85.00	15	75.95	4.9038
13	21	.00	35.00	35	21.19	10.4767
14	21	10.00	30.00	20	23.10	6.6099
15	21	10.00	45.00	35	28.10	8.4374
16	21	10.00	45.00	24	28.33	8.7082
17	21	75.00	100.00	25	87.86	5.6061

The evaluator may find grouping the data in these categories helpful to answer some questions about the program. The evaluator may also find that summarizing the data by category will help the analysis. Table 8-5 provides perhaps a clearer look at the results when the data are grouped and summarized.

The *skills taught* and *efficiency* categories have lower mean scores than the other categories. Although there is a range in the spread for the *efficiency* category, the maximum score is still only 45 percent, which is well below the other categories.

Which evaluation questions can be answered now?

1. Were the business objectives met, and if so, to what extent?
   Sales increased by 250 percent. The survey data indicate that the participants perceived their productivity increased by 76 percent. Productivity would be the best indicator of performance

Table 8-5
Summary for Question Categories

Category	Mean Percent	Minimum	Maximum	Standard Deviation
Confidence	82.14	65	95	7.677
Work Environment Support	78.24	30	100	16.813
Skills	48.71	25	75	9.121
Productivity	75.95	70	85	4.904
Efficiency	25.18	0	45	9.067
Overall	87.86	75	100	5.606

that would improve sales, so the linkage is positive for the program. But the questions on efficiency rated low with an average perceived increase of only 28 percent.

2. Were the performance objectives met, and if so, to what extent?

The survey data show that the participants perceived they were 48 percent proficient in their skills. Next to efficiency, this is the lowest category score.

3. Did the performance vary among the participants, locations, or other identified variables?

Although there was variability among the questions, there was little variability among the participants' responses to each question.

4. What is helping them, or inhibiting them, to perform in their job environment?

The survey questions that asked about the work environment averaged 78%, indicating that the participants generally perceived that their work environment supported their opportunity and ability to use the skills they were taught. *However, question 5 had a mean score of 50 percent, which indicates that the participants did not feel that they necessarily had the necessary equipment and information required to apply the knowledge and/or skills taught in the course.*

Note that at this point in the evaluation, only *results* have been provided. It is important that the evaluator considers and presents all the results before drawing conclusions or making recommendations. To jump to conclusions in this case and declare the program successful based only on the sales data, for example, would be irresponsible when other (perception) data are available. Only by thoroughly examining and analyzing all the data can the evaluation progress to the point where conclusions can be drawn. The conclusions drawn and recommendations that are made for the sales example used in this chapter are discussed in chapter 9.

The intent of this book is not to discuss in detail how to conduct an ROI analysis but rather to take the evaluation to the point where an ROI analysis might be possible. It is evident, however, that this program lends itself nicely to conducting an ROI analysis, because the benefits (sales) are tangible and real rather than perceived. If an ROI analysis were conducted, the calculation would be conducted using the ROI formula (Phillips 1997).

$$\frac{\text{The program benefits (sales increase)} - \text{the program costs}}{\text{The program costs}} \times 100 = \text{ROI}(\%)$$

The results of an ROI analysis would provide the client organization with an idea of the value of their investment in the program. In the sales example this may be an important issue, because the program costs would not only include the cost of the development and delivery of the program but the cost incurred when taking the sales force off the "street" to attend the two-week course. The sales data indeed showed the impact on sales during both the month they attended the training and the month after the training. It is possible that those costs may make the ROI not as high as the client would expect, which would play a part in their decision-making about the continuation of this program. If the ROI is not as high as expected, they may want to consider an e-Learning or computer-assisted event rather than the classroom program used, so participants could learn the skills on their own computer and not have to travel to, or spend the time in, a classroom. Many organizations are considering alternative delivery to cut down on the time participants spend in the classroom. Whenever consideration is given to changing a program, such as using alternative delivery, however, an evaluation should be conducted on the changed program to ensure performance is not sacrificed for potential cost savings.

There is ample room in the world of evaluation to experiment with different types of tools and methodologies to measure job performance. The evaluator can take existing successful approaches and techniques and experiment using them in different ways that work best in their particular environment.

Martineau and Holmes-Ponder (1999), from the Center for Creative Leadership (CCL), used an instrument, REFLECTIONS, to measure individual behavioral change as a result of a leadership development program. Their follow-up process began three months after the development program ended. They mailed each program alumnus a set of ten surveys for their raters. The raters were those people who had been able to observe the participant's behaviors both before and after the program—the participant's boss, those reporting to the participant (direct reports), or the participant's peers. The groups reported their ratings in separate categories on the feedback report. CCL took care to ensure confidentiality, ensuring those in the peer and direct report categories that their confidentiality was guaranteed by having them return the surveys in sealed envelopes. Figure 8-4 is a sample from the REFLECTIONS tool.

CCL performed both quantitative and qualitative analyses of the survey data. To measure quantitative behavior change, data from the REFLECTIONS survey were subjected to descriptive analysis (means, standard deviations) and mean comparisons using t-tests (a statistical test) to determine the behaviors on which participants changed significantly. CCL measured qualitative behavior change by using a qualitative data analysis program known as "QSR NUD*IST" to analyze comments from a supplemental survey. Table 8-6 shows a sample of the results.

Scale:

Not at All 1	To a Minimal Extent 2	To a Small Extent 3	To Some Extent 4	To a Moderate Extent 5	To a Considerable Extent 6	To a Large Extent 7	To a Very Great Extent 8	Completely 9

Behavioral Statement	Before the Program	Now
Is aware of the impact of his/her behaviors on others.	_____	_____
Delegates effectively.	_____	_____
Understands the political nature of the organization and works appropriately within it.	_____	_____

Figure 8-4. Sample REFLECTIONS provided to peers and direct reports.

Table 8-6
Sample Behaviors Showing Strongest Change from REFLECTIONS

Behaviors (listed in descending order of change)	Before Program Mean	New Mean
Are approachable and receptive to others	5.00	6.93
Take more effective actions in your leadership situations	4.56	6.34
Strive to be capable and cool in high-pressure situations	4.57	6.33
Display sensitivity to others, even when you are under stress	4.73	6.43
Are aware of the impact of your behaviors on others	4.24	5.93
Set leadership improvement goals	4.81	6.50
Display patience with others	4.50	6.19
Delegate effectively	5.34	7.01
Avoid agitating others by not spreading tension and anxiety when you are upset	4.34	5.98
Strive to understand the political nature of the organization and work appropriately within it	5.64	7.28
Are not abrasive; do not antagonize	4.66	6.29

In addition to these ratings, both participants and their raters made powerful comments relating to observable improvements in client service, departmental planning and strategizing, and completion of targeted programs and projects. CCL concluded from these results that the participants had become more aware of the impact of their behavior on others, were making adjustments in their interactions with others, and were better able to maintain a necessary amount of composure in situations that required their leadership. They believe their evaluation design and instrumentation were effective in providing critical data about the impact of the leadership development program on the client organization.

Erwin and Graber (1999) found performance evaluation to be an important by-product of the human capital approach to employee development upon which Com Ed's Fossil Division was embarking. They used already available job profile data and multi-rater 360-degree assessments from a system that served many other uses, such as employee selection and development, succession planning, and compensation. This not only saved valuable evaluation resources and time but provided the opportunity to have a control group to test the impact of training and to help isolate the impact of the training versus other factors that could have influenced the skill. The data were already quantified, so they lent themselves to the use of descriptive statistics (means, medians, and range) or statistical significance testing. The evaluators were therefore able to invest their evaluation resources in calculating the cost of skill gap and determining the financial impact of the training.

PRESENTING RESULTS

How results from the analysis are presented is as important as the results themselves. As discussed in chapter 5, data presented incorrectly can tell a misleading story. But unlike learning data, performance data can get rather complicated, and the evaluator must take care to present it in the clearest way possible and in a way that answers the questions asked of the evaluation. Group data in proper categories for easy comparisons. Bolding, shading, and using color are techniques the evaluator can use to distinguish one area of data from another. For example, shading could be used to highlight comparisons that are statistically different. It is the evaluator's job to determine the best way to display results. Clarity is the goal.

Many of the tables in the sales example are used for analysis and would not necessarily be tables provided in the evaluation report for this program. Group the data in whatever way necessary, so that differences and trends are seen. But be careful how the data are presented to the client. Unless the client has an understanding of what a standard deviation means, for example, or has other programs with which to compare different standard deviations, presenting the range (low and high scores) may be more helpful. The graphs used in the sales example (Figures 8-1 and 8-3) may be useful for the client because it provides them with comparisons at a glance. Grouping the data in categories (Table 8-5) to answer specific questions is good for analysis but may also be helpful to the client. The case studies in progress provide examples of different ways data are summarized for analysis and organized for possible client presentation.

Do not provide complex or detailed data in the body of the report; include it either as an appendix, or have it ready for any of those who may want more detail.

CASE STUDIES IN PROGRESS

Let's look at how we analyze the data collected from the job performance measurement tools that were designed in the previous chapter for each of our case studies in progress.

Technical Training Program

The performance objectives for the Technical Training Program case study were to improve warehouse employees' driving skills, particularly as they relate to safety, and warehouse operational skills. By meeting these performance objectives, it is expected that motor vehicle and on-the-job accidents would decrease and customer satisfaction would be improved.

To measure performance, the supervisor maintains logs for sixteen of his employees for six weeks. Each week he turns his logs in to the evaluation group. The evaluation group scores the logs and places the scores into a data spread sheet. The data are separated into two groups, the scores for the eight participants who were in the experimental group (the group that received the training) and the scores for the eight participants in the control group (the group that did not receive the training). The scoring is done as described in chapter 7. Each participant could achieve a maximum score of twenty-two points. Within each group, the data are listed by individuals. It is not necessary in this case to determine percentages—the total points each participant receives each week is used. The means are calculated for each group for each week. Table 8-7 provides the results of the supervisors' ratings for each participant and the calculated mean points.

Because the data set is small, the evaluator sees some results just by looking at the scores before any other calculations or analyses are done. The experimental group has higher scores in every case. Table 8-8 provides the mean scores for each week for each group.

The scores are stable for the control group with the exception of week 3, where they are lower. The scores increase weekly for the

Table 8-7
Technical Training Program Performance Log Results

Experimental Group Points 8 Participants						Experimental Group Mean No. Points 22 Maximum Points	Control Group Points 8 Participants						Control Group Mean No. Points 22 Maximum Points
Week 1	Week 2	Week 3	Week 4	Week 5	Week 6		Week 1	Week 2	Week 3	Week 4	Week 5	Week 6	
15	16	12	20	20	20	17.17	5	6	4	5	7	5	5.33
10	10	7	14	18	18	12.73	8	9	5	10	8	9	8.17
12	12	10	16	16	18	14	7	8	4	9	8	8	7.33
13	14	9	17	16	20	14.83	6	6	3	7	6	7	5.83
9	10	7	14	15	16	11.83	9	8	2	7	9	9	7.3
11	12	6	15	17	19	13.33	7	6	3	8	6	7	6.17
12	13	8	18	20	21	30.67	8	5	2	6	8	7	6
10	12	8	15	19	19	13.83	10	9	7	9	10	9	9

Table 8-8
Technical Training Program Weekly Mean Log Scores

Group Scores	Week 1	Week 2	Week 3	Week 4	Week 5	Week 6
Experimental	11.5	12.38	8.38	16.13	17.63	18.88
Control	7.5	7.13	3.75	7.63	7.75	7.63

experimental group with the exception of week 3. Before doing any statistical analyses, the evaluator can see from the simple calculations that the experimental group performed better than the control group and that their performance improved over time. Something happened in week 3 that brought both groups' scores down. What happened during that week is not important for our evaluation, however, because it happened to the participants in each group, which, as we discussed in our earlier chapters, is one of the advantages to having an experimental versus control group evaluation design. When testing for significance, it is found that the two group's scores were significantly different ($p < .01$).

In addition to the log, weekly riding evaluations are conducted by the supervisors for each participant in both groups. Riding scores are recorded for each individual in the experimental and control groups. The results for that data are provided in Table 8-9.

The riding rating data also show that the experimental group did better than the control group. But it doesn't look like they are as different as indicated in the performance log scores. By calculating the mean ratings, a clearer picture is seen (Table 8-10).

Like the performance log data, the experimental group ratings improved with each week, except for week 3, while the control group data stayed the same, except for week 3. But unlike the performance log data, the experimental group ratings are not higher than the control group ratings for each week. In weeks 1 and 2, they are lower. Again, the evaluator does not need to worry about week 3 because whatever happened to impact the workers' performance was the same for each group. But for weeks 4, 5, and 6, the experimental group ratings are higher than the control group ratings. When testing for significance we find that the overall difference between the groups is significant ($p < .01$).

For the driving rating, the data indicate that it took some time for the participants to apply skills taught in the training to the job. The analyst might expect that week 7 and beyond may show even better performance for the experimental group, as the trend was going

Table 8-9
Technical Training Program Weekly Riding Score Results

Experimental Group Riding Ratings 8 Participants						Mean Rating	Control Group Riding Ratings 8 Participants						Mean Rating
Week 1	Week 2	Week 3	Week 4	Week 5	Week 6	Maximum Rating 100%	Week 1	Week 2	Week 3	Week 4	Week 5	Week 6	Maximum Rating 100%
60%	70%	45%	80%	80%	85%	70%	50%	55%	40%	55%	60%	60%	53.33%
50%	60%	35%	70%	80%	80%	62.5%	55%	60%	30%	60%	55%	60%	53.33%
55%	65%	40%	75%	80%	85%	66.65%	50%	60%	35%	70%	60%	60%	55.83%
60%	70%	50%	80%	85%	90%	72.5%	55%	55%	25%	60%	55%	60%	51.67%
50%	60%	30%	70%	80%	85%	62.5%	65%	65%	40%	60%	70%	65%	60.83%
55%	65%	40%	70%	75%	85%	65%	60%	60%	25%	55%	65%	60%	54.17%
60%	65%	35%	75%	80%	90%	78.33%	65%	60%	40%	55%	50%	65%	55.83%
55%	65%	40%	70%	80%	85%	65.83%	65%	70%	50%	75%	70%	65%	65.85%

Table 8-10
Weekly Mean Riding Ratings

Group Ratings	Week 1	Week 2	Week 3	Week 4	Week 5	Week 6
Experimental	55.62%	65%	39.37%	73.75%	80%	85.63%
Control	65.63%	68.13%	35.63%	61.25%	60.63%	61.88%

upward. In this case study, simply calculating the mean scores for each participant may be misleading. Calculating them for each week and determining significance provides a more accurate picture of what is happening. The evaluator needs to ask questions of the data and conduct whatever additional analyses may be needed to get the clearest possible picture. Drawing conclusions based on the results of this case study will be discussed in chapter 9.

Sales/Customer Service Training Program

The performance objectives for the Sales/Customer Service Training Program case study were to improve customer service representatives' customer relations skills. The expectation was that by doing so, customer satisfaction would increase and call-escalations would be reduced.

Trained observers were able to observe a "before" and "after" call for sixteen participants. Observation checklists were scored as described in chapter 7, resulting in overall percent ratings for each representative. Table 8-11 provides the results for those calls, along with calculated mean scores.

Performance appears to have improved overall. There is a statistically significant difference ($p < .01$) between the "before" scores and the "after" scores. By analyzing each item on the checklist, the evaluator can determine which areas within the program are more effective. That information can be used for improving the course. Conclusions drawn and recommendations made based on these results will be discussed in chapter 9.

This case study is a good example of how beneficial it can be to set up the evaluation program carefully. The observation checklist was tested for reliability and would therefore not be questioned as an effective method for data collection. Also, the scoring scheme (as described in chapter 5) was based upon the realities of the job and the calls that the representatives received. With this preparation, data analysis is easy.

Table 8-11
Results for Sales/Customer Service Training Program Performance
Observations

Representative	Before Training Scores (percent)	After Training Scores (percent)
1	40	62
2	25	80
3	50	90
4	33	75
5	42	82
6	60	85
7	42	88
8	28	75
9	44	62
10	32	85
11	55	68
12	26	56
13	35	75
14	45	89
15	52	90
16	40	100
Mean Scores	41	79

Leadership Development Program

The performance objectives for the Leadership Development
Program case study were to develop or improve supervisory personnel's ability to communicate more effectively with subordinates, conduct more efficient and effective meetings, and
prioritize goals and activities. It was the expectation that, by
developing or improving these skills, turnover would be reduced,
team effectiveness would be increased, productivity would be
improved, and time would be saved by both the supervisor and
his or her subordinates.

To measure developed or improved performance, a follow-up questionnaire was distributed via company email to the participants in the
Leadership Development Program three months after the program. Perhaps because of the advance message from a company executive,

twenty-seven of the thirty-five questionnaires were sent back via the company email, which represented a 77 percent return rate. The questionnaire asked the participants to rate their perceived effectiveness in performing the skills taught in the program. They were also asked how confident they were of their estimates. Then they were asked to rate perceived effectiveness of the program in teaching them each skill. They also were asked to estimate the extent to which several of their work conditions as well as the Leadership Program positively impacted their leadership ability. The follow-up questionnaire used can be found in chapter 7.

Table 8-12 provides the raw percent scores the raters gave for their perception of *their effectiveness performing each listed skill.* The scores have been adjusted to incorporate each participant's level of confidence in his or her estimates. The adjustments were made by multiplying the estimate rating by the percent level of confidence. For example, if the participant rated their effectiveness in performing a skill at 90 percent and the level of confidence for their ratings was 75 percent, the 90 percent is adjusted by multiplying it by 75 percent. The adjusted score is 68 percent.

Table 8-13 provides the raw percent scores the raters gave for their perception of the *program's effectiveness in teaching them each listed skill.*

Table 8-14 summarizes the perceived performance effectiveness data from Table 8-12.

The participants perceived themselves to be fairly proficient in applying the skills and/or knowledge taught in the program (means ranging from 69 percent to 76 percent), with the exception of skills 9 and 10. The minimum rating for questions 9 and 10 was 0 percent, which contributes to the lower mean ratings of 24 percent and 16 percent. To see whether it was an outlier rating that brought those ratings down, we need to look at the raw data in Table 8-12. At a glance, it is apparent that all the participants rated those questions lower than they rated the others, so the outliers are not accounting for the low mean ratings. The mean ratings, therefore, are indicative of the perceptions of the group overall. The skills rated low were:

1. Task team members, based on their individual personality types.
2. Explain to team members how to use personality type indicators to achieve team goals.

Both of these skills address personality types and are the only two skills listed that do so.

Table 8-12
Leadership Development *Performance* Effectiveness Rating Results

Rater		Percent Effectiveness Ratings on Questions											
	Q1	Q2	Q3	Q4	Q5	Q6	Q7	Q8	Q9	Q10	Q11	Q12	Q13
1	65	45	50	40	50	40	70	85	10	20	80	50	70
2	70	50	60	50	40	60	60	80	20	10	60	60	60
3	55	60	60	60	60	60	70	70	30	20	70	50	70
4	60	70	50	70	55	55	60	60	25	25	80	60	60
5	75	80	65	50	60	50	75	75	35	30	65	55	70
6	80	75	65	60	50	50	70	65	10	0	70	60	65
7	75	65	70	75	60	75	65	70	15	15	75	70	75
8	65	70	65	65	70	80	70	75	20	10	65	80	65
9	75	65	70	70	70	70	60	60	30	10	70	70	70
10	65	50	65	80	65	75	70	60	20	10	80	60	70
11	75	60	70	90	70	65	60	70	25	25	90	70	40
12	65	65	75	85	80	80	55	80	40	30	80	85	50
13	70	70	65	90	85	90	60	75	20	15	85	90	60
14	80	80	80	80	80	80	80	80	80	80	80	80	80
15	75	85	75	90	70	75	80	70	25	10	65	85	80
16	75	90	95	50	80	60	90	80	0	0	75	80	80
17	60	80	90	75	80	50	75	85	20	10	75	90	80
18	70	65	80	80	90	60	80	80	10	15	85	85	80
19	80	75	85	80	80	75	80	85	40	30	80	80	75
20	60	70	50	60	60	50	70	70	0	0	70	65	65
21	85	80	90	70	75	60	65	80	10	10	65	75	80
22	65	65	80	65	65	80	80	90	20	10	70	75	65
23	80	85	80	85	80	80	80	80	30	20	80	85	75
24	90	75	75	75	75	85	85	80	20	0	90	85	80
25	80	90	85	80	80	85	80	90	30	20	80	85	80
26	65	85	85	85	80	80	85	70	20	10	10	75	90
27	90	80	75	80	80	80	75	80	30	10	90	80	80

Table 8-13

Leadership Development *Program* Effectiveness Ratings Results

Rater	Percent Program Effectiveness Ratings on Questions												
	Q1	Q2	Q3	Q4	Q5	Q6	Q7	Q8	Q9	Q10	Q11	Q12	Q13
1	90	80	60	80	50	60	80	90	20	40	80	60	60
2	80	60	70	70	50	70	80	80	20	20	90	70	70
3	70	80	70	80	60	80	90	70	30	20	70	80	80
4	80	70	60	85	70	90	85	75	10	15	80	70	70
5	75	65	75	80	60	85	85	80	25	20	75	75	75
6	80	75	75	80	60	80	80	75	10	10	75	75	75
7	80	80	80	75	70	80	75	80	20	20	80	80	80
8	85	90	75	80	75	80	80	75	20	10	90	90	90
9	90	80	80	90	80	70	90	85	20	10	80	80	80
10	85	90	80	80	85	80	80	90	10	10	70	90	90
11	85	80	90	90	80	70	60	80	25	25	60	80	80
12	85	80	85	90	80	85	60	80	30	20	80	85	85
13	70	75	90	90	85	75	60	80	20	10	85	90	90
14	80	80	80	80	80	80	80	80	80	80	80	80	80
15	85	75	90	80	75	75	90	80	20	80	75	90	90
16	85	85	45	75	90	65	90	80	0	0	85	80	80
17	75	80	50	75	80	70	80	80	10	0	85	90	90
18	80	75	65	80	80	60	80	80	10	5	85	80	80
19	90	75	85	90	75	75	85	90	20	20	90	90	90
20	70	70	70	70	60	60	75	70	0	0	75	70	70
21	80	75	80	80	80	70	80	90	10	10	75	80	80
22	75	70	90	85	70	80	80	80	20	10	80	80	80
23	90	85	90	85	90	80	80	80	20	10	90	80	80
24	60	75	80	75	75	85	85	90	10	0	80	80	85
25	80	75	85	80	80	85	80	80	20	10	80	85	85
26	75	80	90	80	90	85	65	65	10	10	75	80	80
27	90	80	80	85	85	80	80	85	20	10	85	75	75

Table 8-14
Summary Statistics for *Performance* Effectiveness Ratings

Question	Number Respondents	Minimum % Rating	Maximum % Rating	Mean % Rating	Standard Deviation
Q1	27	55	90	72.22	9.2334
Q2	27	45	90	71.48	11.9948
Q3	27	50	95	72.59	12.4322
Q4	27	40	90	72.59	13.8932
Q5	27	40	90	70.00	12.3257
Q6	27	40	90	68.89	13.2530
Q7	27	55	90	72.22	9.3370
Q8	27	60	90	76.11	8.9156
Q9	27	0	80	23.52	15.3055
Q10	27	0	80	16.48	15.5548
Q11	27	10	90	73.52	15.1794
Q12	27	50	90	73.52	12.1540
Q13	27	40	90	70.93	10.8342

Table 8-15 summarizes the data for the ratings on the effectiveness of the program in teaching them the listed skills.

Table 8-15
Summary Statistics for *Program* Effectiveness Ratings

Question	Number of Respondents	Minimum % Rating	Maximum % Rating	Mean % Rating	Standard Deviation
Q1	27	60	90	80.19	7.4008
Q2	27	60	90	77.22	6.6986
Q3	27	45	90	76.67	12.2474
Q4	27	70	90	81.11	5.7735
Q5	27	50	90	74.63	11.4292
Q6	27	60	90	76.11	8.3589
Q7	27	60	90	79.07	8.6644
Q8	27	65	90	80.37	6.34
Q9	27	0	80	18.89	14.4338
Q10	27	0	80	14.63	15.9281
Q11	27	60	90	79.81	7.0002
Q12	27	60	90	80.37	7.4583
Q13	27	60	90	79.07	7.0761

The mean scores for program effectiveness range between 75 and 81 percent except again for skills 9 and 10. The mean score for skill 9 is 19 percent and for skill 10 is 15 percent. These ratings are linked closely with the ratings given for skill application.

Table 8-16 provides the results from the question regarding the work environment enablers and barriers.

The participants perceived the *program* was 34 percent responsible for their ability to effectively exhibit leadership qualities. This is the highest percent given to any of the factors.

Part of the survey also included questions regarding the action plans the participants were taught to complete during the program. Table 8-17 provides the results of those questions.

Table 8-16
Contributing Factors for Task Performance Results

Factor	Mean Percent Contribution to Maximizing Effectiveness
Knowledge, skills, or experience you had *before* the leadership program	16
Knowledge, skills, or experience you gained *from* the leadership program	34
Knowledge, skills, or experience you acquired on your own *after* the leadership program	12
Management style, reference materials, or job aides *unrelated* to the Leadership Program, e.g., bulletin boards, methods, and procedure documentation	4
Coaching or feedback from peers	9
Coaching or feedback from your Director	8
Coaching or feedback from your subordinates	7
Observing others	7
Organizational Changes—*Please specify*	1
Market Changes—*Please specify*	0
Other *internal* factors or resources—*Please specify*	1
Other *external* resources (vendors, course, conferences, etc.)—*Please specify*	1
Other—*Please specify*	0

Table 8-17
Action Plan Questions Results

Participant	Number of Actions Established	Percent Completed	Mean Level of Satisfaction (percent)
1	1	100	50
2	2	50	90
3	4	75	80
4	3	33	50
5	2	100	100
6	2	100	90
7	2	50	50
8	3	66	40
9	2	100	100
10	1	0	50
11	2	50	90
12	2	100	100
13	1	100	50
14	4	50	90
15	2	100	100
16	2	50	80
17	1	0	25
18	2	50	100
19	2	100	100
20	1	0	50
21	3	100	80
22	4	75	80
23	2	50	100
24	1	0	20
25	2	100	75
26	2	50	100
27	1	100	80

The participants planned, on the average, to complete two actions. The program did not have objectives for the number of actions the participants were expected to establish, so an average of two actions is not really a result. Each of the twenty-seven partici-

Table 8-18
Leadership Program Action Plan Data Summary

	Mean Percent	Standard Deviation
Actions Completed	64.78	35.8408
Level of Satisfaction	74.81	25.2099

pants planned to complete at least one goal. Table 8-18 provides the summary statistics for the completion and level-of-satisfaction data.

Of the actions planned to be completed by the time the survey was completed, an average of 65 percent were actually completed. On average, the participants were satisfied with the results they achieved for each action completed.

Chapter 9 will present the conclusions drawn and recommendations made based on these results.

SUMMARY

1. Analyzing job performance requires that the evaluator organize the data so the appropriate analysis can be done. Determining the extent to which performance has transferred and conducting further analysis based on the results is part of the evaluation effort. Table 8-19 provides a checklist for analyzing job performance data.

Table 8-19

Checklist for Analyzing Job Performance Data

Question	YES (✓) NO (✓)
1. Is the evaluation based on the key questions the client will ask of the performance data?	
2. Is the evaluation conducted in accordance with the design of the measurement program, i.e., pre-post, post, control vs. experimental group?	
3. Have tables for recording and tabulating the performance data been created so that appropriate statistical analyses of the data can be conducted?	
4. Have the data been summarized for appropriate statistical analysis?	

Table 8-19 (*continued*)

Checklist for Analyzing Job Performance Data

Question	YES (✓)	NO (✓)
5. Has the appropriate statistical test been selected for analysis?		
6. Have evaluation techniques, such as displaying the data in charts, or the use of color or shading, been used to help determine results?		
7. Are the results presented in a way the intended audience can understand?		
8. Are results clearly determined before conclusions are drawn?		

REFERENCES

2. Erwin, R., and J. Graber. 1999. "Human Capital Development: A Good Way to Measure Training." In *In Action: Measuring Learning and Performance*, ed. T. Hodges. Alexandria, Va.: American Society for Training and Development.

3. Martcneau, J.W., and K.M. Holmes-Ponder. 1999. "Measuring the Impact of a Leadership Development Program." In *In Action: Measuring Learning and Performance*, ed. T. Hodges. Alexandria, Va.: American Society for Training and Development.

4. Phillips, J.J. 1997. *Return on Investment*. Houston, Tex.: Gulf Publishing Company.

CHAPTER 9

How to Link Results to Conclusions and Recommendations

Imagine a client being presented with an evaluation report that recommends their program be discontinued. The client, naturally, wants to know what warrants such a recommendation. The individual may have invested a great deal of money and resources planning, designing, and implementing the program. Or, what if the evaluation report recommends that significant changes be made to the program, changes that involve additional investment? The client needs to be assured the recommended changes are necessary. Hopefully, the evaluation report has few if any recommendations for program changes. But even then, the client is entitled to feel certain that the program will, as currently designed and implemented, continue to meet its business and performance objectives.

Recommendations are sound if they are based on conclusions directly linked to the results of the evaluation. It is the evaluator's responsibility to ensure this linkage is made, and it is the evaluator's job to demonstrate to the client that any recommendations made are sound. It is important that the evaluator take the client step by step through the logic for making recommendations, so that by the time they get to them, it is obvious why they have been made. At this point, the client will be more inclined to consider the recommendations.

DRAWING CONCLUSIONS

After analyzing the performance data, the evaluator's next step is to look at the results from the evaluation and determine what

conclusions can be drawn from those results. It may be advanta-
geous for the evaluator to bring the program task force into the
process again at this point to help with this stage of the evaluation. If, for example, the program evaluation shows different
results for groups who reside in different locations, the client may
know of a situation in a particular location that may have influenced the results. Although the planners should have taken into
account all potentially influential variables in the evaluation planning, sometimes events happen that could not have been foreseen.
An additional advantage to having the task force members
involved at this point is that they become part of the process for
drawing conclusions and will, therefore, be more vested in the
final recommendations made for the program. The designers and
trainers can help determine what types of course enhancements
may help and how the changes will be implemented. With or without the program task force involvement, however, the evaluator is
the unbiased source to ensure all relevant factors and results are
interpreted correctly.

The Difference between a Result and a Conclusion

The job performance analysis for the sales example and the
case studies in progress in chapter 9 produced results. The
results in each case are the *outcomes* of the analysis that was
conducted. These outcomes are presented differently for clarity,
but they are still only the outcomes. Drawing conclusions based
on these outcomes or results is taking analysis to the next step of
evaluation. Because evaluation includes making *judgments* about
the results (Hopkins 1998), the evaluator must determine what
the results mean. Unfortunately, few evaluators are trained specifically to do this. If conclusions are provided with few or no
results to support them, it is clear that the evaluation was biased
or subjective. And that is a problem because the client will
become suspicious of every conclusion the evaluator makes. But
it is easy, sometimes, to jump to conclusions when they seem so
obvious. One way the evaluator can be diligent in this step of
evaluation is to think logically about the conclusion(s) being
drawn. Map each conclusion to at least one result. Creating a
logic map will ensure diligence. Table 9-1 provides the beginning
of such a map with three separate example results.

Table 9-1
Sample Logic Map—Conclusions Linked to Results

Result	Conclusion
1. The mean units produced increased by 45 percent with a range of 0–95 percent.	1. The program is more effective for some than for others.
2. A significant correlation was found between estimates of timesaving and the extent of reported improvement in team effectiveness.	2. Improved team effectiveness tends to save time for this group.*
3. No significant difference was found between the control group and the experimental group.	3. The data does not substantiate that training had its intended impact.

*Correlation does not necessarily mean that there is a *causative* relationship between two variables. But if a correlation is statistically significant, one can be confident that there is some degree of true relationship between two variables (Hopkins 1998).

Conclusion Statement

How to state conclusions is based on the intended audience of the evaluation report. Notice in Table 9-1, conclusion statement number three is phrased, "The data does not substantiate that training had its intended impact." The statement could read, "The training had no impact." The second statement is more direct and would be preferable if the intended audience is receptive to that type of direct statement. When a conclusion is known to have serious impact, such as this one, however, the evaluator may want to be more precise. In this case, the evaluator may expect an adverse reaction and believes a more descriptive or causative conclusion statement would be more palatable. If the conclusion is negative, the evaluator may feel that the client will consider the recommendation based on the conclusion if the conclusion sounds more objective.

The examples in Table 9-1 are simple and directly linked. Many times, however, conclusions are drawn on more than one result. They are determined by looking at a combination of several results. Indeed, when drawing conclusions, all evaluation results from a program are considered together. If reaction and learning data were collected, for example, they are included as part of the evaluation. Armed with these data and the results from the performance evaluation, along with any client, designer, or program-implementer insights, the evaluator is in the best position to make sense of it all. If the evaluator is concerned that he or she is not in the best position to draw conclusions because of bias or political pressures, the safest thing to do would be to present the results without conclusions. This would be unfortunate, however, because the evaluator most likely understands the data better than anyone else.

There is no way to prescribe *how to* draw conclusions, as each program evaluation will be different from another. It is an acquired skill that comes with practice. The examples offered in this chapter, including the case studies in progress, provide the benefit of such practice. There are a few tips to keep in mind when drawing conclusions based on results.

Tips for Drawing Defendable Conclusions

1. Ensure that the people conducting the evaluation are not biased for or against the program.
2. Ensure that the evaluator is not so familiar with the data that they cannot see the whole picture.
3. Ensure the evaluator is not compromised in any way by those who will be seeing and acting on the conclusions.
4. Ensure each conclusion is based on at least one result.
5. Use as few qualifiers as possible when drawing conclusions such as, "These results demonstrate a *tremendous* need to change the company policy."
6. State the conclusion in terms the client can understand (Brinkerhoff and Gill 1994).

MAKING RECOMMENDATIONS

Once conclusions are drawn, the next step is for the evaluator to determine if recommendations are warranted. It is a mistake to make recommendations until clear conclusions have been drawn because it does not provide the client with the benefit of the logic behind the recommendation. It may cause the client to question it. Recommendations are offered *only* if the conclusions warrant them. If the evaluator concludes that the program is effective, based on the results and that there are no areas for improvement, no recommendations are needed. If, however, it is concluded that there are areas in which the program is weak, the evaluator has the opportunity and the responsibility to provide specific recommendations based on the conclusions. According to Combs and Falleta (2000), the benefits of the recommendations always outweigh the cost for implementing the changes recommended. Making recommendations requires that the evaluator understand the realities of the client organization, so that the recommendations can be acted on. If, for example, the evaluator concludes that a program is not long enough to effectively teach the skills required, yet the evaluator knows that the client is unable to take people off the job any longer, then the recommendation may be to revise the training to teach the use of job aids rather than to extend the program. The evaluator is never compromised, however, into *not* offering a feasible recommendation that is clearly indicated by the conclusions. To do this would be to ignore the findings of the evaluation. Table 9-2 provides the continuation of the sample logic map in Table 9-1 to include the recommendations that could be made based on each result and conclusion.

Recommendations are made after careful consideration of the conclusions. A few tips for making recommendations based on conclusions are offered.

Table 9-2
Sample Logic Map—Recommendations Linked to Conclusions

Result	Conclusion	Recommendation
1. The mean units produced increased by 45 percent with a range of 0–95 percent.	1. The course is more effective for some than for others.	1. It is recommended that the program target group be more clearly defined and advertised in the curriculum listing.
2. A significant correlation was found between estimates of timesaving and the extent of reported improvement in team effectiveness.	2. Improved team effectiveness tends to save time for this group.	2. No recommendation.
3. No significant difference was found between the control group and the experimental group.	3. The data does not substantiate that training had its intended impact.	3. Training in its current state should be discontinued.

Tips for Developing Logical Recommendations

1. Understand the limitations of the client organization for implementing the recommendations offered (Torres, Preskill, and Piontek 1996).
2. Ensure each recommendation is based on at least one conclusion.
3. State recommendations in language that the client can understand.
4. Do not be compromised into *not* making a feasible recommendation when it is warranted, based on a clear conclusion(s).

Remember that the client and the HRD organization will almost always begin reading the study or briefing by going to the recommendations section first. The study must support the recommendations made.

SALES EXAMPLE

The business objectives for the sales course example used in chapter 8 called for an increase in sales and improved sales associates' efficiency. The associated performance objectives are to improve the sales associates':

- Communication skills
- Ability to manage their accounts
- Ability to uncover business problems
- Ability to effectively delegate
- Leadership skills

The data for actual sales were tabulated, summarized, and analyzed for the participants both before and after the sales course. A follow-up questionnaire was administered to the participants six months after course completion to determine their perceptions of the extent to which the course improved their confidence, efficiency, skills, and productivity. It also asked the participants to rate the extent to which their work environment supported the knowledge and/or skills they acquired in the class and if they would recommend the course to their colleagues. The data from the questionnaire were tabulated, summarized, and analyzed. Both analyses produced the following results:

- Sales data improved by 250 percent.
- The two months with the lowest sales for all participants were the month the associates attended the training and the month after the training.

- Perceived efficiency improved by 28 percent.
- The skills and abilities required to improve sales and efficiency were perceived to have improved by 49 percent.
- The environment was perceived to be supportive of the skills/knowledge taught by 78 percent. However, one question pertaining to the participants having the necessary resources, such as equipment and information required to apply the knowledge and/or skills taught in the course, received a mean rating of 50 percent.
- Perceived productivity improved by 76 percent.
- The participants recommend this course to their colleagues (88 percent).

Table 9-3 provides the conclusions the evaluator draws for the sales course example, based on the results.

Table 9-4 provides the logic map for linking the recommendations with the conclusions made for the sales course example.

Table 9-3
Sales Example Logic Map—Conclusions Linked to Results

Result	Conclusions
Sales data improved by 250 percent.	The course improves sales.
The two months with the lowest sales for all participants were the month the associates attended the training and the month after the training.	Taking the associates "off the street" to attend the training costs the company sales.
Perceived efficiency improved by 28 percent.	The course improves efficiency but not as much as it improves productivity.
The skills and abilities required to improve sales and efficiency is perceived to have improved by 49 percent.	The course improves the skills attributed to improving efficiency and sales.
The environment was perceived to be supportive of the skills/knowledge taught by 78 percent.	The current work environment supports the skills taught in the course.
Question regarding having necessary resources received rating of 50 percent.	Resources to apply knowledge and/or skills taught may be a transfer problem.
Perceived productivity improved by 76 percent.	The course increases productivity.
The participants recommend this course to their colleagues (88 percent).	The course is relevant and useful.

Table 9-4
Sales Example Logic Map—Recommendations Linked
to Conclusions

Results	Conclusions	Recommendations
Sales data improved by 250 percent.	The courses as currently configured improves sales.	
The two months with the lowest sales for all participants were the month the associates attended the training and the month after the training.	Taking the associates "off the street" to attend training costs the company sales.	Alternative delivery that requires fewer hours dedicated to training should be considered.
Perceived efficiency improved by 28 percent.	The course improves efficiency but not as much as it improves productivity.	A calculation should be conducted to determine the financial benefit of the efficiency improvement, to determine if this should continue as an objective for the program.
The skills and abilities required to improve sales and efficiency is perceived to have improved by 49 percent.	The course met is performance objectives.	
The environment was perceived to be supportive of the skills/knowledge taught by 78 percent. Question regarding having necessary resources received rating of 50 percent.	The current work environment supports the skills taught in the course. Resources to apply knowledge and/or skills taught may be a transfer problem.	Management should investigate the equipment or information the associates are provided on the job to determine suitability.
Perceived productivity improved by 76 percent.	The course increases productivity.	
The participants recommend this course to their colleagues (88 percent).	The course is relevant and useful.	

Notice that, unlike conclusions, recommendations are limited to only those activities that can be acted on. The evaluator can conclude overall in this case that the program should continue because it is meeting its business and performance objectives, except in the area of efficiency. The follow-up questionnaire revealed areas where the course can be enhanced, and specific recommendations are made for that enhancement. The client may feel the program can be continued as is, based on the conclusions, keeping the evaluation recommendations in mind for consideration at a later date. Or they may want to begin exploring the recommended changes and implementing them into a new design while the old design continues. When complete, it can then replace the old design.

If an ROI analysis is conducted on this program, different conclusions and recommendations may be made. If, for example, cost figures are tied to the perceived efficiency savings, a higher than 250 percent sales increase benefit may be realized. Also, if the cost to attend the training is included as part of the cost of the program, the cost/benefit ratio may be one that would support the recommendation made above and provide justification for experimenting with alternative delivery methods.

Just as results are stated clearly, conclusions and recommendations need to be concise, with no ambiguity or qualifying descriptors. Qualifying descriptors that are unnecessary may give the reader a feeling that the evaluation is biased. For example, which statement gives the best feeling of a professional, unbiased assessment, "This program was extremely successful" or "This program exceeded its objective of increasing sales while improving efficiency"?

CASE STUDIES IN PROGRESS

Now let's look at conclusions and recommendations made based on the results of the performance evaluations analysis conducted for the different case studies in progress.

Technical Training Program

The performance objectives for the technical training program case study are to improve warehouse employees' driving skills, particularly as they relate to safety, and to improve warehouse operational skills. By meeting these performance objectives, it is expected that motor vehicle and on-the-job accidents will decrease and customer satisfaction will be improved.

To measure performance, an experimental-versus-control-group program evaluation design was used. The experimental group went through the training, and the control group did not. The employees'

Table 9-5
Technical Training Program Weekly Mean Log Score Results

Group Scores	Week 1	Week 2	Week 3	Week 4	Week 5	Week 6
Experimental	11.5	12.38	8.38	16.13	17.63	18.88
Control	7.5	7.13	3.75	7.63	7.75	7.63

supervisor maintained logs for sixteen of his employees for six weeks to measure warehouse operational skills. Each week he turned his logs in to the evaluation group. Table 9-5 provides the results of the weekly log scores.

The difference between the two groups was found to be statistically significant ($p < .01$).

In addition to the log, weekly riding evaluations were conducted by the supervisors for each participant in both groups, to measure driving skills. Riding scores were recorded for each individual in the experimental and control groups. Table 9-6 provides the results for those data.

Again, the difference between the two groups was found to be significant ($p < .01$).

Chapter 7 provides a comprehensive discussion of these results and explores the factors that could have produced these findings. In addition, chapter 5 provides the results of the learning evaluation. Learning did take place with a post test mean score of 79 percent.

Table 9-7 presents the conclusions and recommendations based on the results.

Both the learning and performance evaluations are positive. Learning is taking place, and the learning is transferring to the work environment. If the evaluation design included an ROI analysis, the data from this performance evaluation would have been used to determine the tangible benefits (reduced motor vehicle and warehouse accidents). The tangible benefits would be converted to mone-

Table 9-6
Technical Training Program Weekly Riding Rating Results
(in percent)

Group Mean Ratings	Week 1	Week 2	Week 3	Week 4	Week 5	Week 6
Experimental	55.62	65	39.37	73.75	80	85.63
Control	65.63	68.13	35.63	61.25	60.63	61.88

Table 9-7
Technical Training Program Logic Map—Linking Results, Conclusions, and Recommendations

Result	Conclusion	Recommendation
The experimental group had significantly higher warehouse log scores than the control group.	The trained group performed better in the warehouse than the untrained group.	This program should continue as currently designed and implemented. The results of the evaluation could be advertised to maximize attendance.
The experimental group had significantly higher riding scores than the control group, although the riding scores were not as different as the log ratings.	The trained group performed better on the road than the untrained group.	This conclusion supports the recommendation above.

tary values and the intangible benefits (increased customer satisfaction) would have been quantified or noted. Program cost data (development, delivery, and participant time in the classroom) would be calculated. Using the formula provided in chapter 8, the ROI would then be calculated. But an ROI analysis could not be done until this careful and successful *job performance evaluation* was conducted.

What were the *successful* components of the technical training case study job performance evaluation?

- The experimental-versus-control-group design effectively isolated the impact of the training versus anything else that may have impacted performance. Indeed, something did impact the employees' performance during the third week of this study. The client might be able to inform us what it was that brought the performances down, but whatever it was, it was irrelevant to the study because it impacted both groups' performances.
- The same supervisor rated both groups. Although it is possible that the supervisor may have unconsciously rated the trained group higher, expecting them to perform better, the supervisor was made aware of that possibility, which hopefully helped him keep whatever bias he had in check. In addition, the supervisor had no vested interest in this particular program itself. He wanted the best program possible for his employees—one that would have the

maximum impact on their performance, so rating diligence on his part could be assumed. The fact that the same supervisor rated both groups eliminated any inter-rater reliability problems that could have existed using the performance measurement tool.

- Having a clearly defined warehouse behavioral log provided the supervisor with the opportunity to objectively and quickly measure performance. The behaviors were stated unambiguously. Because the supervisor was familiar with the metrics used for rating, little training was required for its use. Also, the log is designed for easy scoring.

- Using an already established riding rating sheet ensured existing standards were being employed for the evaluation. No additional tasks outside of the normal work situation were added.

- Offering rewards for good driving and placing safety posters in the warehouse to help enable transfer may encourage the members of the control group and future participants to actively learn when they are provided with the online training program.

Some possible *weaknesses* of the evaluation design may include:

- The control group was aware that they were being purposely held back from receiving the training. This may have engendered resentment on their part, which could have created artificial (negative) performance.

- As mentioned above, the supervisor may have been biased toward the trained group in that he may have had expectations for performance. Although steps were taken to mitigate the risk, the risk did exist.

- Offering rewards for good driving and placing safety posters in the warehouse may have influenced the control group. So their behavior is most likely not the same as what it would be normally.

- Because the results of this program were good, learning or reaction data were not necessary for drawing conclusions or making recommendations. If the results were not as good, those two components would become important.

Sales/Customer Service Training Program

The performance objectives for the Sales/Customer Service Training Program case study are to improve customer service representatives'

Table 9-8
Sales/Customer Service Training Program Performance
Observations Results

Representative	Before Training Scores (in percent)	After Training Scores (in percent)
1	40	62
2	25	80
3	50	90
4	33	75
5	42	82
6	60	85
7	42	88
8	28	75
9	44	62
10	32	85
11	55	68
12	26	56
13	35	75
14	45	89
15	52	90
16	40	100
Mean Scores	41	79

customer relationship skills. The expectation is that by doing so, customer satisfaction will increase and call escalations will be reduced.

Trained observers were able to observe a "before" and "after" call for sixteen participants. Observation checklists were used and scored as described in chapter 7, resulting in overall percent ratings for each representative. Table 9-8 provides the results for those calls, along with calculated mean scores.

The differences between the before and after training scores were found to be significant ($p < .01$). Before drawing conclusions based on these results, the analyst decides to break down each behavior area to determine if the participants performed better in one area than another. Table 9-9 provides the percent "yes's," "no's," and "NAs (not applicable)" received for each behavior area on the checklist. (See chapter 7 for the entire checklist.)

These results show areas of performance that were stronger than others. Some of the "yes" percentages are not as high as other scores.

Table 9-9
Sales/Customer Service Training Program Percent Breakdown
by Behavior Area Results

	Percent Breakdown		
Behavior Area	Yes	No	NA
Opening the call (ten behaviors)	98	2	0
Diagnosing problems and identifying needs (six behaviors)	80	10	10
Assessing progress and updating the plan (four behaviors)	60	45	15
Recommending approaches for results (five behaviors)	55	35	20
Closing the call (five behaviors)	98	2	0
Overall listening skills (four behaviors)	75	25	0

Before drawing conclusions about the training program based on the performance data alone, it is helpful for the evaluator to go back to the learning analysis results to see the extent to which learning took place and how the results in Table 9-8 compare with the learning data. Chapter 5 provides the results of the learning evaluation. The mean score of the proficiency test is 86 percent. So learning did take place. But the data was not analyzed by behavior breakdown as was done for the performance evaluation. If the learning data is accessible, the evaluator can go back to it and break it down as done with the performance evaluation. If not, conclusions are made on the performance data breakdown alone. Table 9-10 presents the conclusions and recommendations based on the performance evaluation results.

If the learning data could be broken down into the behavior categories as was done for the performance data, the evaluator may find that one or more of the behavior categories had higher scores than those from the performance evaluation. If that were the case, the conclusions and recommendations would be different. Look at Table 9-11 as a comparison.

These sets of conclusions and recommendations tell a different story and demonstrate how important learning data can be. If a follow-up survey were used in addition to the observations, environmental factors that could be inhibiting those performances not rated high could have been determined.

If an ROI analysis were part of this evaluation, the number of reduced escalations would have been tracked, the value of each

Table 9-10
Logic Map for Sales/Customer Service Program—Linking Results, Conclusions, and Recommendations

Results	Conclusions	Recommendations
There was a significant difference between the behaviors before and after the training.	Sales/customer service performance improved as a result of the training program.	
Opening the call and closing the call had the highest scores with 98 percent "yes" ratings.	The participants were effective at opening and closing calls.	These portions of the training should continue as designed and delivered.
Diagnosing problems and identifying needs had the second highest scores with 80 percent "yes" ratings.	The participants were effective at diagnosing customer problems and identifying customer needs.	These portions of the training should be continued as designed and delivered.
Overall listening had the third highest scores, with 75 percent "yes" ratings.	The participants demonstrated effective listening skills, although there is room for improvement.	The portion of the training should be examined for enhancements.
Assessing progress and updating the plan and recommending approaches had the lowest scores with 60 percent and 55 percent "yes" ratings.	Although the training program improved the participants' ability to assess progress of the call, updating the plan, and recommending approaches to solve customer problems, there is room for improvement in these areas.	This portion of the training should be examined for enhancements.

escalation determined, and a tangible benefit derived. A customer survey may have been given to determine customer satisfaction improvement, and an intangible benefit determined. A Return on Expectation (ROE) interview(s) could have shown an estimated cost-benefit. The costs for the program (development, materials, delivery, and the value of participant time spent in class) would be determined. Using the calculation provided in chapter 8, an ROI for this program would be determined. Unless this is an expensive program, however, an ROI study does not appear to be of value. The learning and job performance evaluation provides sufficient information for ensuring the program's success and providing specific areas for program enhancements.

Table 9-11

Logic Map for Sales/Customer Service Program—Linking Results, Conclusions, and Recommendations Using Both Learning and Performance Data

Results	Conclusions	Recommendations
The mean proficiency score was 87 percent, and there was a significant difference between the job performance behaviors before and after the training.	Sales/customer service performance improved as a result of the training program.	
The mean proficiency scores for opening the call and closing the call behaviors was 92 percent, and these behaviors had the highest on-the-job performance scores with 98 percent "yes" ratings.	The program effectively prepared the participants to effectively open and close calls.	These portions of the training should be continued as designed and delivered.
The mean proficiency score for the diagnosing problems and identifying needs behaviors is 82 percent, and these behaviors had the second highest job performance scores with 80 percent "yes" ratings.	The program effectively prepared the participants to diagnose customer problems and identify customer needs.	These portions of the training should be continued as designed and delivered.
The mean proficiency score for the overall listening behaviors was 60 percent, and these behaviors had the third highest job performance scores with 75 percent "yes" ratings.	The participants did not demonstrate as high a proficiency from the training as the other categories. They demonstrated effective listening skills on the job, although there is room for improvement.	This portion of the training should be strengthened.
The proficiency scores for the assessing progress and updating the plan and recommending approaches for results were 80 percent and 82 percent, respectively, but these behaviors had the lowest job performance scores with 60 percent and 55 percent "yes" ratings.	Although the training program effectively taught the participants how to assess progress of the call and updating the plan and recommending approaches to solve customer problems, the skills did not transfer successfully to the job.	The client organization should investigate what is not happening on the job to support the training given to the participants. Possibilities may include coaching or feedback from peers or from supervisors, or a software package that could provide clues for customer problem resolutions.

What were the *successful* components of the sales/customer service case study performance evaluation?

• The proficiency checklist used was tested for reliability.
• The proficiency checklist was designed to be realistic to the job to ensure transfer.
• The performance results were based on actual, rather than perceived, performance.
• The checklist was designed so the behaviors could be grouped into performance categories for analysis.

Possible *weaknesses* for this evaluation are:

• If a follow-up survey had been administered in addition to the observation, the evaluator could explore reasons for the two lower job performance behavioral categories.
• The learning data analysis should have broken the checklist data into the performance objective categories. The conclusions and recommendations may be different, as seen in Tables 9-10 and 9-11. This demonstrates the importance of putting together a program task force, so that all members are aware of the business, performance, and learning objectives.

Leadership Development Program

The performance objectives for the Leadership Development Program case study are to develop or improve supervisory personnel's ability to communicate more effectively with subordinates, conduct more efficient and effective meetings, and prioritize goals and activities. The program task force expects that by developing or improving these skills, turnover will be reduced, team effectiveness will be increased, productivity will be improved, and time will be saved by both supervisors and their subordinates.

To measure newly acquired or improved performance, a follow-up questionnaire was distributed to participants in the Leadership Development Program three months after the program via company email. The questionnaire asked the participants to rate their perceived effectiveness in performing the skills taught in the program. They were asked their confidence level in their ratings, and the ratings were adjusted accordingly. Then they were asked to rate the perceived effectiveness of the program in teaching them each skill. They also were asked to estimate the extent to which several of their work conditions, as well as the Leadership Development Program, positively impacted their leadership ability.

Table 9-12 provides the results of the questions regarding the participants' perceptions of the Leadership Development Program's effectiveness.

Table 9-13 provides the results of the questions regarding the participants' perceptions of the effectiveness of the Leadership Development Program in teaching them the skills listed.

Table 9-12

Leadership Development *Performance* Effectiveness Results

Question How *effective* are you in performing each of the skills listed?	Minimum % Rating	Maximum % Rating	Mean % Rating	Standard Deviation
1. Communicate using positive language	55	90	72	9.23
2. Determine when subordinates need assistance	45	90	71	11.99
3. Conduct individual meetings so that subordinates' concerns and ideas are accounted for	50	95	73	12.43
4. Open team meetings with clearly stated goals	40	90	73	13.89
5. Encourage group participation using active listening techniques	40	90	70	12.33
6. Keep discussion on track during team meetings	40	90	69	13.25
7. Accomplish stated meeting goals	55	90	72	9.34
8. Close meetings with clearly stated follow-up actions	60	90	76	8.92
9. Task team members based on their individual personality types	0	80	24	15.31
10. Explain to team members how to use personality type indicators to achieve team goals	0	80	16	15.55
11. Prioritize goals and activities	10	90	74	15.18
12. Complete goals and activities in order of priority	50	90	74	12.15
13. Conduct only necessary meetings	40	90	71	10.83

Table 9-13
Leadership Development *Program* Effectiveness Results

Question How *effective* was the training in preparing you to perform each of the skills listed?	Minimum % Rating	Maximum % Rating	Mean % Rating	Standard Deviation
1. Communicate using positive language	60	90	80	7.4
2. Determine when subordinates need assistance	60	90	77	6.70
3. Conduct individual meetings so that subordinates' concerns and ideas are accounted for	45	90	77	12.25
4. Open team meetings with clearly stated goals	70	90	81	5.77
5. Encourage group participation using active listening techniques	50	90	75	11.43
6. Keep discussion on track during team meetings	60	90	76	8.36
7. Accomplish stated meeting goals	60	90	79	8.66
8. Close meetings with clearly stated follow-up actions	65	90	80	6.34
9. Task team members based on their individual personality types	0	80	19	14.43
10. Explain to team members how to use personality type indicators to achieve team goals	0	80	15	15.93
11. Prioritize goals and activities	60	90	80	7
12. Complete goals and activities in order of priority	60	90	80	7.46
13. Conduct only necessary meetings	60	90	79	7.10

Table 9-14
Leadership Development Factor Contribution Results

Factor	Mean Percent Contribution to Maximizing Effectiveness
Knowledge, skills, or experience you had *before* the leadership program	16
Knowledge, skills, or experience you gained *from* the leadership program	34
Knowledge, skills, or experience you acquired on your own *after* the leadership program	12
Management style, reference materials, or job aides *unrelated* to the Leadership Program, e.g., bulletin boards, methods and procedure documentation	4
Coaching or feedback from peers	9
Coaching or feedback from your director	8
Coaching or feedback from your subordinates	7
Observing others	7
Organizational changes–*Please specify*	1
Market changes–*Please specify*	0
Other *internal* factors or resources–*Please specify*	1
Other *external* resources (vendors, course, conferences, etc.)–*Please specify*	1
Other–*Please specify*	0

The participants were also asked to provide estimates of the extent to which various factors served as enablers of skill transfer. Table 9-14 provides the results of those estimates.

Finally, the participants were asked how many leadership-related actions they had planned and how many, up to the point of the evaluation, were completed. Table 9-15 provides results from the action plan questions.

Table 9-15
Leadership Development Program Action Plan Results

	Mean Percent	Standard Deviation
Actions completed	64.78	35.8408
Level of satisfaction	74.81	25.2099

Results from the learning analysis conducted for this program (chapter 5) demonstrated that the program is effective overall in meeting the course objectives. Table 9-16 provides the conclusions and recommendations made for the Leadership Development Program.

There were a few weak components of this evaluation. The task force for the program, which included the client, the program designers, the evaluator, and the trainers, anticipated that a potential barrier to both the learning and job performance would be in the area of personality-type indicator-testing. The trainers and the designers were concerned that there was not enough time in the program to teach this effectively. The client was concerned that this behavior would not take place because there isn't enough time on the job to do individual testing of this complexity. But regardless of these concerns, *no enablers were put into place in either the learning or job environment to overcome the barriers.* It is not surprising, therefore, that the job performance analysis shows this to be a transfer problem. An additional weakness in the evaluation program was that, when the learning analysis was conducted, no effort was made to see if those areas in particular on the posttest were lower than the others. A learning gain of 38 percent was found and the difference was significant ($p < .01$), so everything was assumed to be fine. But fortunately, the job performance analysis was able to identify this area as a learning problem.

An ROI analysis for this program would be challenging. The business objectives were to reduce turnover, save costs due to time savings, and increase productivity. Company records could turn up reduced turnover data for the participants' subordinate groups, but results would not be expected for a longer period of time after the program completion. And leadership may change during that time, so a direct correlation between the management skill and the subordinate may not be possible. Time savings can be tracked and calculated. Increased productivity will vary by individual depending upon the participants' actual job performance goals. Gathering this data might best be done by individual interviews, but that can be costly. Considering that evaluation costs are part of the program costs when calculating an ROI, the evaluator and the client will want to determine if such a complex evaluation process is of value. In this case, the

Table 9-16
Logic Map for Leadership Development Program—Linking Results with Conclusions and Recommendations

Results	Conclusions	Recommendations
The skills pertaining to evaluating and using personality type indicators were perceived to be low, and the program effectiveness in teaching these skills was perceived as low.	The leadership program did not effectively teach the participants how to determine personality types and therefore the participants were unable to use such skills.	It is recommended that the program either be modified to improve this component of the program or the components be eliminated as an objective based on the effectiveness of other results.
All other skills were being practiced effectively and were perceived as having been taught effectively from the program.	The leadership program was effective in teaching the remaining skills as they related to the performance objectives for the program.	
The participants perceived that 34 percent of the credit for their performing effectively as leaders was due to the program, with the second highest impact area being 16 percent.	The leadership program played the most important role in impacting the participants' effectiveness in meeting the performance objectives.	
The participants completed 65 percent of the actions planned.	The action-planning process positively impacted the participants' ability to use action plans effectively.	The action-planning should continue to be used as part of the Leadership Development program. At a later date, the client may want to know if additional long-term actions planned have been completed successfully by this group.
The participants were 75 percent satisfied with the results achieved through the action-planning process.	The action-planning process was useful to many of the participants.	

client may be willing to assume that by meeting the performance objectives, the business objectives will be met.

What were the *successful* components of the Leadership Development Program case study performance evaluation?

- Using the email process for survey distribution and providing advance notice may be responsible for the high survey response rate achieved.
- The skills effectiveness ratings were closely related to the program effectiveness ratings, which is a good indication that the survey instrument is effectively measuring what it was intended to measure.
- The two lowest ratings were on the same topic and were close for effectiveness and program effectiveness, which indicate that the scores are good indicators.
- The confidence rating provided a conservative estimate which may provide a measure of comfort with the "perception" ratings.

Some possible *weaknesses* of the evaluation design may include:

- The data were perception data.
- Not enough time was allowed to determine the full extent of the action-planning process, because the participants may have planned goals that take longer to accomplish.
- Anticipated learning and job performance barriers were not attended to.
- The learning analysis should have considered the barrier issue in its assessment.

SUMMARY

The evaluator must be careful to draw conclusions only after the program analysis has provided clear results. And any recommendations made must be linked to the conclusions. Table 9-17 provides a checklist to use when drawing conclusions and making recommendations.

Table 9-17
Checklist for Drawing Conclusions and Making Recommendations

Question	YES (✓)	NO (✓)
1. Is every conclusion supported by at least one result?		
2. Are results presented along with the conclusions?		
3. Are conclusions based on results only and not by other potentially biased sources?		
4. Are conclusions stated without qualifying descriptors?		
5. Are all data results included in drawing conclusions?		
6. If the client is available, is he or she brought into the conclusions-making process?		
7. Are recommendations based on clearly stated conclusions?		
8. Are recommendations feasible for the client to act on?		

References

1. Brinkerhoff, R.O., and S.J. Gill. 1994. *The Learning Alliance.* San Francisco, Calif.: Jossey Bass Publishers.

2. Combs, W.L., and S.V. Falletta. 2000. *The Targeted Evaluation.* Alexandria, Va.: American Society for Training and Development.

3. Hopkins, K.D. 1998. *Educational and Psychological Measurement and Evaluation,* 8th edition, Boston, Mass.: Allyn and Bacon.

4. Torres, R.T., H.S. Preskill, and M.E. Piontek. 1996. *Evaluation Strategies for Communicating and Reporting.* Thousand Oaks, Calif.: Sage Publications.

CHAPTER 10

How to Effectively Present Evaluation Results

No matter how good the evaluation design or how comprehensive the data analysis, if the results are not presented well, the effort (and expense) could be wasted. Even if conclusions and recommendations are logically mapped to the results, if they aren't presented well, they may not be heeded.

The "who, what, where, and how" principle may serve the evaluator well when planning the best way to present evaluation results.

DETERMINE *WHO* WILL RECEIVE THE REPORT

Combs and Falletta (2000) recommend using the matrix in Table 10-1 to help plan for communicating the results. Establishing feedback mechanisms to assess the effectiveness of the communication later is an interesting example of the evaluator evaluating his or her own effectiveness.

If the audience is made up of company executives or senior managers who are interested in the extent to which the business objectives have been met, the evaluation report should be brief and to the point. If the audience includes those who work with the program participants, they will most likely be interested in the extent to which the performance objectives have been met and how the environment can best support that performance. They probably will want more details about the results and conclusions. Program designers, however, probably will be more interested in what led up

Table 10-1
Matrix for Communication Planning

Audience	Objectives of the Communication	Audience Needs	Political Sensitivities	Content of the Message	Medium	Timing and Sequencing	Feedback Mechanism
Executives/Business Owners							
Senior Managers							
Individuals Directly Affected by the Intervention							
Individuals Indirectly Affected by the Intervention							

to the recommendations. It is possible this audience may be sophisticated in measurement and evaluation and most interested in the details of the study.

DETERMINE WHAT WILL BE REPORTED

After the audience is identified, the evaluator can determine what information to provide. The executives will most likely want to see monetary benefits, or other business benefits, that were derived from the program. If an ROI or cost-benefit analysis was conducted, they will want to see those results. If other intangible benefits were derived, such as increased customer satisfaction or employee motivation, they will want to know the extent to which the program achieved those benefits. They will want to know if the program was successful and if it should be continued.

The audience representing the program participants will want to know which behaviors were improved, or which performance objectives were met, and which were not. Enablers and barriers to performance will be important. If they can do something to reinforce or support the behaviors, they will want to know what that is.

The program-designers will want to know which course or program objectives were met as demonstrated by the learning data and how the learning transferred to the job. They will be most interested in recommendations that they can act on—such as revisions in course material, instruction, or courseware.

If it is anticipated that the audience will question the evaluation design or calculations, details of the reasoning behind the evaluation design may be needed. The client may want exact program cost figures and their origins or to know how calculations were conducted and the assumptions made for the financial analysis.

DETERMINE WHERE THE REPORT WILL BE PRESENTED

This may or may not be a critical element in the reporting process for the evaluator, depending upon the organization. But if the results are being presented in a formal briefing, the evaluator will want to have a computer slide presentation, such as a Microsoft PowerPoint presentation, prepared in a professional, attractive manner, with back-up slides that anticipate questions the audience may have about particular portions of the evaluation. If the report is going to be distributed in a paper or electronic medium without an opportunity for the evaluator to answer questions, it should include back-up material, such as appendices, which include the data collection instruments used.

DETERMINE *HOW* THE REPORT WILL BE PRESENTED

When selecting the best way to present the results, the evaluator considers both the audience(s) and the complexity of the study. Remember to report findings so the client can "hear" them (Brinkerhoff and Gill 1994). The way in which the information is conveyed influences how, and to what extent, the audience hears it.

Slide Presentation

For the executive audience, the evaluator may find a slide briefing most beneficial. The briefing includes (but may not be limited to) the following:

- One slide on the background or the purpose of the evaluation
- One slide on the evaluation design, stated in nontechnical terminology
- Two or three slides providing the results of the evaluation
- One or two slides on the conclusions drawn based on the results
- One slide on the recommendations based on the conclusion

If assumptions have been made that are important to the results achieved or conclusions made, the evaluator includes a slide for those as well. Another technique to help ensure actions will be taken based on the recommendations is to offer a last slide entitled, "Action Plan." This would help the presenter facilitate a discussion of what needs to take place as a result of the evaluation and identify the parties responsible for those actions.

Executive Briefing

An executive briefing can be a stand-alone document or the first page of a full report. An executive briefing is concise and powerful. The executive briefing has two purposes: (1) to provide just enough information, so the reader knows exactly what happened as a result of the evaluation, and (2) to entice the reader to "look inside for some real good stuff." Notice how the last sentence in the following executive summary example in Figure 10-1 encourages the reader to examine the reasons for the findings.

Executive Summary

A cost-effectiveness analysis was performed for the Computer-Based Training (CBT) portion of the XXX software system-training program, which supports Company XXX sales. The analysis compared the CBT plus 5-day leader-led course with an 8-day leader-led course. The results showed the CBT providing 35 percent savings in year 1, and 48 percent savings in years 2 and 3. The performance data showed that the training was successful in general. Posttest scores were high, and follow-up evaluations conducted one to three months after the training demonstrated successful performance using the XXXX system. When examining the data for different variables, several trends were found. Those participants who used the CBT more than the others rated its contribution to their XXX performance more highly and took less time on the posttraining test. After one-to-three months on the job, those participants who used the CBT more rated their effectiveness in accessing correct screens slightly higher than those who used the CBT less, their estimate of errors made were fewer, their effectiveness updating records higher, and the time to complete orders lower.

Figure 10-1. Example executive summary—Example 1.

Figure 10-2 provides another example of an executive summary that bullets the results.

Evaluation Report

A traditional evaluation study report could mirror the organization of the Measurement Plan provided in chapter 7. Whatever format is used, the evaluation report offers the following information.

1. Introduction or Background
    This paragraph provides a program description along with the business objectives for the program. It describes who the program participants are and how their job functions relate to the business objectives. It also discusses the purpose of the evaluation.
2. Evaluation Objectives
    This section lists the specific objectives for the evaluation. The performance objectives that are mapped to the business objectives are listed. This discussion will establish the expectations for the report, because these are the objectives that are measured.

> ### Executive Summary
>
> XXX Group purchased and implemented the "XXXX" training curriculum designed to provide representatives with advanced training in customer service skills. This training curriculum was ultimately expected to reduce the number of call escalations and improve customer contact interviews. An impact study conducted by the evaluation organization prior to, and after, the training event for three sample sites concluded the following.
>
> - The representatives did not *perceive* that their skills had increased as a result of the training.
> - The team coaches *perceived* some skill increase as a result of the training.
> - The representatives were *observed* to have no skill increase as a result of the training.
> - The training can expect to produce a negative ROI both for year 1 (–85 percent) and year 2 (-54 percent).
>
> The XXX Impact Study Report provides a description of the methodology used for the study, a detailed explanation of the results, the conclusions reached, and the recommendations made by the evaluation organization.

Figure 10-2. Example executive summary—Example 2.

3. Methodology

This section describes the study design and how the data was collected. It should include the following subparagraphs:

3.1 *Reaction Data.* If reaction data were collected for this program, the method used to collect the data and the period used for the data collection are provided.

3.2 *Learning Data.* If learning data were collected, the method for measurement is described.

3.3 *Job Application or Performance Data.* This paragraph describes in detail how these data were collected.

3.4 *Business Impact Data.* If business impact data were used for evaluation, this section would describe the business metrics collected and how they were collected. If the plan was to conduct an ROI analysis or cost-benefit analysis, the formula and the cost data that were used are provided.

3.5 *Analysis.* This paragraph discusses briefly the type of analysis that was conducted on the data.

4. Results

This section provides the results of the analysis. It includes the following subparagraphs:

4.1 *Reaction Data Results.* The results for the reaction-data are provided. Normally, tables or graphs are not necessary for this data if a simple scale such as "strongly disagree"-to- "strongly-agree" is used. But if it would make the results clearer, providing a table may be beneficial. If participant comments are deemed important to the results, the evaluator will provide them in a way they can be read easily. Figures 10-3 and 10-4 provide examples of ways reaction-data results can be presented.

4.2 *Learning Data Results.* The results from the learning data analysis are provided. Again, tables are provided if it helps to make the results clear. Figures 10-5 and 10-6 are examples of learning data analysis-results write-ups.

During 1998, 674 graduates completed post-course questionnaires for this course. Upon completion of training, graduates were generally satisfied as evidenced by their overall ratings for the following areas shown in the table below.

Rating Area	Mean Rating 1 = Strongly Disagree to 5 = Strongly Agree
My knowledge/skills increased as a result of this course.	4.34
The knowledge and/or skills gained through this course are directly applicable to my job.	4.22
I feel confident of my ability to apply what I learned in this course.	4.20
The course was valuable as a development experience for future work.	4.34
Overall, I was satisfied with the course.	4.36

Verbatim comments on post-course questionnaires received during the fourth quarter of 1998 (161 questionnaires) were reviewed to determine graduates' opinions of training impact and barriers to transfer. Few comments were offered (less than ten per question). No themes or patterns emerged from the comments.

Figure 10-3. Reaction data analysis-results—Example 1.

For the self-directed course sessions ending between July and December 1999, eighty reaction questionnaires were received for Phase 1 and fifty-six for Phase 2. Table 1 presents the mean scores, using a scale ranging from 1 (Strongly Disagree) to 5 (Strongly Agree). Notable findings have been shaded. As Table 1 shows, questions 10 and 11 are the only questions that did not achieve a mean score of greater than 3.0.

Table 1.   Mean Reaction Scores

Rating Scale		Self-Directed Course	
1. . . . . 2 . . . . 3 . . . . . .4. . . . .5 Strongly Strongly Disagree Agree		Phase 1 ($n = 80$)	Phase 2 ($n = 56$)
1. It was easy to make arrangements to take this course.		3.92	3.73
2. I had the skills and/or knowledge required to start this course.		4.31	4.43
3. The facilities and equipment were favorable to learning.		3.81	3.34
4. The equipment required for this course was functioning properly.		3.62	3.21
5. I was able to take this course when I needed it.		3.97	3.68
6. I clearly understood the course objectives.		3.96	4.04
7. The course met all of its stated objectives.		3.90	3.59
8. The way this course was delivered (such as classroom, computer, video) was an effective way for me to learn this subject matter.		3.58	3.20
9. Participant materials (handouts, workbooks, etc.) were useful during the course.		4.00	3.75
10. I had enough time to learn the subject matter covered in the course.		3.24	3.00
11. The course content was logically organized.		3.09	2.95
12. The course content was neither too easy nor too difficult.		3.67	3.16
13. The instructor's(s') words and interactions showed respect for different ideas or points of view.		4.51	4.38
14. I was satisfied with the level of feedback/coaching I received.		4.46	4.55
15. The instructor(s) were knowledgeable about the subject.		4.66	4.54

Figure 10-4. Reaction data analysis-results—Example 2.

16. Overall, I was satisfied with the instructor(s).	4.61	4.57
17. My knowledge and/or skills increased as a result of this course.	4.31	4.39
18. The knowledge and/or skills gained through this course are directly applicable to my job.	4.40	4.42
19. I feel confident of my ability to apply what I learned in this course.	3.96	3.68
20. This course was valuable as a development experience for future work.	4.13	4.13
21. Overall, I was satisfied with the course.	3.90	3.64
Overall Mean	4.00	3.83

Figure 10-4. Reaction data analysis-results—Example 2 (Continued).

Course participants in the combined sample achieved a mean Mastery Test score of 91.5 percent and a mean Proficiency score of 94.5 percent, indicating successful mastery and demonstration of course skills at course completion.

Figure 10-5. Learning data analysis-results—Example 1.

Learning data lend themselves to bar charts as well, as demonstrated in chapter 5.

4.3 *Job Application or Performance Data Results.* This section is the "meat" of the report. Chapters 8 and 9 have provided a variety of ways results from performance evaluations can be presented. These will vary depending upon the measurement tools used, the amount and complexity of the data, and the type of analysis conducted.

4.4 *Business Impact Data Results.* If the study analyzed business impact data, this section would include the results of one or more of the following:

- Intangible benefits, such as increased or decreased employee motivation
- Tangible benefits, such as positive or negative ROI or cost-benefit calculations
- Return on expectation (ROE) or other formal interview estimates

Mean test scores from all available regions were collected and are presented in the table below. *Test scores were low, with several regions reporting mean scores below 70 percent. Across regions, test scores ranged from 40 percent to 100 percent, with 75 percent being the most frequently achieved test score.* Anecdotal evidence from the employee who scored the tests indicated that errors on test items tended to be randomly distributed. A copy of the test is located in Appendix C.

Region	Number of Tests Returned	Mean Test Score (in percent)
1	18	77
2	3	72
3	7	61
4	7	74
5	8	75
6	13	67
7	7	67
8	18	69
9	9	73
10	7	64
Overall	97	70

Figure 10-6. Learning data analysis-results—Example 2.

5. Conclusions

Provide the conclusions in this section. They are based on the results provided in the previous section. Bullet each conclusion. A number of example conclusion statements are offered in chapter 9.

6. Recommendations

If the conclusions warrant recommendations, put them in this section. Again, bullet each recommendation.

Appendices

The report may or may not have appendices, depending on the evaluation design and the intended audience for the report. Appendices could include:

• Objective maps
• ROE interview reports
• Measurement tools used
• Data summary tables

- Tables of data from individual regions or groups if they were combined in the body of the report
- Results of previous relevant studies

Use whatever format works best for the audience. Combs and Falletta (2000) offer the following general suggestions for preparing an evaluation report.

Tips for Preparing Evaluation Reports

1. Use a conversational writing style, so that the report is easy to read and understand.
2. Use text boxes, bullets, headings, subheadings, and transitions to organize and simplify the material.
3. Use visual aids—tables, charts, matrices, diagrams, and illustrations—to present the evaluation data in meaningful formats.
4. Define acronyms and abbreviations on the first mention and include these in a glossary.
5. Avoid using technical terms; if their use is necessary, they should be fully explained on the first mention and included in the glossary.

CASE STUDIES IN PROGRESS

Now let's look at how the results from the case studies in progress are presented.

Technical Training Program

The performance objectives for the technical program case study are to improve warehouse employees' driving skills, particularly as they relate to safety, and warehouse operational skills. By meeting these performance objectives, it is expected that motor vehicle and on-the-job accidents will decrease and customer satisfaction will be improved. The audience for the presentation of the results, conclusions, and recommendations for this program are senior executives who are interested in whether the program met its business objectives. They have limited time to study the results from the evaluation but want to feel comfortable with the conclusions. Figures 10-7 through 10-13 provide a slide briefing prepared for the executives.

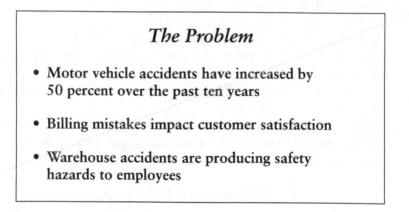

Figure 10-7. Technical training program introductory slide.

The Problem

- Motor vehicle accidents have increased by 50 percent over the past ten years

- Billing mistakes impact customer satisfaction

- Warehouse accidents are producing safety hazards to employees

Figure 10-8. Technical training program background slide.

Evaluation Design

- Compared trained and untrained employee driving skills during driving evaluations

- Compared trained and untrained employee warehouse skills using daily performance logs

Figure 10-9. Technical training program evaluation methodology.

Results

- The trained group had significantly higher warehouse log scores than the untrained group

- The trained group had significantly higher riding scores than the untrained group

Figure 10-10. Technical training program results.

Conclusions

- The trained group performed better in the warehouse than the untrained group

- The trained group performed better on the road than the untrained group

Figure 10-11. Technical training program conclusions.

Expected Impact

- On-the-job accidents will be reduced

- Motor vehicle accidents will be reduced

- Customer satisfaction will increase

Figure 10-12. Technical training program conclusions.

Recommendations

- The training program should continue as currently designed

- The evaluation results should be advertised to maximize attendance

---

Figure 10-13. Technical training program recommendations.

These slides provide a very brief synopsis of the evaluation. The evaluator will be prepared to answer questions or provide specific information, as the audience needs.

Sales/Customer Service Training Program

The performance objectives for the Sales/Customer Service Training Program case study are to improve customer service representatives' customer relations skills. The expectation is that by doing so, customer satisfaction will increase and call escalations will decrease. The audience for the presentation of the results, conclusions, and recommendations is the client organization—the participants' management. When the customer service representatives are taken off the job to attend the training, they are missed—it means extra workload for the other representatives and poorer customer service. They are making a huge investment. This group, therefore, is particularly interested in how effective the training is and if the team leaders can do anything to support it. A full report with an executive summary will provide this audience with the specific data they need to support the recommendations made. The evaluator prepares a full report using the format discussed in this chapter. The report will include both Tables 10-2 and 10-3 to present the results from the performance analysis.

Notice in Table 10-3 the areas that were discussed as problem areas in chapter 9 are shaded. This helps to reinforce the discussion the report provides about the results.

Table 10-2
Results of Sales/Customer Service Training Program
Performance Observations

Representative	Before-Training Scores (in percent)	After-Training Scores (in percent)
1	40	62
2	25	80
3	50	90
4	33	75
5	42	82
6	60	85
7	42	88
8	28	75
9	44	62
10	32	85
11	55	68
12	26	56
13	35	75
14	45	89
15	52	90
16	40	100
Mean Scores	41	79

Table 10-3
Sales/Customer Service after Training Percent Breakdown
by Behavior Area

Behavior Area	Percent Breakdown		
	Yes	No	NA
Opening the Call (ten behaviors)	98	2	0
Diagnosing Problems & Identifying Needs (six behaviors)	80	10	10
Assessing Progress & Updating the Plan (four behaviors)	60	45	15
Recommending Approaches for Results (five behaviors)	55	35	20
Closing the Call (five behaviors)	98	2	0
Overall Listening Skills (four behaviors)	75	25	0

CONCLUSIONS

The following conclusions are drawn based upon the results of this study.

- Sales/customer service performance improved as a result of the training program.
- The participants were effective opening and closing calls.
- The participants were effective diagnosing customer problems and identifying customer needs.
- The participants demonstrated effective listening skills, although there is room for improvement.
- Although the training program effectively taught the participants how to assess progress of the call and updating the plan and recommending approaches to solve customer problems, the skills did not transfer successfully to the job.

RECOMMENDATIONS

The following recommendations are offered based on the conclusion.

- That the training program strengthen the module on effective listening skills.
- That the management looks at ways it can reinforce the training the participants receive for assessing progress and updating plans and recommending approaches for results. Coaching in this area from team coaches may be of benefit, and/or software could be built into the representatives' system that would provide clues for customer problem resolutions.

Figure 10-14. Sales/customer service presentation of conclusions and recommendations.

The observation checklist used for measurement is offered in an appendix. After these results are presented, the conclusions and recommendations are offered. Figure 10-14 exhibits how these are presented.

A report such as this provides compelling information. Management will most likely be convinced to act on the recommendations made. Because the recommendations made in this case study are ones that the client *can* act on, and because they are clearly supported by the conclusions and the results, the chances that this evaluation will have a positive impact are good.

Leadership Development Program

The performance objectives for the Leadership Development Program case study are to develop or improve supervisory personnel's ability to communicate more effectively with subordinates, conduct more efficient and effective meetings, and prioritize goals and activities. It is expected that by developing or improving these skills, turnover will be reduced, team effectiveness will be increased, productivity will be improved, and time will be saved by both supervisors and subordinates. The audience for the presentation of the results, conclusions, and recommendations are the program designers. They expect this program will be offered to all management personnel and want to ensure that all aspects of it are effective. The design of this program evaluation was fairly complex (see chapter 7) and the analysis leading to the results, conclusions, and recommendations was involved (see chapters 8 and 9). The audience will want to see the data presented in a full report but may get lost in the details. The tables created in chapter 9 would be appropriate for the report but the evaluator wants to present the results in a way that can lead the reader carefully through the results section of the report. One technique would be to highlight or bold or box in each result followed by the appropriate explanations and supporting data. Figures 10-15 through 10-18 provide result statements presented in a way the audience will be able to follow and understand.

By highlighting each result, the evaluator can take the reader through a complex report or presentation step-by-step, so that by the time the discussion of conclusions is reached, the reader clearly understands the results and can better consider the evaluator's conclusions and recommendations.

The results of the questions regarding the participants' perceived effectiveness of the Leadership Program were that the skills pertaining to evaluating and using personality type indicators were perceived to be low. All other skills were perceived to be effectively practiced.

Question: How *effective* are you in performing each of the skills listed?	Minimum % Rating	Maximum % Rating	Mean % Rating	Standard Deviation
1. Communicate using positive language.	55	90	72	9.23
2. Determine when subordinates need assistance.	45	90	71	11.99
3. Conduct individual meetings so that subordinates' concerns and ideas are accounted for.	50	95	73	12.43
4. Open team meetings with clearly stated goals.	40	90	73	13.89
5. Encourage group participation using active listening techniques.	40	90	70	12.33
6. Keep discussion on track during team meetings.	40	90	69	13.25
7. Accomplish stated meeting goals.	55	90	72	9.34
8. Close meetings with clearly stated follow-up actions.	60	90	76	8.92
9. Task team members based on their individual personality types.	0	80	24	15.31
10. Explain to team members how to use personality type indicators to achieve team goals.	0	80	16	15.55
11. Prioritize goals and activities.	10	90	74	15.18
12. Complete goals and activities in order of priority.	50	90	74	12.15
13. Conduct only necessary meetings.	40	90	71	10.83

Figure 10-15. Leadership program skill effectiveness result presentation.

The results of the questions regarding the participants' perceived effectiveness of the Leadership Program in teaching them the skills listed were that the participants rated the program low in effectiveness in teaching the skills pertaining to evaluating and using personality indicators. The program was perceived as effective in teaching all other skills.

Question: How *effective* are you in performing each of the skills listed?	Minimum % Rating	Maximum % Rating	Mean % Rating	Standard Deviation
1. Communicate using positive language.	60	90	80	7.4
2. Determine when subordinates need assistance.	60	90	77	6.70
3. Conduct individual meetings so that subordinates' concerns and ideas are accounted for.	45	90	77	12.25
4. Open team meetings with clearly stated goals.	70	90	81	5.77
5. Encourage group participation using active listening techniques.	50	90	75	11.43
6. Keep discussion on track during team meetings.	60	90	76	8.36
7. Accomplish stated meeting goals.	60	90	79	8.66
8. Close meetings with clearly stated follow-up actions.	65	90	80	6.34
9. Task team members based on their individual personality types.	0	80	19	14.43
10. Explain to team members how to use personality type indicators to achieve team goals.	0	80	15	16.93
11. Prioritize goals and activities.	60	90	80	7
12. Complete goals and activities in order of priority.	60	90	80	7.46
13. Conduct only necessary meetings.	60	90	79	7.10

Figure 10-16. Leadership development program effectiveness result presentation.

The participants perceived that 34 percent of the credit for their performing effectively as leaders was due to the program, with the second highest impact area being 16 percent.

Factor	Mean Percent Contribution to Maximizing Effectiveness
Knowledge, skills, or experience you had *before* the leadership program.	16
Knowledge, skills, or experience you gained *from* the leadership program.	34
Knowledge, skills, or experience you acquired on your own *after* the leadership program.	12
Management style, reference materials, or job aides *unrelated* to the Leadership Program, e.g., bulletin boards, methods, and procedure documentation.	4
Coaching or feedback from peers.	9
Coaching or feedback from your Director.	8
Coaching or feedback from your subordinates.	7
Observing others.	7
Organizational Changes—*Please specify.*	1
Market changes—*Please specify.*	0
Other *internal* factors or resources—*Please specify.*	1
Other *external* resources (vendors, course, conferences, etc.)—*Please specify.*	1
Other—*Please specify.*	0

Figure 10-17. Leadership development contributing factors result presentation.

The results from the action plan questions were that sixty-five percent of the actions planned by the participants were completed and the participants were satisfied with the action-planning process.

	Mean Percent	Standard Deviation
Actions Completed	64.78	35.8408
Level of Satisfaction	74.81	25.2099

Figure 10-18. Leadership development program action plan result presentation.

Table 10-4
Checklist for Presenting Evaluation Results

Question	YES (✓)	NO (✓)
1. Has the audience for the presentation been considered?		
2. Is the slide presentation brief with back-up slides prepared?		
3. Is an executive summary concise but powerful?		
4. Does the report provide all relevant data, that is, reaction, learning, performance, and impact?		
5. Will tables and figures used, be clear to the audience?		
6. Are all results supported?		
7. Is each conclusion supported?		
8. Is each recommendation supported?		

SUMMARY

The evaluator takes particular care in deciding how best to present results from learning and performance analyses. Providing a powerful and meaningful report that is accepted by the audience can be a rewarding experience for the evaluator and demonstrates the evaluation value to the organization. Table 10-4 provides a checklist to use when preparing presentations of evaluation results.

REFERENCES

1. Brinkerhoff, R.O., and S.J. Gill. 1994. *The Learning Alliance,* San Francisco, Calif.: Jossey-Bass Publishers.

2. Combs, W.L., and S.V. Falletta. 2000. *The Targeted Evaluation Process.* Alexandria, Va.: American Society for Training and Development.

CHAPTER 11

Now What? How to Maximize Evaluation Results

The program has been evaluated. It is either the strong, healthy, fruit-producing tree we hoped for, or it is one with areas of weakness. The evaluator provided guidance where needed, recommending a careful needs-assessment to determine what type of tree was needed and conducting formative evaluations to ensure proper growth and longevity. The evaluator put together a team of experts to determine business, performance, and program objectives and ensure they are clearly defined so they can serve as a strong trunk—or foundation—for the program. The team fertilized the tree with enablers to aid its growth. The evaluator developed measures to determine the extent to which learning occurred and tested the strength of the measures. Once the program was initially established, the evaluator measured the extent to which job performances were transferred to the job. If weaknesses were found, they were uncovered and described. Hopefully, the tree is producing the flowers or fruit intended and the organization is able to benefit from them. It has been a journey, growing this tree. But it has been a journey that the evaluator has taken with all the guidance, tools, and assistance available.

But now what? What role does the evaluator play at this point? Does he or she report the findings and move on to another project or stay actively involved in implementing the recommendations from the evaluation?

Post-Program Evaluator Roles

The role the evaluator plays at this point may be dependent on the structure of the organization and where the evaluator is situated in that structure. It may be dependent on the part the evaluator played on a program task force. Or the evaluator may be in a position to decide what function to assume. There are several roles this individual can play at this stage of the evaluation. Some of them are:

- The decision-making partner
- The enabler
- The consultant
- The enforcer

Each of these roles could be played distinctly, or aspects of each could be combined.

The Decision-Making Partner

This is a desirable role for the evaluator. Combs and Falletta (2000) define "evaluation utilization" as the effective use of evaluation results for decision-making. The client organization may be counting on the evaluator to be an integral part of not only deciding the fate of the program but providing specific recommendations in which they will put a great deal of credence. This role requires that the evaluator be completely familiar with the program and the organization it has been designed to support. This is often the case if the evaluator is part of the design or delivery team. It is particularly critical that data collection tools used for the evaluation produce clear results to ensure decisions made are not questioned. Action planning, for example, will produce results that require obvious decisions. If the evaluator is on the team for making decisions for the program based on the evaluation results, they may want to consider the following suggestions.

Tips for the Decision-Making Partner

1. Understand the stakeholder or client's expectations for the program.
2. Ensure the team understands the results from the evaluation.

3. Ensure the team agrees with the conclusions made based on the results.
4. Facilitate brainstorming sessions to uncover all possible program decision options and consider them all.
5. Document all assumptions made for each decision.
6. Plan a follow-up evaluation for programs where the decisions change the program in any significant way.

The Enabler

This is one of the most enviable roles for the evaluator. It can be a rewarding experience to have the opportunity to help ensure that the evaluation results are incorporated in such a way that the program can be enhanced. If the evaluator is a member of the program task force, he or she will be in the position of being a team player from the start of the evaluation. The evaluation program itself may have been one that included continual involvement from the client organization, again a desirable situation. Often, however, if the organization is large and the evaluation group is small, this level of involvement may not be realistic, because the evaluator may be conducting several programs at the same time or may be "charged" with determining impact after the program has begun. If there is the possibility that the evaluator can play this role, here are a few tips to keep in mind.

Tips for the Enabler

1. As discussed in chapter 6, involve the team in as many aspects of the evaluation as possible. Develop a program task force that includes the client, the designers, the participant group, and the trainers.
2. Help the task force identify all potential barriers to transfer prior to the program initiation to identify ways to remove the barriers.
3. Become completely familiar with the key components of the program design.
4. Become completely familiar with the client organization and the program users and their environment.
5. Understand the client's expectations for the program.
6. Remain unbiased throughout the program design and evaluation.

7. Incorporate team-building activities to establish trust among the task force members.
8. Get continual "buy-in" from the team members throughout the evaluation.

The Consultant

Robinson and Robinson (1989) distinguish three types of consulting styles that the HRD consultant can use: the *expert style*, the *pair-of-hands style*, and the *collaborator style*. The *expert style* has the consultant put on the hat of the expert, identifying the cause of the problem and the solution. In this role, the consultant decides what needs to be done, how, and when. A risk to the consultant using this style is that he or she may receive no support from managers for decisions they were not involved in making. Additionally, the client may feel little ownership in the program. The consultant using the *pair-of-hands style* does not make decisions but simply implements the decisions of the client. This individual has no active role in helping the client make decisions. When the consultant uses a *collaborator style*, he or she is seen as an equal partner in diagnosing the problem and determining the solution. Whether an external or internal consultant, the evaluator strives to use the collaborator style of consulting. External consultants often find themselves in a difficult position when having to deliver "bad" news from an evaluation, however. They want to be brought in to do future work with the organization and don't want to be seen as negative, but they are expected to be completely unbiased and, therefore, provide the evaluation results without qualification. An internal consultant could be seen as someone who will deliver the news and be on his or her merry way, not caring about what is left behind. The consultant must work hard to develop the collaborative approach, establishing rapport with the stakeholders or clients and ensuring their buy-in for the evaluation in the early stages of the evaluation planning. They need to ensure they are seen as a team player and a partner—someone who cares about the program's success.

Tips for the Consultant

1. Conduct interviews with program stakeholders early during the evaluation-planning stage.
2. Involve members of the task force in developing the measurement or data collection plan or in some way get their buy-in for it.

3. Invest time to meet with the client organization as often as possible, rather than breezing in and out.
4. Establish yourself as part of the organization, using the words "we" and "us."

The Enforcer

Measurement is done to improve the process, not to blame or punish (Brinkeroff and Gill 1994). The evaluator spends a great deal of time and effort to reinforce this principle. That is why being an enforcer is the least desirable role for the evaluator to play, but often, either because of the political situation surrounding the program or the way in which the organization is structured, this is the role he or she must play. The client organization may believe that the evaluator is unbiased, is most familiar with the results of the evaluation, and/or has the least to gain or lose from decisions made about the program. They believe, therefore, that the evaluator is in the best position to take a stand on ensuring something is done as a result of the evaluation. There may be cases when the evaluator knows nothing will be done with the results unless he or she takes action to ensure something happens. The following tips are offered for the evaluator to make the "enforcer" role work.

Tips for the Enforcer

1. Focus on action items that can be started or completed right away.
2. Focus first on those actions that can be done most easily.
3. Offer assistance to accomplish action items resulting from the evaluation.
4. Emphasize the benefits that can be expected from taking the actions recommended.
5. Always use an encouraging, positive tone rather than an authoritarian, or "policeman," tone.

USING EVALUATION RESULTS FOR ORGANIZATIONAL TRENDING

In addition to striving to ensure that each evaluation program has impact, the evaluator can also provide a valuable service by developing a method for analyzing and presenting trends seen from many evaluation programs. For example, it could be found that reaction, learning, and performance data are continually lower when the program has been developed by an outside vendor. It could also be found that detailed comparisons show that computer-assisted programs achieve higher results than instructor-led programs. These are important findings on which the company can base major business decisions. Tracking learning data can provide an organization with ongoing information about the success of individual programs. Comparisons can be made with different user groups or different regions. Decisions regarding instructors, vendors, or program material can be made. Tracking job performance data may show overall company strengths and weaknesses that can be compared with results seen from other companies in benchmarking efforts. The evaluator can focus on ways in which this information can best be provided to those leaders in the organization who can make best use of it.

USING BENCHMARKING DATA FOR CONTINUOUS IMPROVEMENT

Because the HRD community is just beginning to become familiar with the value of evaluations, many are not used to using the results from them. As more and more organizations use evaluation, the evaluation role will, hopefully, grow into one that has continual and meaningful impact. It is important that the evaluator benchmark and network with other evaluators from different organizations to stay current in evaluation and to demonstrate to their own organization the value others are seeing from their evaluations. One such organization is the ROI Network™—a group of evaluation practitioners from various organizations and countries. The American Society for Training and Development (ASTD) is becoming more active in providing evaluation support and works with others such as the Network to develop avenues for imparting evaluation knowledge. The Evaluation Consortium is a group of evaluation specialists from corporations. The field of evaluation is leaving the schoolroom and entering and thriving in small and large organizations in many types of businesses.

CASE STUDIES CONCLUDED

Throughout this book, three case studies have been developed using the information and techniques provided in that chapter. These case studies included a technical training program, a sales/customer service program, and a leadership program. Let's conclude each case study by imagining how the evaluator ensured that the results of each of these evaluations has impact on the organization.

Technical Training Program

The performance objectives for the technical training program case study are to improve warehouse employees' driving skills, particularly as they relate to safety, and warehouse operational skills. By meeting these performance objectives, it is expected that motor vehicle and on-the-job accidents will decrease and customer satisfaction will improve. It was concluded that the program successfully met its performance and business objectives based on the results of the evaluation. It was recommended to senior executives that (1) the program continue as designed, and (2) the results of the evaluation be advertised in order that it be fully maximized.

The evaluator has happily taken on the role of *the enforcer* by suggesting ways in which the evaluation results can be advertised. It is decided that the results will be advertised in the company database with the course description. A brief mention will be made that the course was evaluated to be successful. Also, each warehouse supervisor across the company footprint is sent an email message from the vice president with the results of the study and a request that each supervisor arrange to have their warehouse employees attend the training within the next year. A follow-up study is not considered necessary, but the senior executives want motor vehicle accident and customer satisfaction metrics to be monitored on a regular basis.

Sales/Customer Service Training Program

The performance objectives for the Sales/Customer Service Training Program case study are to improve customer service representatives' customer relations skills. The expectation is that when this is done, customer satisfaction will increase, which will reduce call escalations. The evaluation results for the program were good, but a few areas of weakness were discovered. It was recommended to the design group that certain areas of the program design be strengthened. It was recommended to the client organization that management look for ways the field can better support the training program, in order that it have its full impact.

The evaluator has assumed the role of *the enabler* and will work with the design group to help identify those areas of the program that can be enhanced. The evaluator may choose to pilot the course after revisions are made and analyze reaction and learning data to check for effectiveness. The evaluator also assumes the role of a *consultant* by conducting interviews with field supervisors and evaluating the representatives' systems. The evaluator may want to put together a report of this field assessment for the client organization to include recommendations. After the course has been revised and the field staff support and/or systems modified, the evaluator will conduct a follow-up evaluation with the same evaluation design to determine the extent to which the program has improved.

Leadership Development Program

The performance objectives for the Leadership Development Program are to develop or improve supervisory personnel's ability to communicate more effectively with subordinates, conduct more efficient and effective meetings, and prioritize goals and activities. It is expected that developing or improving these skills will lead to reduced turnover, increased team effectiveness, improved productivity, and time for both supervisors and subordinates.

The evaluation found that all aspects of the program were successful except for one module. The evaluator plays the role of *the decision-making partner* by pointing out how successful the program is in meeting its business and performance objectives and the expense for having this level of employee attend each hour of the program. The evaluator suggests that the program objectives be modified to eliminate that portion of the program that was unsuccessful. This will reduce the time for participant attendance in the program by three hours. The program will, therefore, still meet its objectives while saving the valuable time for future attendees. A follow-up evaluation is not considered necessary.

SUMMARY

In order for an organization to receive the maximum impact from its evaluation programs, the evaluator must ensure that results are presented well and to the right people. The evaluator may need to assume different roles to ensure the results are heard and heeded and must ensure all necessary follow-up actions are taken. Table 11-1 provides a checklist to ensure the evaluator maximizes on evaluation program results.

Table 11-1
Checklist for Maximizing Evaluation Results

Question	YES (✓)	NO(✓)
1. Has the role for the evaluator at this stage been determined?		
2. Does the evaluator feel comfortable with the role he or she is taking?		
3. Has the evaluator planned for this role and included the appropriate people in the planning at the most opportune times?		
4. Has the evaluator included necessary organizational members in deciding upon actions to be taken as a result of the evaluation?		
5. Is it determned if follow-up evaluations are necessary?		
6. Are actions taken as a result of the evaluation been documented and advertised as appropriate?		
7. Are evaluation results across the organization tracked and trended?		
8. Are results of trends provided to those in the best position to take the action necessary to benefit the organization?		
9. Is the evaluator staying current on what other practitioners are accomplishing with their evaluation efforts and ensuring success stories are provided to their organization?		

REFERENCES

1. Brinkerhoff, R.O., and S.J. Gill. 1994. *The Learning Alliance.* San Francisco, Calif.: Jossey Bass Publishers.

2. Combs, W.L., and S.V. Falletta. 2000. *The Targeted Evaluation Process.* Alexandria, Va.: American Society for Training and Development.

3. Robinson, D.G., and J.C. Robinson. 1989. *Training for Impact.* San Francisco, Calif.: Jossey-Bass Publishers.

Example Action Plans

Example 1*
Apple Computer
ACTION PLAN FOR TRAIN-THE-TRAINER PROGRAM
Sample

Name _____ Instructor Signature _____ Follow-up Date _____

Objective: To apply skills and knowledge from the Train-the-Trainer Program Evaluation Period: _____ to _____

Improvement Measures: Productivity; Labor Efficiency; PPA Failures; Quality; Communications; Customer Response; Other

Action Steps	Analysis
As a result of this program, what specific actions will you apply based upon what you have learned? 1. _____ 2. _____ 3. _____ 4. _____ 5. _____ 6. _____	What specific unit of measure will change as a result of your actions? A. What is the unit of measure? (example above) B. As a result of the anticipated changes above, please estimate the monetary benefits to your line or department over a **one-month period**. $ _____ C. What is the basis of your estimate? (How did you arrive at this value?) _____ _____ D. What level of confidence do you place in the above information? (100% = Certainty and 0% = No Confidence) _____ %

Intangible Benefits:
_____
_____

Comments _____
_____

*Reprinted with the permission of the American Society for Training and Development (ASTD). Burkett, H. 1999. " Measuring a Train-the-Trainer Approach to Support Build-to-Order Capabilities." In *In Action: Measuring Learning and Performance*, ed. T.K. Hodges, Alexandria, Va.: Figure 2, pg. 35.

Example 2*

CECU ACTION PLANNING DOCUMENT

Name _____

_____ Manager's Name _____

Course(s) Taught: Electric Systems Fundamentals   Evaluation Period: _____ to _____

New Skills Application	Business Results
Based on what you learned in this class, please list at least three new skill applications you will apply back on the job within the next 30 days. Example: Be able to identify and accurately complete documents used for inspecting transmission lines. 1. _____ 2. _____ 3. _____ 4. _____	*Please describe what you to improve back on the job because of applying each of these new skill applications (examples: # of customer contacts per day, customer responsiveness, increase customer satisfaction, reduce customer complaints). How will you measure each of them?* Example: Reduce customer complaints by proactively inspecting transmission—thereby resolving problems I see before customer is affected. 1. _____ 2. _____ 3. _____ 4. _____

1. By applying these skills and making the performance improvements above, how much money (in dollars) will you save or make the company? Explain.
$ _____

2. Express in percent how confident you are that the savings or revenue generation will occur _____ %

3. Please identify at least one skill you feel you could improve with more training. Describe how that skill would enhance your job performance.

∧ ∧

4. Please list any barriers you may face in trying to implement these skills.
☐ ☐ ☐

*Reprinted with the permission of the American Society for Training and Development (ASTD), Whalen, J.P. 1999. "Enhancing Job Performance Through Technical Training and Education." In *In Action: Measuring Learning and Performance*, ed. T.K. Hodges, Alexandria, VA.: Figure 1, pg. 91.

Example 3*

HEALTHSEARCH PHARMACEUTICAL, INC.

Name _____   Instructor Signature _____   FLM Signature _____

PLAN OF ACTION: Salustatin Promotion Program (SPP)

Current # of HPI prescriptions in the market _____
# of HPI prescriptions necessary to achieve goals _____

Part I – Sales Representative Key Behavior/Skill	Part II – Sales Representative Action Steps (from key behavior/skill)
Date of First Follow-up _____ 1. Setting specific call objectives............... 2. Communicating the core promotional message......... 3. Use of support brochures/materials............. 4. Handling objections............... 5. Command of product knowledge..............	**Keep Doing This** ↓ ↓ **Reinforce of Improve** 1. _____ 1. _____ 2. _____ 2. _____ 3. _____ 3. _____ 4. _____ 4. _____ 5. _____ 5. _____
Date of Second Follow-up _____ 1. Setting specific call objectives............... 2. Communicating the core promotional message......... 3. Use of support brochures/materials............. 4. Handling objections............... 5. Command of product knowledge..............	**Keep Doing This** ↓ ↓ **Reinforce of Improve** 1. _____ 1. _____ 2. _____ 2. _____ 3. _____ 3. _____ 4. _____ 4. _____ 5. _____ 5. _____
Date of Third Follow-up _____ 1. Setting specific call objectives............... 2. Communicating the core promotional message......... 3. Use of support brochures/materials............. 4. Handling objections............... 5. Command of product knowledge..............	**Keep Doing This** ↓ ↓ **Reinforce of Improve** 1. _____ 1. _____ 2. _____ 2. _____ 3. _____ 3. _____ 4. _____ 4. _____ 5. _____ 5. _____

Your Signature _____   Supervisor's Signature _____

Part III PLAN OF ACTION — Salustatin Promotional Program (SPP)   Page _____ of _____

Circle the appropriate answers under each key behavior/skill. Circle more than one if appropriate:

Legend: Y = Yes   N = No   NS = Not Sure/Do Not Know

☞ How did sales representative's behavior/skills influence physician's decisions?	1. Call Objectives	2. Core Message	3. Promotional Support	4. Handling Objections	5. Product Knowledge	6. Other
A. Physician is a better listener?	N Y NS	N Y NS	N Y NS	N Y NS	N Y NS	N Y NS
B. Physician is ready to extend meeting time?	N Y NS	N Y NS	N Y NS	N Y NS	N Y NS	N Y NS
C. Physician is using the representative as a resource?	N Y NS	N Y NS	N Y NS	N Y NS	N Y NS	N Y NS
D. Physician better understands the benefits of Salustatin?	N Y NS	N Y NS	N Y NS	N Y NS	N Y NS	N Y NS
E. Physician is more convinced that Salustatin is superior?	N Y NS	N Y NS	N Y NS	N Y NS	N Y NS	N Y NS
F. Physician is more convinced that representative understands the needs of his/her practice?	N Y NS	N Y NS	N Y NS	N Y NS	N Y NS	N Y NS

☞ In my view, my contact with physicians during this reporting period will result in: *Check only one response below:*

☐ No change in physician prescribing behavior

☐ A modest improvement in physician prescribing behavior in favor of HPI

☐ A significant improvement in physician prescribing behavior in favor of HPI

☞ **The behavior/skill that has worked best for me:** _____

Your Signature: _____

Supervisor's (FLM) Signature: _____

Comments: _____

*Reprinted with the permission of the American Society for Training and Development (ASTD). Stone, R.D. 1999. "Successful Use of Action Planning to Measure the Impact of Training." In *In Action: Measuring Learning and Performance*, ed. T.K. Hodges, Alexandria, Va.: Figure 1, pg. 189, 190.

Example 4*
Bell Atlantic

ACTION PLAN WORKSHEET

Protégé	Protégé Dept.	Mentor	Mentor Dept.	Date
Protégé Phone			Mentor Phone	

Write your Major Goal in the box below.
(If you have more than 1 Major Goal, Please complete a separate Action Plan for Each Goal.)

Instructions: Using the ideas from your **Brainstorming Worksheet**, write down the **Action Items** that need to be accomplished to reach your Major Goal. Write down each Action Item below with a target date for completing it. Please construct each Action Item according to the **Action Item Guidelines** below:

Action Item Guidelines: Make sure each Action Item is specific, detailed, and includes observable behavior(s) to be accomplished. It helps to begin each item step with an action verb. For example, "Talk to Mr. Smith in Marketing," or "Send Mr. Smith a resume." Make sure to come up with at least some Action Items that can be completed within the next 6–10 weeks. ACTION ITEMS DO NOT NEED TO BE COMPLETED IN ANY PARTICULAR ORDER.

NO.	ACTION ITEMS (What Steps will be taken)	Person Responsible (Mentor or Protégé)	Target Date for Completion (When)	Actual Date Completed
1				
2				
3				
4				
5				
6				
7				

Protégé Signature _____

Mentor Signature _____

Sign this Action Plan after the Major Goal and Action Items have been Agreed Upon

PLEASE UPDATE THIS ACTION PLAN AS YOU ACCOMPLISH EACH ITEM AND SAVE THIS FORM. IT WILL BE REQUESTED LATER ON AS PART OF THE MENTORING PROGRAM EVALUATION PROCESS

BRAINSTORMING WORKSHEET FOR YOUR ACTION PLAN

Protégé	Protégé Dept.	Mentor	Mentor Dept.	Date

| Protégé Phone | | Mentor Phone | |

Directions: Your and your Mentor must agree upon a Major Goal(s) to be accomplished as a result of your Mentoring Partnership. You and your Mentor must also agree upon the Action Items you will undertake in order to accomplish this Goal(s). If you have not had a chance to meet with your Mentor and to decide on a Major Goal(s), simply choose a primary goal now that you would like to accomplish and use it for this brainstorming activity and your Action Plan on the next page.

The purpose of this activity is to practice coming up with as many ideas, activities, or resources as possible that might help you to accomplish your Major Goal(s). After choosing a Major Goal, use the following Brainstorming Rules to guide you and your Mentor (if present):

Brainstorming Rules	Write your Major Goal Here
1. Propose as many ideas as quickly as possible in the space below	
2. Write down ANY outlandish ideas because they may trigger other ideas	
3. Don't criticize or evaluate your ideas right now	
4. Be creative! You never know what ideas may be reasonable after all.	

More Directions before leaving this page:

After brainstorming, **review your ideas** with your Mentor and **ask for your Mentor's input** if he/she was not present during the Brainstorming activity. Once you and your Mentor have brainstormed your Action Items, **jointly decide** which items are feasible and decide on a logical order for accomplishing them. Proceed to the final Action Plan . . . →

─────────────

*Source: With permission from Toni Hodges, Manager, Measurement and Development, Bell Atlantic, 1999.

APPENDIX B

Example Follow-Up Questionnaires

Example 1*
Healthsearch Pharmaceutical, Inc.

THE ESSENTIAL SELLING SKILLS TRAINING PROGRAM IMPACT QUESTIONNAIRE

1. Listed below are the objectives of the training. After reflecting on this course, please indicate the degree of success in meeting the objectives: *Check the appropriate box for each item.*

Objective	Very Little Success	Limited Success	Generally Successful	Completely Successful
A. Recall of a working definition of market share	☐	☐	☐	☐
B. Describe why it is important to grow market share	☐	☐	☐	☐

*Reprinted with the permission of the American Society for Training and Development (ASTD). Stone, R.D. 1999. "Successful Use of Action Planning to Measure the Impact of Training." In *In Action: Measuring Learning and Performance,* ed. T.K. Hodges, Alexandria, Va.

C. Use country-specific
data to define the
value of increasing
market share   ☐   ☐   ☐   ☐

D. Use country-specific
data to define the
number of
prescriptions
necessary to move
market share   ☐   ☐   ☐   ☐

E. Establish specific
call objectives for
every Salustatin
physician   ☐   ☐   ☐   ☐

F. Relate strategic call
objectives to
physician
prescribing
behavior   ☐   ☐   ☐   ☐

G. Use the sales
brochure that
supports core
promotional
message   ☐   ☐   ☐   ☐

H. Deliver the core
message   ☐   ☐   ☐   ☐

I. Handle physicians'
objections   ☐   ☐   ☐   ☐

2. Please rate, on a scale of 1–5, the relevance of each of the program elements to your job, with (1) indicating no relevance, and (5) indicating very relevant.

_____ Role-playing
_____ Coaching
_____ Feedback using videotape
_____ Core promotional message brochures
_____ Other (specify)

3. How has the training helped you to improve your ability to do your job? Please use the following scale to rate your frequency of job application of each skill/behavior and the extent to which the training has helped to improve your job effectiveness.

Scale	1	2	3	4	5
Frequency of Application:	Rarely (once a month)	Seldom (once every 2 weeks)	Occasionally (1-2 times per week)	Frequently (once per day)	Very Frequently (several times per day)
Improved Job Effectiveness:	Not Much Improvement	Somewhat Improved	Moderately Improved	Definitely Improved	Significantly Improved

For each item below, check the appropriate box in each of the two columns to the right.	Frequency	Effectiveness
	How frequently do you apply this skill/behavior in your job?	As a direct result of the training, how much has application of this skill/behavior improved your job effectiveness?
The Skill/Behavior Learned from the Essential Selling Skills Training	1 2 3 4 5	1 2 3 4 5
A. Setting market share goals	☐ ☐ ☐ ☐ ☐	☐ ☐ ☐ ☐ ☐
B. Setting strategic call objectives	☐ ☐ ☐ ☐ ☐	☐ ☐ ☐ ☐ ☐
C. Forming and using questioning techniques	☐ ☐ ☐ ☐ ☐	☐ ☐ ☐ ☐ ☐
D. Communicating the core promotional message to customers	☐ ☐ ☐ ☐ ☐	☐ ☐ ☐ ☐ ☐
E. Uncovering hidden objections	☐ ☐ ☐ ☐ ☐	☐ ☐ ☐ ☐ ☐
F. Handling objections	☐ ☐ ☐ ☐ ☐	☐ ☐ ☐ ☐ ☐

4. Indicate the extent to which you think this training has had a positive influence on the following measures in your own work or your work unit. *Check one box for each item as appropriate.*

	No Influence	Little Influence	Some Influence	Moderate Influence	Significant Influence
A. Increased revenue from the sales of Salustatin	☐	☐	☐	☐	☐
B. Increase in market share	☐	☐	☐	☐	☐
C. Increase in sales of other HPI prescription products	☐	☐	☐	☐	☐
D. Improved customer satisfaction	☐	☐	☐	☐	☐
E. Increase in quality time with customer	☐	☐	☐	☐	☐
F. Increased confidence level of sales representative	☐	☐	☐	☐	☐
G. Improved relationship between representative and physician	☐	☐	☐	☐	☐
H. Improved job satisfaction	☐	☐	☐	☐	☐
I. Closer partnership between sales manager and sales representative	☐	☐	☐	☐	☐
J. Improved ability to sell as a team	☐	☐	☐	☐	☐
K. Reduction in sales rep voluntary turnover	☐	☐	☐	☐	☐

(continued)

	No Influence	Little Influence	Some Influence	Moderate Influence	Significant Influence
L. Improved my ability to influence physician-prescribing behavior	☐	☐	☐	☐	☐
M. Improved my ability to adapt to changing needs and business issues of physicians	☐	☐	☐	☐	☐
N. Improved my ability to tailor sales situations and activities to individual physician needs	☐	☐	☐	☐	☐
O. Other (Please specify) _____	☐	☐	☐	☐	☐

Please cite specific examples or provide more details:

_____

_____

_____

5. Several factors often contribute to performance improvement. In addition to the Essential Selling Skills training, we have identified some of the other factors below. Look at the factors and indicate what percentage you attribute to each as appropriate. Reflect on your own performance improvement as a gauge. If you feel that some of the factors are not appropriate, then do not assign them a percentage.

Please select the items that you feel are appropriate by writing in your estimated percentages as they apply.	Percentage Improvement Attributed to:	Comments?
A. Physician seminars promoting Salustatin	_____ %	
B. Other local promotions of Salustatin	_____ %	

C. Essential Selling Skills training for sales representatives	_____ %	
D. Coaching by my sales manager	_____ %	
E. Salustatin physicians seeing more patients with associated indications	_____ %	
F. Improved sales brochures supporting the core promotional message	_____ %	
G. Lack of competing products from our competitors	_____ %	
H. Other training initiatives–*Please specify*	_____ %	
I. Other–*Please specify*	_____ %	
Total of all selected items must = 100 percent	**Total 100%**	

Comments:

_____

_____

_____

6. Please identify any specific job accomplishments or improvements you have achieved that you can link to the Essential Selling Skills training, and comment on your impact on increased sales. *Think about new behavior you have applied or the application of skills as a result of the training (e.g., improved assessment of physicians' needs, improved handling of objections, better questioning techniques, more quality contact time with physicians, improved ability to influence physician prescribing behavior, sales successes that resulted directly from more effectively planning for sales calls, etc.).*

*_____

_____

_____

7. An inherent part of the SPP initiative is the coaching process practiced by sales managers. *Using the scale below, rate the frequency at which your manager applies the coaching behavior. Then rate the performance of your manager in each area of coaching. Circle your choices.*

Frequency of your manager's application:

1. Never
2. Infrequently
3. Occasionally
4. Often
5. Most of the time

Level of your manager's effectiveness:

1. Not Very Effective
2. Somewhat Effective
3. Moderately Effective
4. Effective
5. Very Effective

* My Sales Manager:	How Often Does Your Manager Apply This Practice?					Manager's Level of Effectiveness?				
	1	2	3	4	5	1	2	3	4	5
A. Helps me plan sales calls	☐	☐	☐	☐	☐	☐	☐	☐	☐	☐
B. Reviews call strategy with me	☐	☐	☐	☐	☐	☐	☐	☐	☐	☐
C. Goes with me on calls to evaluate my skills	☐	☐	☐	☐	☐	☐	☐	☐	☐	☐
D. Gives me feedback on the effectiveness of sales calls	☐	☐	☐	☐	☐	☐	☐	☐	☐	☐
E. Challenges me to achieve my objectives	☐	☐	☐	☐	☐	☐	☐	☐	☐	☐
F. Identifies effective actions to repeat	☐	☐	☐	☐	☐	☐	☐	☐	☐	☐
G. Identifies ineffective actions to improve in the future	☐	☐	☐	☐	☐	☐	☐	☐	☐	☐
H. Reviews my action plan with me	☐	☐	☐	☐	☐	☐	☐	☐	☐	☐
I. Suggests improvements to my action plan when necessary	☐	☐	☐	☐	☐	☐	☐	☐	☐	☐

Comments:

_____

_____

_____

8. What barriers, if any, have you encountered that have prevented you from using skills or knowledge gained in the training program? *Check all that apply. Please explain, if possible.*

❑ I have no opportunity to use the skills _____
❑ Not enough time _____
❑ My work environment does not support these skills _____
❑ My manager does not support this type of course   _____
❑ This material does not apply to my job situation   _____
❑ Other (Please specify) _____

9. Do you think the training represented a good investment for
Healthsearch Pharmaceutical Incorporated?   Yes ❑   No ❑
Please explain.

_____

_____

_____

10. What suggestions do you have for improving the training?
Please specify.

_____

_____

_____

Example 2*
Apple Computer

TRAIN-THE-TRAINER
IMPACT QUESTIONNAIRE
(SAMPLE AREAS)

1. Listed below are the learning objectives from the Train-the-Trainer
program. After reflecting on this training one month later, please
use the following scale to show the degree to which your skills and

---

*Reprinted with the permission of the American Society for Training and
Development (ASTD). Burkett, H. 1999. "Measuring a Train-the-Trainer Approach
to Support Build-to-Order Capabilities." In *In Action: Measuring Learning and
Performance*, ed. T.K. Hodges, Alexandria, Va.

knowledge have been enhanced or changed as a result of this training.

5   Completely Enhanced/Greatly Changed
4   Very Much Enhanced/Significant Change
3   Moderately Enhanced/Some Change
2   Somewhat Enhanced/Little Change
1   No Change
NA   No Opportunity to Use Skill

Objective						
Assessing Learners' Working Style	1	2	3	4	5	NA
Designing an SOJT Plan	1	2	3	4	5	NA
Applying Adult Learning Theory to SOJT	1	2	3	4	5	NA
Analyzing Job/Task Requirements	1	2	3	4	5	NA
Sequencing Job Tasks	1	2	3	4	5	NA
Demonstrating Steps for Effective OJT Delivery	1	2	3	4	5	NA
Communicating Process Requirements	1	2	3	4	5	NA
Identifying Errors in a Work Process	1	2	3	4	5	NA

2. Did you implement your on-the-job action plan for this program?

   Yes_____   No_____

   If yes, please describe the results. If not, please explain your reasons.

3. Please rate the extent to which this program has positively influenced each of the following measures of your work unit.

   5   Completely Influenced
   4   Significantly Influenced
   3   Moderately Influenced
   2   Somewhat Influenced
   1   No Influence

Improvement Measure					
Productivity	1	2	3	4	5
Labor Efficiency	1	2	3	4	5
Process-Induced Failures	1	2	3	4	5
Quality	1	2	3	4	5
Communications	1	2	3	4	5
Customer Response	1	2	3	4	5
Other (please name)	1	2	3	4	5

4. List behaviors, materials, or skills you've used on the job as a result of this program.
5. What has changed about your work as a result of this program?
6. Please identify any accomplishments or improvements you've made personally or to your line's performance that you can link to this program (specific behavior change, action items, new projects, etc.).
7. What specific value in dollars can be attributed to the above improvements?

$: _____

Basis of Estimate:

8. *Your degree of confidence* in the above estimate, based on a percentage.

_____ %

(0% = No Confidence and 100% = Full Confidence)

9. Other factors, besides training, may have influenced your improvements. Please list any other factors (i.e., change in management, attention to the program) that might have influenced you and estimate the percentage of its influence.

Other factor (specify): _____ %

Other factor (specify): _____ %

10. Please indicate the percent of your improvements or accomplishments that you consider to be *directly related* to the Train-the-Trainer program.

_____ %

NOTE: The total percentage for items 9 and 10 cannot exceed 100%.

11. Do you think the Train-the-Trainer program represented a good investment for Apple?

    Yes_____   No_____

    Please explain.

12. What barriers, if any, have you encountered in trying to apply skills or knowledge gained in Train-the-Trainer? List all that apply. Please explain, if possible.

13. How would you describe management support of this program, based upon your experience?

14. One month later, what suggestions do you have that would improve Train-the-Trainer going forward? Be specific.

15. Other Comments:

_____

_____

_____

Example 3[*]
General Electric Corporation

SAMPLE LIST OF FOLLOW-UP QUESTIONS

---

1. *Based on the action plan and discussion you had with your manager, what specific action steps have you completed? What action steps still need to be completed?*
2. *How are you specifically applying what you learned as a result of attending the ESF course?*
3. *How have you and your job changed as a result of attending the ESF course?*
4. *What is the impact of these changes to the customer and the organization?*
5. *What barriers (if any) inhibited you from applying what you learned?*
6. *List any skills you did not have an opportunity to apply in the evaluation timeframe.*

Note: The series of questions relating to actual business scenarios and performance data is not included in this sample list.

[*]Reprinted with the permission of the American Society for Training and Development (ASTD). Whalen, J. P. 1999. "Enhancing Job Performance Through Technical Training and Education." In *In Action: Measuring Learning and Performance,* ed. T.K. Hodges, Alexandria, Va.

Example 4*
Nextel Corporation

Performance Management (PM) Program Evaluation

When completing the following questions, keep in mind . . .

➤ *the information covered in the Performance Management class, which included goal setting using Target-Action-Impact and SMART criteria, communication skills, giving feedback, coaching, creating employee working files and performance journals, conducting interim performance reviews (IPRs), conducting annual performance reviews (APRs), and development planning*

➤ *the action plan on page 48 of your Performance Management manual that you completed at the end of the program*

➤ *any actions you have taken that were the result of something you learned during the PM program*

1. Listed below are some things you should be able to do after taking the Performance Management (PM) class. Since the class, have you used the following behaviors or skills?

BEHAVIORS/SKILLS

   i. Update employee objectives to meet the SMART criteria within 90 days of class.

        Yes No
        ❑   ❑

  ii. Coach employees on an ongoing basis to ensure continuous performance improvement.

        Yes No
        ❑   ❑

 iii. Create working files for all employees in your organization within 90 days of class.

        Yes No
        ❑   ❑

---

*Reprinted with the permission of Lynn Schmidt, Director, Training and Education, Nextel Communications, 2001.

   iv. Conduct an Interim Performance Review
       for all employees.   Yes No
                                                 ❏   ❏

    v. When preparing for Annual Performance
       Reviews, do you review an employee's
       working file, gather additional information,
       review past performance, and set future
       goals and objectives?   Yes No
                                                 ❏   ❏

   vi. Implement the development planning
       process for each employee.   Yes No
                                             ❏   ❏

1a. **Estimate the extent to which the following factors contrib-
uted to your use of the above behaviors and skills** *(indicate a
percentage from zero to 100 on each line such that they total
100%).*

    The Performance Management (PM) class   _____%
    Other programs completed prior to attending
    the PM class   _____%
    Other programs you began subsequent to
    attending the PM class   _____%
    Organizational changes (e.g., staff, structure)   _____%
    Interactions with/advice from your manager,
    colleagues, others   _____%
    Other   _____%

                                      Total: 100%

2. **Think about what has changed about** *you* **and** *your work* **as a
result of participation in the Performance Management (PM)
class. List specific behaviors that you have stopped, started, or
increased back on the job since taking the PM class.** *(For example: increased delegation to employees, coached employees regularly, or any other action items.)*

ACTIONS TAKEN Related to the Performance Management Program
(list all that apply)

1.
_____

2.
_____

3. _____

4. _____

2a. What are the RESULTS of the actions you listed in question 2?

Results of Actions Taken *For example: business outcomes, job performance changes, productivity improvements, time savings (cycle time, your time, your employee's time, coaching time)*, costs *(turnover, recruiting, hiring)*, or quality *(improved work quality, more occasions of getting it right the first time)*	Estimate how much money this saves/makes Nextel on a *quarterly* basis.	How did you arrive at this value? *Please indicate the assumptions you made and the specific calculations you performed to arrive at the value.*
EXAMPLE: Decreased the amount of time spent per employee creating annual performance reviews from average of 4.5 hours per review to .75 hours per review.	EXAMPLE: $1,875	EXAMPLE: Before: 4.5 hours per review. After: .75 hours per review. Preparation Time Saved: 3.75 hours @ $50/hr for each of 10 employees
1.	$	
2.	$	
3.	$	
4.	$	

2b. What level of confidence do you place in the above estimations?   ____%
  (0% = no confidence/certainty; 100% = total confidence/certainty)

3. Which of the following aspects of your job were most improved by the behaviors and skills you learned in the class? *(check all that apply)*

Relationships Improved	Business Results Achieved	Personal Outcomes Realized
❏ Manager	❏ Cost reductions/cost efficiencies	❏ Increased job satisfaction
❏ Direct reports/team	❏ Productivity increases	❏ Increased organizational commitment
❏ Peers	❏ Improved quality	❏ Reduced stress
	❏ Increased customer satisfaction	❏ Increased / better quality personal time
	❏ Top line, revenue generation	❏ Improved family relationships
	❏ Bottom line, profitability	

4. What additional benefits have been derived from this class? *These might include things such as work habits, work climate, attitudes, new skills, customer service and satisfaction, employee development and advancement, initiative, innovation, etc.*

_____

_____

_____

5. What barriers, if any, have you encountered that have prevented you from using, or fully utilizing, the skills or knowledge you learned in this program? *Please explain.*

_____

_____

_____

Focus Group Tools

Focus Group Checklist

❏ Advance notice
- Contact participants by phone 1–2 weeks prior to session
- Send letter of invitation—explain purpose
- Include list of questions
- Give each participant a reminder call

❏ Begin the focus group
- Welcome group
- Provide brief overview of topic and process
- Explain importance of input, how the data will be analyzed, who will see the data, and what actions will be taken as a result
- Set the ground rules (time limit, full participation, confidentiality, and summary of results)

❏ Questions
- Questions should flow in a logical sequence (as planned)
- Key questions should focus on the critical issues
- Consider probing for clarification
- Use "think back" questions as needed
- Provide equal time for input from each participant

❏ Logistics
- Room should be comfortable, with appropriate number of tables and chairs
- Meeting room should be private
- Background noise should be minimal and not interfere with discussions

- Key questions should be listed on flip chart or whiteboard
- Provide paper and pencils for participants if necessary
- Provide light refreshments
- Have assistant (meeting recorder) take notes

❏ Tips for facilitator
- Be well rested and alert for focus group session
- Practice the introduction
- Ask questions with minimal reference to notes
- Avoid head-nodding
- Avoid comments that signal approval (like "great," "I agree," etc.)
- Avoid giving your opinion

❏ Meeting Dynamics
- Limit individual time to avoid excessive input from talkative participants
- Allow, encourage, or maybe require everyone to participate
- Use silence as a way to seek input
- Ask for details and examples from individuals who "agree with everyone"
- Ask for clarification and supporting data from those who "disagree with everyone"
- Keep meeting on focus, on track, and on schedule

❏ Tips for Meeting Recorder
- Use "Notes and Quotes" paper for recording discussion and comments
- Record useful content issues under "Notes"
- Use any appropriate shorthand technique to capture information (abbreviations, phrases, symbols, etc.)
- Capture potential quotes under "Quotable Quotes." These may be usable anecdotes in impact study report
- Do not link a name with specific information
- Review the data at the end of the session to ensure that recorded information is understandable

❏ At the end of the focus group
- Summarize key points and process
- Check to see if there are other comments
- Thank the group for participating
- Tell the group when they will see the results in the summary report

Date of Focus Group:
Location of Focus Group:
Number of Participants:
Facilitator:

Focus Group Notes & Quotes

Q1

Notes	Quotable Quotes

Source: Krueger, R.A. 1994. *Focus Groups: A Practical Guide for Applied Research*. Second edition. Thousand Oaks, Calif.: Sage Publications.

Index

The Value of Belonging

ASTD membership keeps you up to date on the latest developments in your field, and provides top-quality, *practical* information to help you stay ahead of trends, polish your skills, measure your progress, demonstrate your effectiveness, and advance your career.

We give you what you need most from the entire scope of workplace learning and performance:

Information
We're your best resource for research, best practices, and background support materials – the data you need for your projects to excel.

Networking
We're the facilitator who puts you in touch with colleagues,experts, field specialists, and industry leaders – the people you need to know to succeed.

Technology
We're the clearinghouse for new technologies in training, learning, and knowledge management in the workplace – the background you need to stay ahead.

Analysis
We look at cutting-edge practices and programs and give you a balanced view of the latest tools and techniques – the understanding you need on what works and what doesn't.

Competitive Edge
ASTD is your leading resource on the issues and topics that are important to you. That's the value of belonging!

For more information, or to become a member, please call 1.800.628.2783 (U.S.) or +1.703.683.8100; visit our Website at **www.astd.org**; or send an email to customercare@astd.org.

Linking People,
Learning & Performance

Yarn—The Things It Makes and How to Make Them

Yarn—The Things It Makes and How to Make Them

Carolyn Meyer

Illustrated by Jennifer Perrott

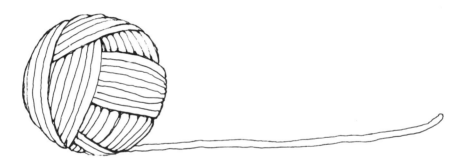

Harcourt Brace Jovanovich, Inc.
New York

Contents

For
CHERYL
and
JANINE

Introduction

In the days before man began to write his own history, he survived in the simplest ways he could. He lived in a cave, ate what he found, and used the skins of animals to keep himself warm.

But people have always wanted to improve their ways of doing things. They built shelters and raised plants and animals for food. They discovered how to twist together animal hairs or plant fibers to make strong, flexible threads, and they learned to cross the threads over and under each other to make cloth.

Weaving is one of the most ancient of crafts. Knitting, which is another way of making cloth by connecting a series of loops with long needles, is a more recent invention, although no one seems to know just when it began. The origin of crocheting, drawing one loop through another with a hook to form a lacy kind of fabric, is also difficult to trace. Macramé, tying knots in yarn and cord to make decorative designs, is a newcomer. It is only about seven centuries old, and we know that it started in Arabia.

Although today most cloth is made on computer-controlled high-speed machinery, weaving, knitting, crocheting, and tying macramé knots by hand are still very popular. Many people have discovered the pleasure of using their hands to create things to wear and to use that are more beautiful than any machine can produce.

CHAPTER 1

Crocheting

Crochet (pronounced *kro-SHAY*) is a French word meaning "small hook." It is not hard to learn, and the basic materials required are a crochet hook and some yarn. Crocheting is fun, too. Once you have developed the knack of moving the hook with the yarn, the design grows quickly.

There are only a few basic stitches in crocheting, and they all begin with the *chain*. Single Crochet and Double Crochet are the two stitches used most often. They can be put together in almost endless combinations, to make circles and squares and rectangles, airy, open patterns, fanciful designs, and tight, close patterns.

Although some historians believe that crocheting is one of the very early crafts, the kind of crocheting we know today is only about four hundred years old. It was developed by European nuns who were experts in making lace. A hook—actually a wire with a bent end —was one of the many tools used in making lace. But the nuns created a great variety of designs using just that one simple tool. For a long time crocheting remained a "convent art," and the nuns of Ireland were especially famous for their work.

Some early American colonists knew how to crochet, but the craft didn't really become popular in the United States until the immigrants began to arrive from Ireland in the 1840s. Irish girls who had been taught to crochet by nuns brought to this country their handwork and their skill.

At one time crocheting was worked with very fine thread and was used mainly to make elegant tablecloths and curtains and delicate trimmings for handkerchiefs, dresses, and baby clothes. Today all kinds of yarn, and sometimes string and straw, are used to crochet all kinds of things, from a sturdy rug to a complete wardrobe.

What You'll Need

CROCHET HOOKS: They are made of plastic, aluminum, steel, or bone. Sizes range from a very fine size A to a large size J, or from a very fine size 0 to a large size 14. Sizes are sometimes different, depending on what the hook is made of. The kind of hook you use is up to you, but the size should depend on the thickness of the yarn. The smallest hook is used to crochet fine cotton thread into delicately lacy old-fashioned doilies. The largest hooks are used with thick yarns for rugmaking.

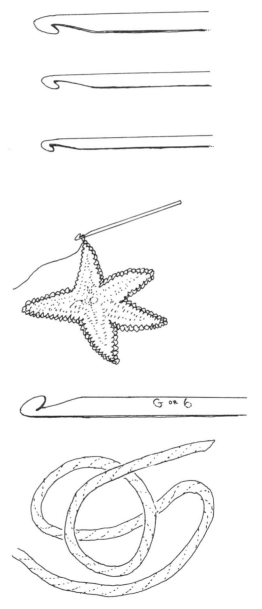

A medium-sized hook, such as a G or a 6, is the best for learning to crochet.

YARN: Use whatever yarn you have. Knitting worsted, a medium-weight yarn, is a good kind to begin on. It is the right weight for a size G hook. You will be able to see your stitches more clearly if you use light-colored yarn.

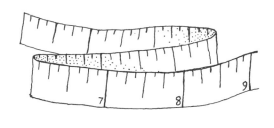

RULER: Measuring is an essential part of crocheting. A tape measure is useful, too.

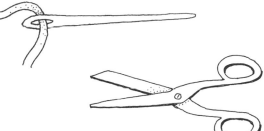

NEEDLE: A blunt-end needle with an eye large enough for yarn to pass through is used for sewing together the parts you crochet.

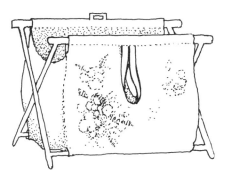

SCISSORS: A small pair for cutting yarn is good to have.

NEEDLEWORK OR YARN BAG: A place for everything. Perhaps you'll want to make one, but in the meantime use whatever you have.

Getting Started

Crocheting always begins with a single loop made this way: Make a loop with your yarn, as though you were writing a small letter "e." Write another "e" next to it.

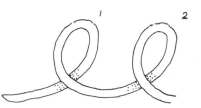

Slide the second loop under the first loop and pull it through. This makes a slipknot.

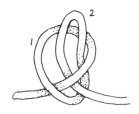

13

Put the loop on the end
of your crochet hook.

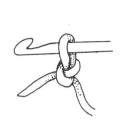

Pull both ends of the yarn.
Pulling one end will tighten
the slipknot. Pulling the
other end will make the loop
smaller. But be careful
not to make it too small.
You should be able to slide the
hook easily in and out of the loop.

Your two hands work together. The right hand moves the hook (if
you are right-handed), and the left hand controls the yarn. It is
important to learn to hold hook and yarn the right way from the
beginning.

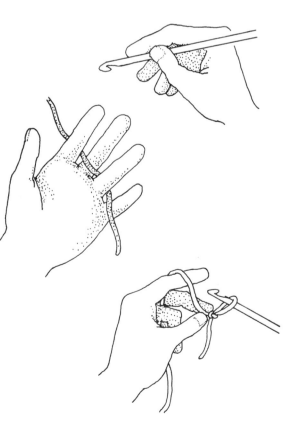

Hold the hook like a pencil
in your right hand.
Hold your left hand
with the palm toward you.
Lace the yarn through
your fingers this way:
In front of your little finger,
behind your ring finger,
in front of your middle finger,
behind and around
your index finger.

Pinch the slipknot between
the thumb and middle finger
of your left hand.
As you go along, always keep
those fingers close to the
loops nearest the hook.

14

The yarn should be stretched firmly between your index finger and the hook.

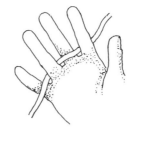

If you are left-handed, you will do everything just the opposite way: Hold the hook in your left hand. Lace the yarn through the fingers of your right hand. Pinch the slipknot between the thumb and middle finger of your right hand.

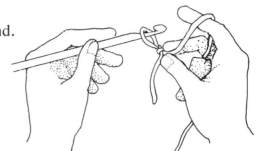

Now you are ready to begin pulling one loop through another to make a chain.

You already have one loop on the hook. Push the hook through that loop a little way, so that the yarn from the slipknot is behind the hook. Then move the hook so that the yarn wraps over it and catches in the hook at the end.

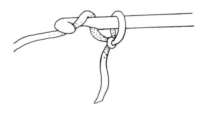

Now pull the yarn through the loop on the hook to form a new loop. Let the first loop drop off.

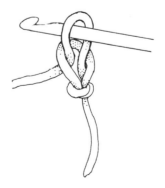

Chaining

A chain is a series of plain loops, each pulled through

15

the one before it. The chain is the base on which all other crochet stitches are made. Just keep pulling each new loop through the one before it, letting that one drop off. Make the loops rather loose. Practice chaining until you can handle the hook easily and make loops that are even in size.

When you are following directions in crocheting, the symbol for chaining is *ch*. The direction *ch* 12, for instance, means "make a chain of 12 loops."

Making a Yarn Necklace

You can make a handsome necklace by chaining. Just *ch* as many loops as you need to make the chain as long as you want it. Heavy yarn works best. But you can make several chains of the same length with light-weight yarns, maybe using a different color for each chain.

Slide a medal or other piece of jewelry, or even a pretty button, onto the chain before you knot the ends together.

Single Crochet

Single Crochet stitches are the smallest and closest together of all crochet stitches. To begin the Single Crochet, *ch* 12. That is, make a loop for the hook and chain a series of 12 loops. Make them rather large and loose.

Row 1: Skip the chain loop
next to the hook. Push the
hook down through the center
of the *next* chain loop,
the second from the hook.

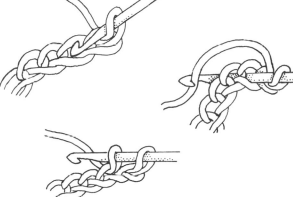

Wrap the yarn over the hook
and pull it back through
the center of the chain loop.
Then you will have two loops
on the hook.

Wrap the yarn over the hook again
and pull it through *both* loops
on the hook. This leaves one
loop on the hook and makes
one Single Crochet.
The symbol for Single Crochet is *sc*.

When you have completed any crochet stitch, there will always be
only one loop left on the hook.

Push the hook through the
center of the next chain
loop to begin the next *sc*.
Wrap the yarn over the hook
and pull it back through
the center of the chain loop.

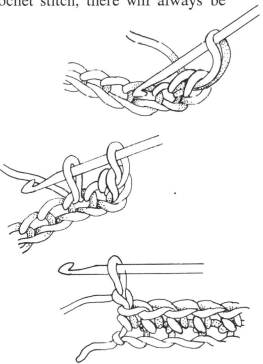

Sc in each chain loop.
When you have crocheted in the
last chain loop, make one extra
chain loop. The extra loop
makes a step up to begin
the next row.

17

Then turn your work—that is, hold the hook still and just turn the finished stitches from right to left so that the reverse side of the work is toward you.

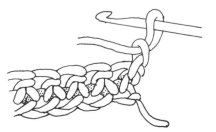

When you are crocheting, the side of the work facing toward you is always called the *front*. The side of the work facing away from you is always called the *back*. And all of this has nothing to do with the right or the wrong side, or the inside or the outside.

The first row probably seemed very awkward to you. But you'll find that the second row and the ones that follow it seem easier.

Row 2: Skip the chain loop next to the hook. Instead of pushing the hook through the center of each loop, as you did in Row 1, do it this way: From the *front* of your work, slide the hook beneath the two top strands of the first stitch in Row 1.

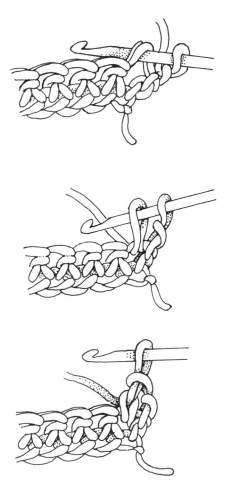

Wrap the yarn over the hook and pull it through the two strands. You'll have two loops on the hook.

Wrap the yarn over the hook again and pull it through both loops on the hook. This leaves one loop on the hook and completes one *sc*.

18

Sc in each of the stitches of Row 1, always sliding the hook beneath the two top strands of each stitch. Make sure not to miss the last stitch in the row. It is not as easy to see as the other stitches. Remember to keep your work pinched between the thumb and middle finger of your left hand. At the end of the row, *ch* 1 to make the step up to the next row. Turn your work, skip the first chain loop, and begin Row 3 in the second loop from the hook. Keep working one row after another until you begin to feel confident with that stitch.

Fastening Off

When you have worked several rows of the practice piece, make the last stitch and cut the yarn. Leave a tail about 2 inches long. Pull the tail through the last loop. Then, with your hook, weave the tail in and out, going under the two top strands of the last row of stitches. Clip the yarn close to your work. Then weave in the other tail at the beginning of your work.

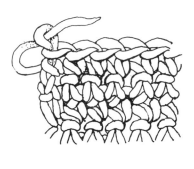

Making a Headband

By the time you have finished a practice piece of Single Crochet, you will feel a bit more comfortable in handling the hook and yarn. The more you do, of course, the more confident you'll become and the faster you can go. Making a headband in Single Crochet will help you gain even more speed and confidence.

19

First, measure around your head where the headband will go to find out how long to make it. Then *ch* enough loops to measure the width of the band, about 1½ inches, unless you would prefer to make it wider. The number of loops you will need depends on the size of the hook you are using and the thickness of the yarn. It also depends on your "gauge," or the way you have of crocheting, whether it's tight or loose or somewhere in between. If you are using a size G hook with knitting worsted, you will probably make the headband five stitches wide. That means that you will *ch* 5, plus one more loop for turning—the "step up" to begin the next row—making 6 loops altogether.

Row 1: Skip the loop next to the hook and *sc* in each loop to the end of the chain. When you reach the end, *ch* 1 and turn your work.

Row 2: Skip the loop next to the hook and *sc* in each stitch of Row 1, sliding your hook under the two top strands of that row. At the end of the row, *ch* 1 and turn.

Repeat Row 2 as many times as you need to, until the piece is long enough. Fasten off. Cut two pieces of ribbon, each about 6 inches long, for tying. With an ordinary needle and thread, sew a piece to each end of the headband. Make a few extra stitches on top of each other, and cut the thread close to your work.

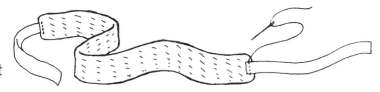

Double Crochet

Double Crochet stitches have more loops than Single Crochet, so there are more steps in making each stitch. But Double Crochet forms a more open pattern, and the work goes faster than it does with Single Crochet.

To begin the Double Crochet, *ch* 12—that is, make a loop for the hook and then make a series of 12 loops.

20

Row 1: Wrap the yarn over the hook. Count 4 chain loops from the hook. Push the hook down through the center of the fourth loop.

Wrap the yarn over the hook again and pull it back through the center of that fourth chain loop. Then you will have 2 regular loops with a "yarn over" loop between them, making 3 loops on the hook altogether.

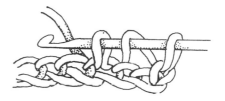

Wrap the yarn over the hook again and pull it through one regular loop and the "yarn over" loop. Then you'll have 2 loops on the hook.

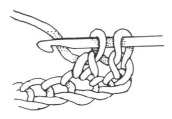

Wrap the yarn over the hook one last time and pull it through *both* remaining loops. This leaves just one loop on the hook and makes one Double Crochet.

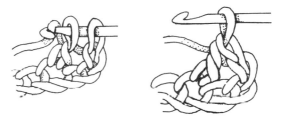

Just as in Single Crochet, there is only one loop left on the hook after each stitch is completed. The symbol for Double Crochet is *dc*.

To make the second *dc*, wrap the yarn over the hook and push the hook through the center of the next chain loop.

21

Wrap the yarn over the hook
again and pull it back through
the center of the chain loop.

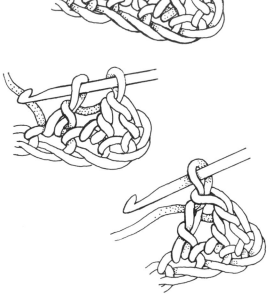

Wrap the yarn over the hook
again and pull it through
one regular loop and the
last "yarn over" loop.

Wrap the yarn over the hook
once more and pull it through
both loops. This leaves one loop
on the hook and completes
the second Double Crochet.

At first it all seems very complicated, but as you do each stitch, it will
become easier and you will not have to think so hard about each step.

When you come to the end of the chain, make 3 extra chain loops
for the step up to the beginning of the next row. Turn your work—
hold the hook still and just turn the finished stitches from left to right.

In directions for crocheting, the symbol *y.o.* means "yarn over" or
"wrap the yarn over the hook." You will find the symbol often in the
directions for Row 2.

Row 2: Begin with *y.o.* hook.
Then from the front of your work
(the side facing you) skip the
3 chain loops and slide the hook
beneath the two top strands of the
fourth loop from the hook in Row 1.

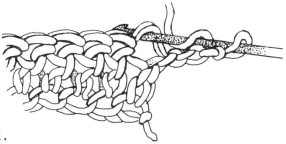

22

Y.o. hook and pull it through the two strands. Then you will have 3 loops on the hook—two regular and a *y.o.* loop between them.

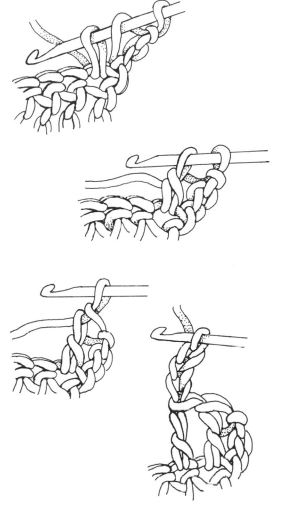

Y.o. hook again and pull it through one regular loop and the *y.o.* loop in the middle.

Y.o. hook again and pull it through both loops on the hook. This leaves one loop on the hook and completes one Double Crochet.

Make a *dc* in each stitch to the end of the row. Make 3 extra chain loops for the step up to the beginning of the next row.

Turn your work and begin Row 3.

Making a Belt

When you made the headband in Single Crochet, you first made a short chain and then worked dozens of short rows of stitches. When you make the belt in Double Crochet, however, you can try a different approach: make a very long chain—long enough to go around your waist, plus 12 more inches for tying. Then you make only a few *dc* rows—just as many as you need to make the belt as wide as you want it. If you like, you can change colors every few rows, or you can alternate two colors.

To change to another color,
simply pull a loop of the second
color through the last loop
made with the first color.
Leave a 3-inch tail.
Then cut the first color, also
leaving a tail. Later, when
you have finished crocheting
the piece, go back and weave
the tails in and out of a few stitches.
Clip yarn close to your work.

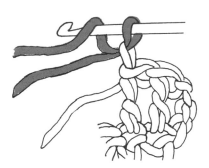

Making Fringe and Tassels

You can decorate the ends of your belt, and many other yarn
projects, with fringe or tassels. They are not hard to make, and they
can turn a simple thing like a belt into something quite special.

To make fringe, cut pieces of yarn that are a little more than twice as
long as you want the fringe to be. If you want a 2-inch fringe, then
cut pieces of yarn that are about 4¼ inches long.

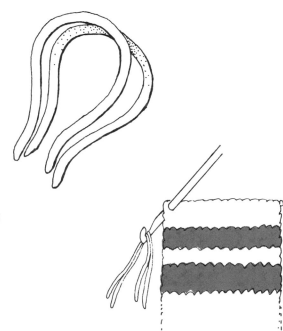

Put two pieces of yarn
together and fold them in
half to form a big loop.

Push your crochet hook
through the two top strands
of yarn at the very end row
of stitches of the belt.

Use the crochet hook
to pull the loop of yarn
through your work halfway.
Then use the hook to pull
the four ends of yarn
through the loop.
With your fingers, pull on
the ends to tighten the loop.

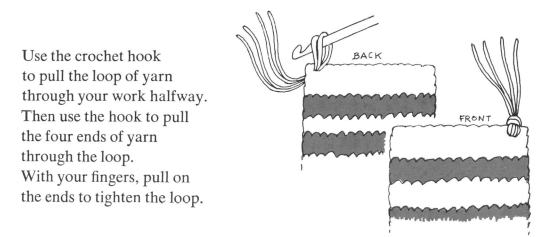

Then take two more pieces of yarn and make another loop of fringe
next to the first one. Keep making loops across the end of the belt.
When you have finished, you can trim the fringe with scissors to
make it even.

To make tassels, decide how long
you want them to be and cut
a piece of cardboard to that size.
Then wrap yarn around the
cardboard to make a fat bundle
of yarn. Start wrapping
from the bottom end of the
cardboard and end at the bottom.
How many times you wrap the yarn
depends partly on how thick
the yarn is. (Knitting worsted,
for example, needs to be wrapped
around about twelve times
to make a really fat tassel.)

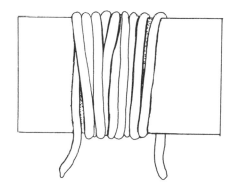

Now cut two pieces of yarn,
each about 4 inches long.
Slide one piece under the yarn
wrapped around the card.
Pull the piece up to the top
and tie it.

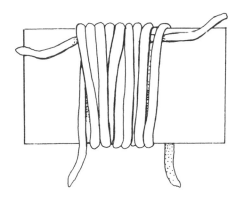

Cut through the yarn at the bottom of the cardboard, a few strands at a time.

Take the second 4-inch piece of yarn and wrap it several times around the bundle of yarn about ½ inch below the top. Tie it and trim the ends.

Now the tassel is ready to be sewn on. Tassels work best on the ends of a narrow belt. You should first gather each end of the belt before you sew on the tassels. Thread a blunt-end needle with yarn and fasten the yarn at one corner of the belt.

Sew in and out of the stitches at the end of the belt by making three or four stitches, one on top of the other.

Pull the yarn to gather the end of the belt, and fasten the yarn at the opposite corner by taking three or four stitches. Sew the tassel to the belt with several stitches through the top of the tassel.

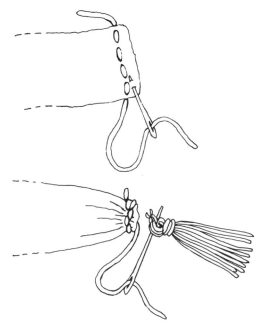

26

Making a Crocheted Pillow

You can design a handsome crocheted pillow made of patches. Work the patches in Single Crochet or Double Crochet or some of both. Use two colors of yarn, or make each patch in a different color. This is a good way to use up leftover yarn, providing it is all about the same thickness.

It's easier to make a cover to fit a pillow you already have than to try to find or make a pillow for a cover after you've made it. Measure the pillow and decide how many squares you need to crochet to cover it.

For instance, if your pillow is 12 inches wide and 12 inches long, you could crochet nine squares, each one 4 inches wide and 4 inches long.

But if the pillow is 16 inches wide and 9 inches long, you might want to crochet 12 rectangles, each 4 inches long and 3 inches wide.

You may think of still another way to do it.

Sewing the Patches Together

When you have crocheted enough patches to complete your design, you are ready to join them together. Lay out the pieces the way you want them to go. Then thread a blunt-end needle with yarn and weave each seam like this:

27

Lay the two patches close together with the edges touching. Come up with the needle from the wrong side close to the edge of the first patch. Then cross over to the second patch. Go down with the needle close to the edge of the second patch.

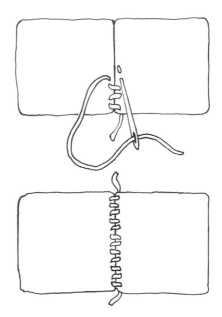

Make one stitch on the second patch and cross over again to the first patch. Keep crossing back and forth, making one stitch on each side, to the end of the seam.

Make three or four extra stitches, one on top of the other, at the end of the seam. Then weave the rest of the patches together the same way.

Finishing the Pillow

The design that you have crocheted is the front of your pillow. You can also crochet the other side, but most people use a plain piece of cloth for the back. Try to find a piece that goes with the colors you have used.

Measure your crocheted work. Then cut a piece of cloth that is 1 inch longer and 1 inch wider than the crocheted piece.

Use a ruler to measure ½ inch from each edge of the cloth for a seam, and mark it on the right side with chalk or pencil.

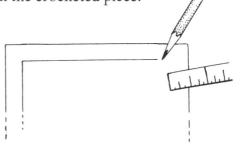

Fold the seam toward the wrong side. Pin it and baste it, with long running stitches. Use a sharp needle and ordinary thread.

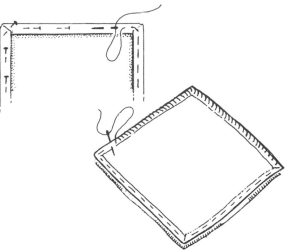

Put the right sides of the cloth and the crocheted piece together. With needle and thread sew around three sides of the pillow with an overcast stitch. Pull out the basting stitches.

Turn the pillow cover right side out and put the pillow inside. Sew the open side of the cover with overcast stitches. If you like, you can make a tassel to sew on each corner of the pillow.

Crocheting in the Round

So far you have been crocheting back and forth on a straight piece, building each row on the row before it. But crochet stitches can be worked in circles as well as in squares. And these circles can become bright designs to be used by themselves or on a headband or belt. Or they can be sewn together to decorate something else that you have crocheted or knitted or sewn. Crocheting in the round is only a little more complicated than straight crocheting. But you have a lot more freedom to experiment with your ideas.

A Small Closed Circle

To begin, make a loop for your hook and *ch* 4. Now push the hook through the first loop you made. Then you'll have two loops on the hook.

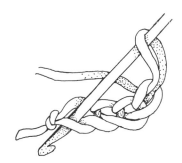

29

Y.o. hook (that is, wrap the yarn over the hook) and pull the yarn through both loops. This is called a Slip Stitch, and the symbol is *sl st*. You will have one loop on your hook, and the chain will form a small ring. This ring is the center around which all the stitches are made.

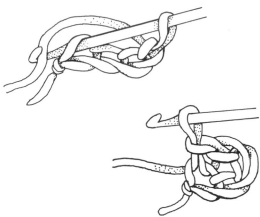

When you are working around a ring, each row is called a *round*. The symbol is *rnd*.

Rnd 1: *Ch* 2 to make a step up. Then make a *dc* stitch this way:

Y.o. hook, slide the hook through the center of the ring, as though the ring were a stitch.

Y.o. hook again, and pull the yarn back through the ring, making three loops on the hook.

Y.o. hook again, and pull the yarn through one regular loop and the *y.o.* loop in the middle.

Y.o. hook again, and pull the yarn through both loops on the hook. This leaves one loop on the hook and completes one *dc*.

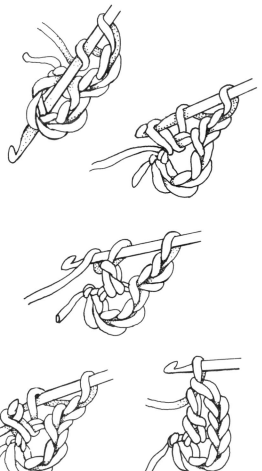

30

Make another *dc,* again
sliding the hook through the
center of the original ring, as
though the ring were a stitch.

Make 12 *dcs* all together,
always going through the center
of the same ring, crowding
the stitches around the ring
to form a circle.

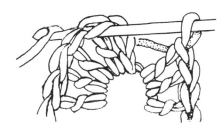

When you have made the last *dc,*
push the hook through the
top loop of the first *dc.*
Join the 2 *dcs* with a *sl st.*

To fasten off, cut the yarn, leaving a tail about 2 inches long. Pull the
tail through the *sl st.* Then with your hook weave the tail in and out
of the tops of the first few stitches. Clip the yarn close to your work.
Weave the other tail around the ring and trim it.

You can make a larger circle
by adding another round.
Ch 3 for the step up.
Work around the outside of *Rnd* 1,
sliding the hook in the space
between each stitch in the round.

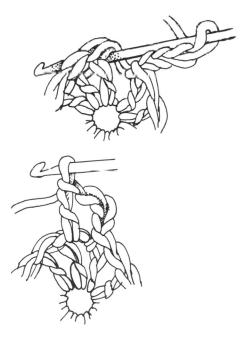

But as you add each round,
you must also add more stitches
in order to make the circle
lie flat. One way to add
more stitches is to work
two stitches in each space
between the stitches of *Rnd* 1.

Another way to add more stitches
is to make a *ch st* between each *dc*.
If you make several *ch sts*
between each *dc,* the *ch sts* and the
dcs will form open petals around
the center of *dcs,* and you'll
have something like a sunflower.

A Big Sunflower

First make a Small Closed Circle: To begin, *ch* 4 and join with a *sl st*
to form a center ring. **Rnd 1:** *Ch* 2, then work 12 *dc* in the ring. Join
the last *dc* to the first *dc* with a *sl st*. This completes the center.

Rnd 2: *Ch* 1. Then work 1 *dc,*
sliding the hook in the space
between the first and second *dc*
in *Rnd* 1. *Ch* 5 and work another *dc*.

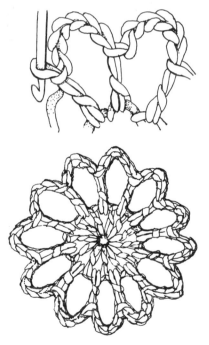

Go all around the center,
making 5 *chs* between each *dc*.

When you have gone all the way
around, *ch* 5 again, and fasten the
last chain loop with a *sl st*
to the first *dc* in the round.
Then fasten off.

You can also try making Sunflowers using *sc* instead of *dc*. Or use
single in one round and *double* in the other. You can make more
stitches in the first round, or you can have fewer stitches. You can add
more chain loops between each crochet stitch to make bigger, more
open petals. Or you can work only two or three chains.

e, you could hang
ght-colored Sun-
a Yarn Necklace.

ng a few small
ifferent kinds
ted belt or headband.

ugh small circles to go
the neck of a sweater
d each cuff.

me circles on the pocket
or jacket.

ouquet of crocheted
Cut pieces of wire
. Insert one end of
near the center opening.

opposite end of the wire
stems" are of different
Put the flowers in a
a small opening. Try to
the flowers closely in a
o the wire stems don't show.

ne design on each
of a crocheted pillow.

collection of circles in
rner of a plain cloth pillow.
er the entire pillow with
of circles.

An Open Center Design

You can make a design with an op
around which to work the stitches.
sections around an open center.

To begin, *ch* 6 and join with
a *sl st* to form a center ring.
Rnd 1: Make 2 *scs* in the
ring. Then *ch* 5.

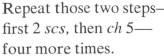

Repeat those two steps—
first 2 *scs,* then *ch* 5—
four more times.

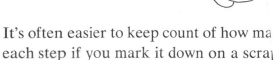

It's often easier to keep count of how ma
each step if you mark it down on a scra

At the end of the last *ch* 5, join the *ch* t
fasten off.

You can try making this Open Center De
center, just by adding or taking away chai
can use *dc* instead of *sc*. Try working mc
stitches—or more *dcs* between the chains.
sections, or six sections instead of five. Eac
will create a slightly different kind of design

Arranging Your Designs

After you have made several different kind
all sorts of ways of using them imaginatively.

33

For instanc
a single bri
flower fron

Or try sew
circles of c
to a croch

Make end
all around
and arou

Scatter sc
of a dress

Make a l
flowers.
for stem
the wire

Bend th
so the "s
lengths.
vase wi
arrange
bunch s

Stitch c
square

Stitch
one co
Or cov
masse

34

Make a wall hanging with
round crocheted flowers blooming
in a straight crocheted vase.
Use plain cloth for a background.
Draw the stems with a felt-tipped
marking pen.

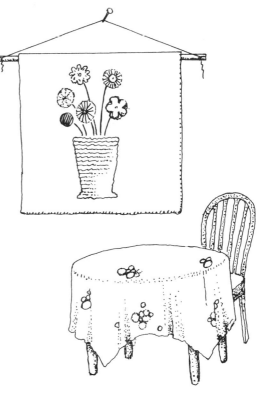

Try planting a whole garden
of flowers on a small blanket
or tablecloth.

Sewing on Your Designs

The way you sew on the designs depends on the kind of material you
are sewing them to. If it's crocheted or knitted material, use a blunt-
end needle and yarn that matches the designs.

Come up with the needle
from the wrong side, and
make a few small stitches
to hold the design firmly
in place. You do not need
to sew all around the outside
of each design (unless you
want to). Try to hide your
stitches so they don't show.

If you are sewing the designs on woven cloth, it is easier to use an
ordinary needle and sewing thread that matches the designs.

35

Making a Round Mat

Once you have mastered the small round crocheted pieces, you will have enough experience to work a bigger, more complicated project. You can crochet a mat, which could also be made into a pillow cover, a hat, or almost anything else you want to use it for.

To begin, *ch* 3 and join with a *sl st* to form a center ring. **Rnd 1:** *Ch* 3, then work 8 *dcs* in the ring. Join the last *dc* to the first *dc* in the round with a *sl st*. *Ch* 3 to step up to the next *rnd*.

Rnd 2: Work 2 *dcs* in every other stitch of the previous round and 1 *dc* in each of the alternate stitches, always sliding the hook in the space between each *dc*. When you come to the end of this *rnd* and all the other *rnds,* join the last *dc* to the first *dc* with a *sl st*. Then *ch* 3 to step up to the next *rnd*.

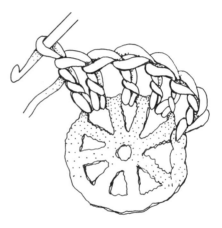

(In *Rnd* 2 you added 8 extra *dcs* by working 2 *dcs* in some of the stitches. You will find that crocheting 8 extra *dcs* evenly spaced in each *rnd* will be enough to keep the piece flat as you add round after round.)

Rnd 3: Work 1 *dc* in each of the first two stitches of the previous *rnd*. Work 2 *dcs* in every *third* stitch. Join the first and last *dcs* with a *sl st*. *Ch* 3.

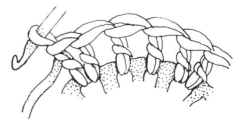

36

Rnd 4: Work 1 *dc* in each of the first three stitches of the previous *rnd*. Work 2 *dcs* in every fourth stitch. Join the first and last *dcs* with a *sl st*. *Ch 3*.

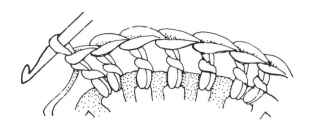

Now you can see that in *Rnd 5* you'll work 2 *dcs* in every *fifth* stitch, and in *Rnd 6*, 2 *dcs* in every *sixth* stitch, and so on for each round. It's easier to keep count of the number of stitches if you write it down. But if you do sometimes lose count and make a mistake, it won't matter very much.

Keep adding rounds until the piece measures about 12 inches across. If you wish, you can change colors at the beginning of a round. Fasten off.

Now let your imagination run free. You can use the piece as a placemat or as a mat under a potted plant or a vase of flowers.

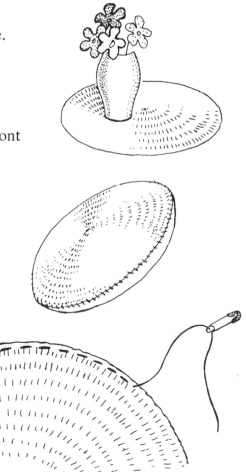

Use your crocheted work as the front of a cover for a round pillow.

To make a hat for yourself, measure around your head with a tape measure. Then cut a piece of narrow elastic or elastic thread to the right length. Fasten a small safety pin to the end of the elastic and use that to weave the elastic through the spaces between the stitches. Sew the ends of the elastic together with several stitches.

37

If you don't have any elastic, you can use a piece of yarn or ribbon, but the hat will not fit as well or as comfortably.

Granny Squares

Not all crocheting "in the round" is actually round. Sometimes it turns out to be square. This is a very popular square design that your grandmother may have used to make an openwork blanket called an afghan. Today these Granny Squares are also used to make table-cloths and pillow covers, ponchos, jackets, and skirts. And afghans, too.

You will notice as you go along that groups of 3 *dcs* are worked in the open spaces of the previous round. Each *dc* group is joined by a bridge of *ch* 3 that forms the open spaces for the next round. But in each corner you'll make two groups of *dcs* joined by *chs*. This is what keeps the corners square. As you step up to the next round, you will *ch* 3 to take the place of a *dc* stitch at either the beginning or the end of the round.

To begin, *ch* 5 and join with a *sl st* to form a center ring.

Rnd 1: *Ch* 3, then make 2 *dcs* in the ring. (The *ch* 3 takes the place of the first *dc*.) This forms one group. *Ch* 3 for a bridge.

38

Make 3 *dcs* in the ring for the second group. *Ch* 3 for the bridge. Make 3 *dcs* again for the third group. *Ch* 3 for the bridge. Make 3 *dcs* for the fourth group. *Ch* 3 and join the last *ch* to the first group with a *sl st*.

Rnd 2: *Ch* 6 (3 *chs* to take the place of the last *dc* in this *rnd;* 3 more to make a bridge).

Now you are ready to turn Corner #1. Work 3 *dcs* in the space, *ch* 3, 3 *dcs* again in the same space. *Ch* 3 for the bridge.

1

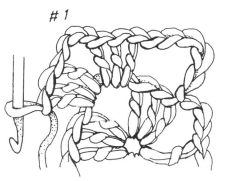

Corner #2 is the same as #1. *Ch* 3 for the bridge. Corner #3 is the same. *Ch* 3 for the bridge.

For Corner #4, work 3 *dcs* in the space, *ch* 3, then only 2 *dcs* in the same space. Insert your hook in the third chain loop, the middle of the *ch* 6 made at the beginning of the *rnd,* and join with a *sl st*.

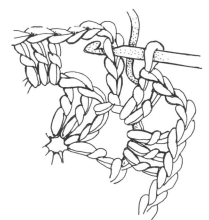

39

Rnd 3: *Ch* 3, work 2 *dcs* in the open space, *ch* 3 for the bridge. Work Corner #1 as you did in *Rnd* 2.

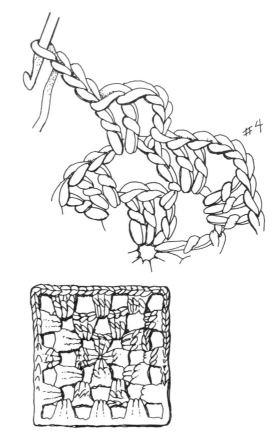

Ch 3, 3 *dcs* in open space, *ch* 3. Work Corner #2.
Ch 3, 3 *dcs* in open space, *ch* 3. Work Corner #3.
Ch 3, 3 *dcs* in open space, *ch* 3, Work Corner #4.
Ch 3 for the bridge and join with a *sl st* to the first group of *dcs*.

Now you can either fasten off or continue to add more rounds. Remember to work 3 *dcs* in the open spaces and *ch* 3 for bridges between, except at the corners. At each corner there are always two groups of 3 *dcs,* with *ch* 3 bridges.

Making a Granny Skirt

If you have about ten ounces of yarn (it doesn't have to be all the same color, but it should be the same thickness), you can make yourself a skirt of Granny Squares. It will take some time to do, but you can do a square now and then when you have a few minutes, and it will be finished before you know it.

To decide how many squares you'll need, measure around the widest part of your hips. Add another 2 inches or so for comfort, more if you want a fuller skirt. Then measure from your waist to where you want the skirt to come. Finally, measure your sample square.

For example, suppose your hip measurement is 30 inches and you add an extra 2 inches. And suppose you've decided to make the skirt 14 inches long. That means you'll need enough squares to form a rectangle 32 inches by 14 inches. Then, if your square measures about 4 inches, you'll have to make 24 squares—8 to go around you multiplied by 3 to make it 12 inches long. After you have sewn the squares together, you can crochet a few additional rows at the top and bottom to make the skirt exactly the length you want.

You can crochet all the squares in the same color, or you can make them in different colors. You can also use several colors in each, the way the old-fashioned Granny Squares were made.

When you have made as many squares as you need, sew them together like this:

Lay two squares right side down, next to each other with the edges together. Thread a blunt-end needle with yarn and weave back and forth through the top loop of each *dc* and *ch* along one side of the last *rnd*.

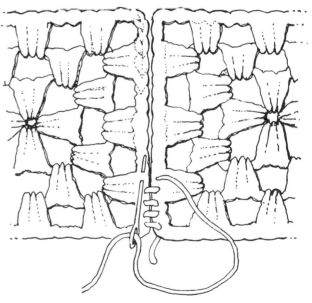

Join enough squares to make a row. Then sew the rows together, to make a rectangle, being careful to match the corners of each square.

If you need to make the skirt longer,
now or as you grow taller,
crochet several more rows around
the waist. Work 3 *dcs* in each
open space with *ch* 3 between
for bridges. Sew the open seam.

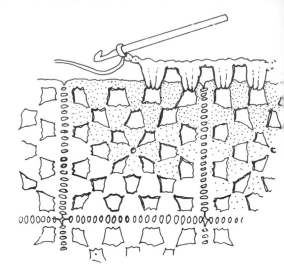

Cut a piece of ribbon long enough to go around your waist, plus another 18 inches for tying. Weave the ribbon in and out of the open spaces around the waist.

Or you can crochet a tie. Cut two pieces of yarn three and a half times longer than you need to go around your waist and tie.

Put the two pieces together,
and *ch* as if they were
one piece.

Weave the crocheted chain
in and out of the open spaces
around the top of the skirt.

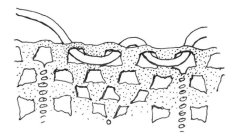

Make a tassel for each end (the directions are on page 25).

42

CHAPTER 2

Knitting

Knitting comes from an Old English word, *cnyttan,* which means "to tie" or "to knot." In an ancient Egyptian tomb scholars have found what they claim are thick knitted wool socks, but the kind of knitting we know about did not become popular until the late fourteenth century in England and Scotland. At first, loops were formed on the fingers or on a series of pegs. Then knitters began to use two long rods—knitting needles—to make rows of interlocking loops of yarn.

The next step was a machine for knitting. In 1589 William Lee, an English clergyman, became annoyed with the young lady he was courting because she paid more attention to her knitting than she did to him. The machine he invented only made his problems worse. Queen Elizabeth, fearing that it would put the hand-knitters out of work, refused year after year to grant him a patent for his machine. Mr. Lee died lonely and poor. Eventually, of course, knitting machines *were* accepted. Modern ones that make stockings and underwear produce a million stitches a minute, compared to a hundred stitches by hand.

Knitting is especially good for making things to wear. Because of its loop construction, it is very elastic. That stretchiness makes knitted clothes fit your body better than woven cloth. They keep you warmer, too. A great variety of designs and textures can be produced with two needles, some yarn, and just two simple stitches.

43

What You'll Need

Tools for knitting are almost the same as the tools for crocheting, listed on pages 12–13, except:

KNITTING NEEDLES: Like crochet hooks, knitting needles come in several materials—plastic, aluminum, steel, and bone. They range from a very fine size 0 to a large size 15. The size of the needle should depend on the thickness of the yarn and on what you are making. Needles also come in different lengths. Ten-inch and 14-inch lengths are most common. Long needles are needed for making big things, like coats and blankets, but short needles are much easier to handle.

A medium-size needle, such as a size 7, is a good size for learning to knit. Try to find 10-inch long needles.

Getting Started

Knitting always begins with a series of loops on one needle. Begin with a single loop, made this way:

About 12 inches from the end of the yarn, make a loop with your yarn as though you were writing a small letter "e."

Write another "e" loop next to it.

Slide the second loop under the first loop and pull it through. Put it on the end of one needle.

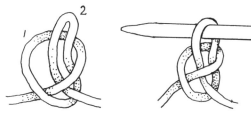

44

Pull on both ends of the yarn. Pulling one end will tighten the slipknot. Pulling the other end will make the loop fit the needle.

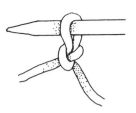

Casting On

"Casting on" is the term knitters use for making the beginning series of loops on one needle.

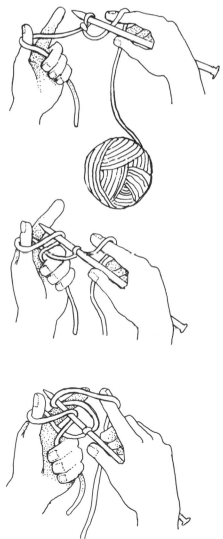

Hold the needle in your right hand, the way you hold a knife for cutting meat. Keep your index finger free and loop around it the yarn that comes from the ball.

Wrap the tail of yarn around your left thumb to form a loop. Hold the yarn securely with the fingers of your left hand, to keep the thumb-loop from unwinding.

Slide the needle through the loop, too, so that both your thumb and the needle are in the loop.

With the free index finger of your right hand, bring the yarn up between the needle and your thumb. Then bring it across the needle. This is what makes the next loop on the needle.

45

Now slip the thumb-loop off
your thumb and onto the
end of the needle.

Pull the tail of the yarn
to tighten the loop.

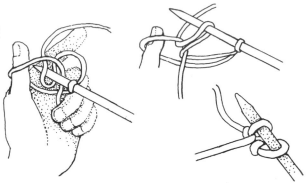

Wrap the tail of yarn over your left thumb to begin the next loop.
When you have learned to cast on with one needle, try it again using
two needles held together in one hand. Form the loops exactly the
same way. Casting on over two needles held together in one hand
makes loops that are bigger and an edge that is stretchier and easier
to work with. When you have finished casting on two needles as
many stitches as you need, slide out one needle. Spread the loops out
on the remaining needle to tighten the loops a little and to make
more space between each one.

To Knit

Cast on about 20 loops over two needles. Slide out one needle and
spread out the loops. Hold the needle with the loops in your left
hand. Hold the empty needle in your right hand. When you are
knitting, the side of the work facing toward you is always called the
front. The side of the work facing away from you is always called
the *back*. And all of this has nothing to do with the right or wrong
side, or the inside or the outside.

Slide the point of the right
needle through the front side
of the first loop on the left
needle. The right needle goes
from the front of the work
to the back, and it goes under
the left needle.

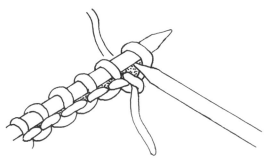

46

Hold the yarn from the ball
in your right hand, hooked
over your index finger. Keep
the yarn in *back* of your work.

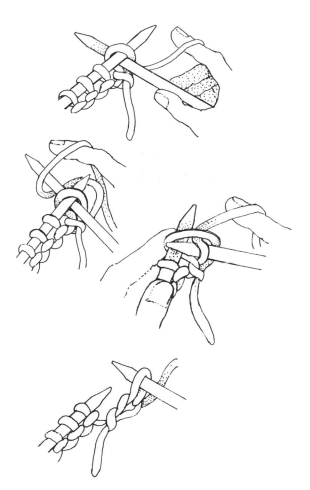

Use your finger to bring the yarn
up between the two needles. Then
bring it across the right needle
to form the first new loop
on that needle.

Now pull the right needle
toward you just enough so that
the loop on the left needle passes
over the point of the right needle.
Move the right needle and slide
the old loop off the left needle,
so that the loop drops to the back
of your work.

This *knits* one stitch.

Knit each stitch on the left needle in the same way, until all the
newly made stitches are on the right needle and the left needle is
empty. Remember always to keep the yarn from the ball in *back* of
your work. Then put the empty needle in your right hand and the
needle with the stitches in your left. Knit the next row of stitches
in the same way.

The symbol for knit is *k*.

Garter Stitch

Knitting each stitch in each row
for several rows is called

47

the Garter Stitch. The back and the front of a piece worked in the Garter Stitch look exactly the same. Keep knitting one row after another, until you begin to feel comfortable with the needles and the yarn.

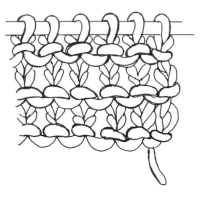

Binding Off

When you have knitted as many rows as you want, you are ready to finish the piece by *binding off*. It is important to bind off very loosely so that the last row will be as stretchy as the rest of the piece.

Knit the first two stitches. Then slide the left needle into the first stitch that you knitted on the right needle and carefully lift that stitch *over* the second stitch and let it drop off the needle.

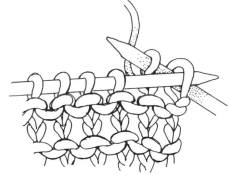

To keep the second stitch from sliding off the needle when it should stay in place, you will have to keep a tight hold on the yarn from the ball. If you pull on that yarn, it will hold the second stitch in place while you lift the first stitch over it.

Now knit another stitch. Again, slide the left needle into what is now the first stitch on the right needle and lift it over the second stitch.

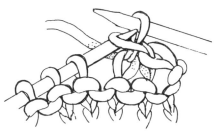

Work all the way across the row, remembering to keep the stitches loose. When there is only one stitch left on the right needle, cut the yarn, leaving a 2-inch tail. Make the loop larger and take it off the needle. With your fingers or with a crochet hook, pull the tail through the loop. With a crochet hook, weave the tail in and out of the top strands of the bound-off stitches. Cut the yarn close to your work.

Finding Your Gauge

To decide how many stitches you will need to cast on to make a piece as wide as you want it, you must first determine your gauge. The size of the needles and the thickness of the yarn, together with your own particular way of knitting—whether it's tight or loose or somewhere in between—is your gauge. Measure an inch across on the sample piece you have just finished, and count the bumps—stitches—in that inch. That tells you how many stitches you must cast on for each inch of width. This is the most important part of your gauge. To find out how many rows you must knit to make an inch, measure an inch along the length of the piece. In the Garter Stitch, each row of bumps means that two rows have been knitted.

Making a Case for Glasses

You can knit a case for regular glasses or sunglasses by using the Garter Stitch. The case is really just one knitted piece folded in half and stitched along the sides. To make a case that measures 6½ inches long and 3 inches wide, knit a piece that is 13 inches long and 3 inches wide.

Find out your gauge with the yarn and needles you are using, and cast on as many stitches as you will need to make a piece 3 inches wide.

Knit in the Garter Stitch until the piece measures 13 inches long. Bind off and weave in the tails.

49

But before you sew up the sides, try decorating the glasses case with embroidery stitches or small crocheted flowers. Fold the finished piece in half.

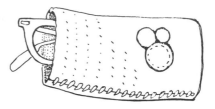

Then with yarn and a blunt-end needle, sew up the sides of the case with overcast stitches.

Making a Baby Bunting

You can knit a sleeping bag or bunting for a doll, or even for a real baby, using the Garter Stitch and almost the same design you used for the glasses case. Actually, a sleeping bag is really one knitted piece that you fold and stitch along the sides.

The size of the doll (or the baby) will determine how big a piece you will need to knit. If your doll is medium-sized (about 14 inches tall), you should knit a piece about 24 inches long and about 9 inches wide. If you're making a bunting for a brand-new baby, knit a piece about 48 inches long and about 15 inches wide.

Find out your gauge with the yarn and needles you are using, and cast on as many stitches as you will need to make a wide enough piece. Knit in the Garter Stitch until the piece is as long as you want to make it. Bind off. Weave in the tails.

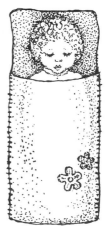

Fold the finished piece so that the back extends about 5 inches above the front for a doll bunting and 6 inches or more for a real baby. Before you sew up the sides, you can decorate the bunting, either with embroidery or with little crocheted flowers scattered and stitched over the front.

50

Then, with yarn and a blunt-end needle, sew up the two sides with overcast stitches.

Knitting a Scarf

If you have several different colors of yarn that you want to use, you can make a gaily striped scarf. Use the Garter Stitch, because both sides will always look nice, no matter which way you wrap the scarf. Make it as wide and as long as you want—as long as you have enough yarn. And the yarn should be all the same thickness, even when the colors are different.

To change to another color of yarn or to add another ball of yarn, knit to the end of the row and cut the yarn you're now using, leaving a 3-inch tail.

Tie a second color to the first color as close to your work as you can. When you begin to knit the next row with the new yarn, be careful not to pull the knot through the first few stitches.

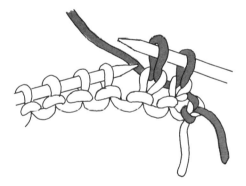

When you come to the end of the scarf, bind off and weave in all the tails. Trim them close to your work. You can make a fringe along both ends, following the directions on page 24.

To Purl

Although you can make many pretty things using just the knit stitch, learning the *purl* stitch will let you make a huge variety of patterns.

51

Cast on about 20 stitches over two needles. Slide out one needle and spread out the loops on the other needle.

Hold the needle with the loops in your left hand. Hold the empty needle in your right hand. Remember that the side facing toward you is the *front* of your work and the side facing away from you is the *back* of your work.

Slide the point of the right needle through the front side of the first loop on the left needle, going through the loop from the *back* of the work toward the *front*.

Keep the yarn in *front* of your work. Use your right index finger to bring the yarn around the right needle, from right to left. Wrap it around the right needle to form the first new loop on that needle.

Now move the two needles so that the loop from the left needle goes over the point of the right needle and slides off the left needle.
This *purls* one stitch, which drops to the front of your work.

Purl each stitch on the left needle until all the newly made stitches are on the right needle. The symbol for purl is *p*.

Stockinette Stitch

Knitting each stitch in one row and then purling each stitch in the next row is called the Stockinette Stitch. It is probably the best-known and most-often-used stitch. The right side is flat and smooth, and all the bumpy loops are on the wrong side.

To remember whether you are on a knit row or a purl row, hold the needles ready to begin. If the front of the work facing you is smooth, you will *knit* this row. If the front of the work is bumpy, it is a *purl* row.

Making a Stocking Cap

Try making a warm stocking cap in the Stockinette Stitch.

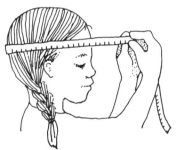

First, measure around your head with a tape measure where the cap will go. This measurement will tell you how wide to make the piece you are knitting.

Next you must determine your gauge, depending on the yarn and needles and your way of knitting, to find out how many stitches to cast on for the width.

After you have cast on the stitches over two needles held together in one hand, *knit* the first row, *purl* the second row, and continue working in Stockinette Stitch for 3 inches, ending with a *knit* row. This forms a turn-up cuff.

Then, with the wrong side toward you, begin with a *knit* row and work the rest of the cap in Stockinette Stitch for about 12 inches, or as long as you want to make it. Knit it all in one color or in gay stripes. Bind off, leaving a tail about 6 inches long.

Then weave the back seam like this:
Bring the sides of the piece together
so that they are touching but not
overlapping. Come up with the
needle from the wrong side close
to the left edge. Then cross over
the seam and go down with the
needle close to the right edge.

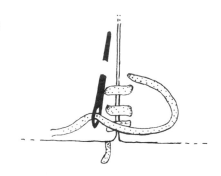

Make one stitch on the right
and cross over again to the left.
Keep crossing back and forth
to the end of the seam.
Make three or four extra stitches,
one on top of the other,
at the end of the seam.

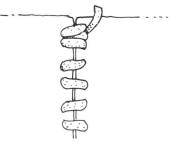

Draw the end of the stocking cap
together like this:
Thread a blunt-end needle
with the tail of yarn.
Weave the needle in and out
of the bound-off edge.
Pull the yarn to gather the edge
as tight as you can, and fasten
the yarn with four or five
stitches on top of each other.

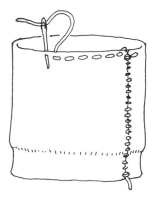

Make a fat tassel (see page 25
for directions) and sew it
to the gathered end.
If you want, you can crochet
a chain and attach one end
to the cap and the other end
to the tassel. Turn up the cuff.

54

This kind of stocking cap is popular with males and females of all ages for skiing, skating, and just keeping warm.

Stretchy Ribbing

To make the piece you are knitting very elastic and stretchy, you can knit a Ribbing Stitch. Stretchy Ribbing is used especially around cuffs of sweaters and of mittens so that the hand can go through easily but the cold air cannot. It is also used on the tops of socks and around the necks of sweaters to make them fit better.

To knit ribbing, cast on an even number of stitches. *Knit* the first two stitches. The yarn is in the back of your work when you knit. Bring the yarn to the front of your work and *purl* the next two stitches. Move the yarn to the back of your work again and knit two more stitches. Continue to *k* 2, *p* 2 across the row. If you end with *p* 2, start the next row with *k* 2. But if you end the row with *k* 2, start the next row with *p* 2.

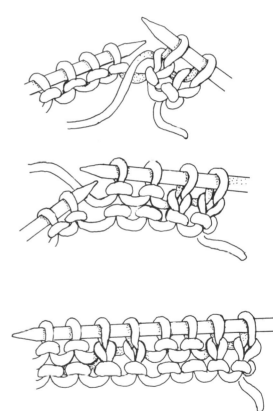

After you have knit a few rows you will be able to see the ribbing pattern and to feel its stretchiness. Ribbing is a slower stitch to make than Garter or Stockinette, because the yarn must constantly be moved back and forth from *knit* to *purl*.

Increasing and Decreasing Stitches

Very often in knitting you will find that you must either add some stitches or take some away. Adding stitches is called *increasing* (the symbol is *inc*). Taking away is called *decreasing* (*dec*). Neither is hard to do, and both are useful to know for when you need to shape something, such as a curving edge.

To *decrease,* just knit two stitches together, usually at the beginning and the end of a row.

If you are decreasing gradually, you will knit two stitches together once in every few rows, and the narrowing will be gentle. If you are decreasing quickly, you will knit two stitches together at the beginning and end of each row.

To *increase,* make two stitches out of one, this way: Begin as though you were knitting a normal stitch, but instead of sliding the knitted stitch off the left needle and letting the loop drop in back of your work, leave it in place.

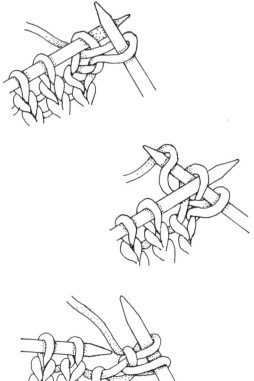

Then slide the right needle through the *back* of the stitch still on the left needle and knit again.

This way you make two new stitches out of one old stitch, first knitting in front of the old stitch, then knitting in back.

56

Making a Pair of Mittens

You can make a pair of mittens for yourself or for someone else. If you knit the whole mitten, and not just the cuff, in Stretchy Ribbing Stitch, it will fit hands of several different sizes.

First, measure your hand from your wrist to the end of your middle finger (or guess how long someone else's hand might be, if you're making a gift). Then measure around your knuckles.

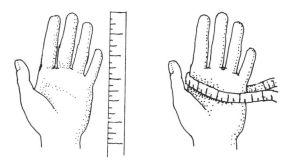

Next, check your gauge, depending on the yarn and needles, to find out how many stitches to cast on. If the measurement around your hand is about 7 inches, for instance, each half of the mitten—the front and the back—should be about 3½ inches wide. If your gauge is about 5 stitches to the inch, you need to cast on 18 stitches. (Remember to cast on an even number of stitches for ribbing).

Making the mitten for the right hand:
Because Stretchy Ribbing is the same on both sides, you knit the right and left mittens the same, but fold and sew them differently. Start at the bottom of the mitten. After you have cast on the number of stitches needed, work in *k* 2, *p* 2 Ribbing Stitch for 4 inches. Knit to the last 8 stitches of the row. Cut the yarn, leaving a 3-inch tail.

Slide the 8 stitches from the left needle onto a stitch-holder or a big safety pin. These stitches will be used to make the thumb after you have finished the rest of the mitten.

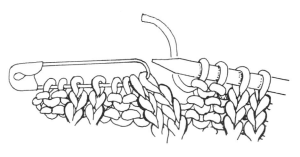

57

Now you must cast on more stitches to take the place of the ones on the stitch-holder. Cast 8 stitches on the empty needle for the first part of the row and continue to knit the stitches still on the other needle for the other part of the row. Be sure to follow the ribbing pattern.

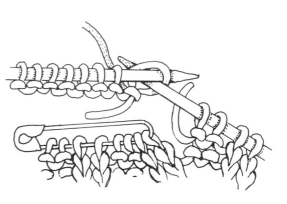

Continue knitting in Ribbing Stitch the length of your hand plus 1 inch. If your hand is 6½ inches long, knit 7½ inches.

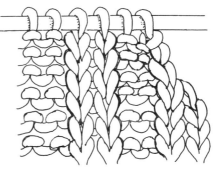

Then begin shaping the top of the mitten. Being careful to follow the ribbing pattern, *decrease* one stitch at the beginning and end of every other row, until you have 10 stitches less than you started with.

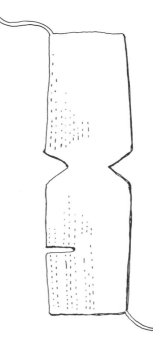

Now continue knitting the back of the mitten. *Increase* one stitch at the beginning and end of every other row, until you have the same number of stitches you started with. Knit in Ribbing Stitch until the back of the mitten is the same size as the front. Bind off.

58

Making the thumb:
Slide the 8 stitches from the stitch-holder back onto the needle. Those 8 stitches are the front part of the thumb.

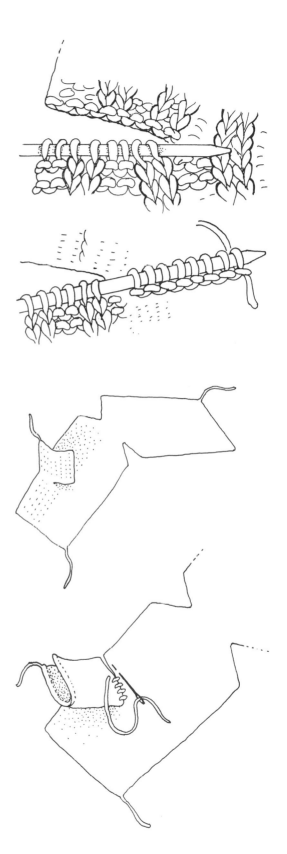

Cast on 8 more stitches for the back part of the thumb.

This makes 16 stitches on your needle. Knit in Ribbing Stitch for 2½ inches. Make sure the ribbing in the thumb matches the ribbing of the rest of the mitten.

Bind off, leaving a 3-inch tail.

Putting the mitten together:
You now have a rather odd-looking piece to sew together.

Fold the thumb section in half. Thread a blunt-end needle with yarn and sew the back half of the thumb section to the mitten, weaving the seam as well as you can. If it is a little awkward to do and if it doesn't look as neat as you'd like, don't worry—it won't show.

Next weave the seam
at the side of the thumb.
Thread the needle with the tail
at the top of the thumb.
Weave the tail in and out
around the opening and pull it
to draw the opening together.
Fasten it with several
stitches on top of each other.

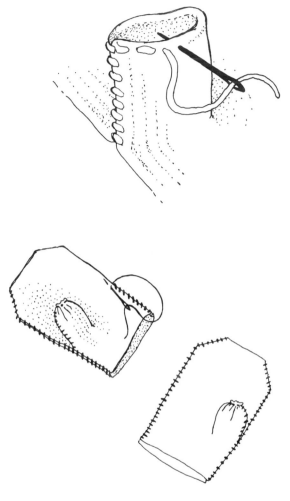

Weave the side seams of the
mitten. Weave in the tails
inside the thumb to keep them
from pulling loose.

Fold the other mitten so that
the thumb is on the opposite
side and so that you have one
right mitten and one left
mitten.

Fancy Ribbing

Not all ribbing is done *knit* 2, *purl* 2, although that is the most common because of its stretchiness. Other kinds of ribbing are not so
elastic, but they look very nice. For example, a pretty Ribbing Stitch
can be created with a *knit* 5, *purl* 2 pattern.

To work this pattern, cast on a number of stitches that can be
divided by 7, plus 2 extra. For example, try it with 23 stitches (3 ×
7 + 2).

60

Row 1: *P* 2, *k* 5 across the row and end with *p* 2.
Row 2: *K* 2, *p* 5 across the row and end with *k* 2.
Repeat these two rows.

Another Fancy Ribbing Stitch is the *purl 5, knit 1* pattern, using the *p* 5, *k* 1 side as the right side. Cast on a number of stitches that can be divided by 6, plus 1 extra. For example, 19 stitches (3 × 6 + 1).

Row 1: *K* 1, *p* 5 across the row and end with *k* 1.
Row 2: *P* 1, *k* 5 across the row and end with *p* 1.
Repeat these two rows.

Try using either of these two Fancy Ribbing Stitches in place of the Stockinette Stitch.

Seed Stitch

The Seed Stitch is also sometimes called the Moss Stitch or the Rice Stitch. The names give you an idea of its interesting texture. Like the Garter Stitch and Ribbing Stitch, it looks the same on both sides, which makes it especially good for scarves and things in which both sides show.

Cast on an uneven number of stitches. *Knit* one stitch, *purl* one stitch, all the way across the row.
K 1, *p* 1 for each row.

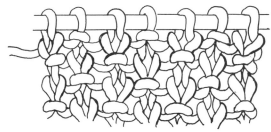

This is a rather slow stitch to make because you must change the yarn from front to back and from back to front between each stitch,

61

as you change from *knit* to *purl*. But it is worth the trouble because it is so pretty.

Making a Shoulder Bag

You can knit a shoulder bag, using the Seed Stitch, either by itself or with Fancy Ribbing. If you use heavy yarn and thick needles, the work will go quickly and the texture will be very interesting.

To make a shoulder bag that is about 12 inches square with a long strap, knit a rectangle about 12 inches wide and 26 inches long.

You can knit it all in the Seed Stitch, or you can knit an inch or two of Seed Stitch followed by an inch or two of Fancy Ribbing to make a striped effect.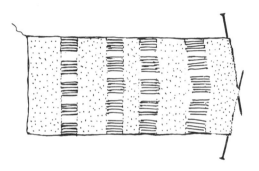

Knit a 2-inch wide strap long enough to go from the bottom of the bag, over your shoulder, and back down to the bottom of the bag.

Weave each end of the strap to the center of each long side of the rectangle. Then weave the sides of the rectangle to the sides of the strap.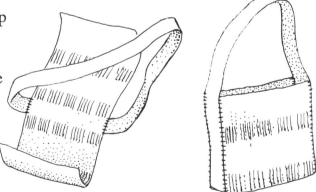

Block Stitch

Knit and *purl* stitches combined in groups of fours make an interesting pattern of smooth and bumpy "blocks" that looks the same on both sides.

62

Cast on a number of stitches that can be divided by 8. Either 16 or 24 stitches are good for a practice piece. *Knit* the first 4 stitches, then *purl* the next 4 stitches. K 4, p 4 across the row for four rows. That makes the first series of blocks.

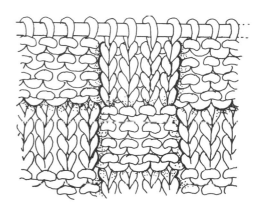

Reverse the pattern for the next series: *p* 4, *k* 4 across the row for four rows. This puts a bumpy block above each smooth block, and a smooth block above each bumpy one.

The next series is again reversed: *k* 4, *p* 4 for four rows.

Making a Small Blanket or Scarf

The Block Stitch looks handsome on any straight piece of knitting. You could add a border on all four sides in Stockinette Stitch.

First, decide what size to make the piece and approximately how many stitches you will need. It should be a number that can be divided by 8. For example, you might plan to cast on 48 stitches— 32 for the Block Stitch, plus 8 more on each side to make a border in Stockinette Stitch.

Cast on the stitches. Knit the border in Stockinette Stitch for an inch or more, ending with a *purl* row. The bigger the piece you are making, the wider the borders can be.

63

For the best effect, use the wider stripes for elaborate pattern stitches, like Fancy Ribbing and Block Stitches, and separate them with stripes of Stockinette and Seed Stitch. Here is a sample:

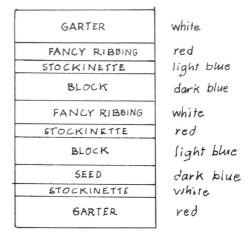

GARTER	white
FANCY RIBBING	red
STOCKINETTE	light blue
BLOCK	dark blue
FANCY RIBBING	white
STOCKINETTE	red
BLOCK	light blue
SEED	dark blue
STOCKINETTE	white
GARTER	red

Cast on as many stitches as you need to make the width you want, and begin to knit. When you come to the pattern stitches, like the Block Stitch, you'll find that the number of stitches doesn't always work out evenly. Divide the extra stitches between the beginning and the end of the rows and knit them in a plain stitch. For instance, you might have 50 stitches instead of 48. In that case, knit one extra stitch on the end of each row.

Knit the two rectangles and join them the way you did the newspaper patterns. Sew the pieces together with yarn.

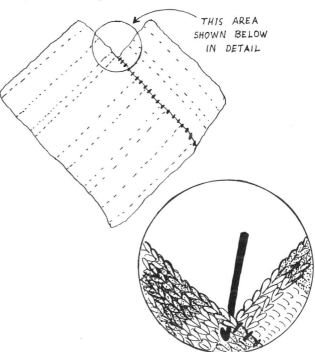

THIS AREA SHOWN BELOW IN DETAIL

Starting at the center of the V neck, slide a crochet hook through the last stitch of each row of knitting and go all around the edge with Single Crochet. Join the last *sc* to the first *sc* with a *sl st*. *Ch* 1 and work another round of *scs*. Add as many rounds as you want.

66

Then *sc* all around the
outside edge. Make 3 *scs*
in each corner. Join the
first and last *sc* with a
sl st. Work as many rounds
as you want.

If you like, you can add a fringe
(see page 24 for directions).
For a 5-inch fringe,
cut pieces of yarn
about 10½ inches long.
(If you are running short
of yarn, make a shorter fringe.)
Attach the pieces of yarn
about an inch apart all
around the edge of the poncho.

CHAPTER 3

Weaving

Although weaving is a much older craft than knitting or crocheting, it is more complicated than either of them in the equipment you need, the methods you learn, and even the words you use to describe the loom and weaving.

The first looms were very crude affairs. The up-and-down threads, called the *warp,* hung from a tree limb to which they were tied. The back-and-forth threads, called the *woof* or *weft,* were pulled over one warp thread and under the next. Even today Indian rugs and blankets are woven on vertical looms in much the same way.

Eventually a loom was developed with the warp threads stretched out horizontally, instead of being allowed to hang. Levers were added for raising groups of threads so that the weaver could pass the shuttle with the woof through them more easily. In 1785, Edmund Cartwright invented the first practical power loom. After that, technical advances came rapidly. Today most weaving, like knitting, is done on fully automated machinery.

The looms still used by hand-weavers are big and complex, and they require a great deal of study and patience and practice to operate well. But someone who wants to learn about weaving can buy or even make a simple little loom for weaving squares or small pieces and then sew the woven pieces together. Or she can try weaving techniques on a piece of plain coarse cloth to make something decorative and unusual.

Weaving on Cloth

One way to get an idea of what weaving is like is to weave yarn on burlap with a blunt-end needle. You could also use linen or homespun or hopsacking or some other kind of plain cloth woven of thick threads.

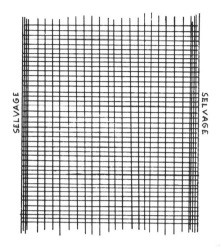

If you have a large piece of burlap or similar cloth, first take a look at how it was woven. The smooth, tightly woven sides of the cloth are called the *selvages*. The threads that run lengthwise, in the same direction as the selvages, are called the *warp*. The threads that run crosswise, from selvage to selvage, are called the *woof* (*weft* is another name for the cross threads).

Look at how the woof passes over one warp thread and under the next, over and under, all the way across. When the cloth was woven, the warp was put on the loom first. This is called *dressing* the loom, and weavers say it is a long and rather tedious job. Then the woof was wound on a shuttle. By a series of mechanical devices, one group of warp threads was raised—in a plain weave like burlap, every other thread is raised—so that the shuttle could pass through with the woof. Then the second group of warp threads was raised and the shuttle passed through again. This is what gives the burlap the "over one, under one" pattern.

Now cut a practice piece of cloth a few inches square. With a small crochet hook or a blunt-end needle, pull out one of the woof threads. Once you get it started, either from the end or from somewhere in the middle, the thread will pull out rather easily. Pull gently so that the warp threads aren't disturbed.

69

Take out four or five more woof
threads next to the first one.
After the first one has been
pulled out, the others will come
out easily. This leaves you an
open space on the practice
piece with only warp threads.
You are going to weave in
the new woof threads in yarn
of a different color.

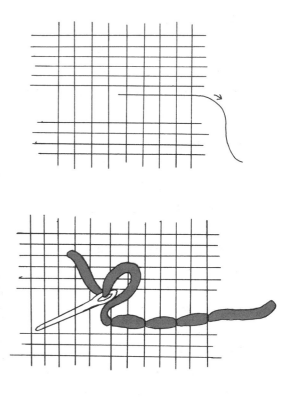

Thread a blunt-end needle
with yarn. It will be your
shuttle. Begin to weave
with the needle from right
to left. Go over one thread
and under the next, over
and under, over and under.

As you go along, use your needle
to push each woof thread
close to the last one woven.
A real loom has a *beater* to push
the woof into place after the
shuttle has passed through once.
This is called *battening*.

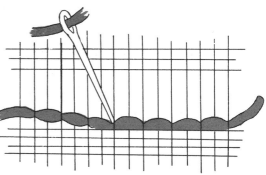

Turn the cloth around and
weave back to the other side.
Go over the threads you went
under before. Go under
the threads you went over
before. Keep on weaving
with the needle and yarn
until the space from which
you pulled out the woof
is filled with yarn.

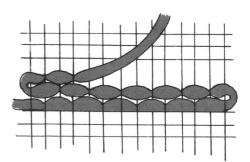

70

Weaving a Bookmark

Cut a piece of burlap (or other plain cloth with heavy threads) about 12 inches long and 3 inches wide. You can weave on the cloth either crosswise or lengthwise or both.

First pull out a few threads. Then thread a blunt-end needle with yarn and weave the yarn in and out, back and forth.

If you are planning to weave lengthwise, pull the warp threads out of the center of the strip.

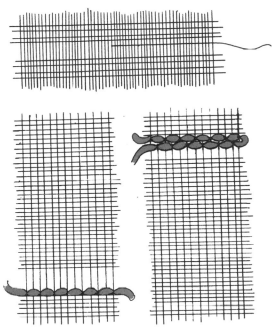

If you are going to weave several stripes across, or reweave the entire strip, start about an inch from the end and pull out just a few threads at a time.

Turn the strip around, from top to bottom, so that you are always weaving from right to left.

If you are planning to weave in both directions, up and down, and back and forth, it will be easier to weave the lengthwise threads first and then do the crosswise threads.

Try not to use too many different kinds and colors of yarn if you are weaving in both directions. Try to put together simple combinations. For instance, if you have a piece of red burlap, try weaving a narrow white stripe down the center and a wide blue stripe across both ends.

After you have woven the
bookmark the way you want it,
turn a little bit of the long
edge to the wrong side (whichever
you decide is going to be the
wrong side). Press with your
fingers and turn again to make
hems. Then turn under the short
edges in the same way. Sew
around all four edges with
hemming stitches so small
that they barely show
on the right side.

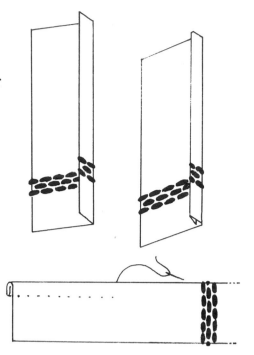

Variations in Weaving

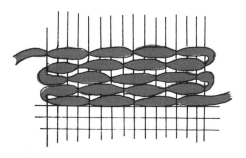

After you have practiced the plain "over one, under one" weave,
you can try more elaborate weaving patterns.

Try going over three, under one.
Or over one, under three.
If you move the pattern
one thread to the left each
time you begin at the edge,
you will create a twill design.

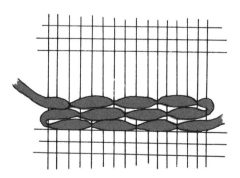

And if you move the pattern one
thread to the left three or four
times and then move back one thread
to the right three or four times,
you will create a herringbone design.

72

Making a Placemat

You can make a placemat and napkin with colorful woven borders by pulling out some of the woof threads and reweaving them with yarn. To make a placemat 16 inches long and 12 inches wide when it is finished, cut a piece of cloth 18 inches by 14 inches. Use plain cloth woven with heavy threads. Linen or a linen-like fabric would be perfect. The extra inches are for a hem on each edge.

Measure 4 inches from the two 14-inch sides of the cloth and pull out a woof thread. Take out as much of the woof as you want in order to weave in a new pattern. If you are planning to make very wide borders, pull out and weave in only a few woof threads at a time.

After you have woven a bright band on each end of the placemat, hem the mat on all four edges. On the wrong side of the mat, measure ½ inch from each edge and make marks to show you where to fold it.

First fold the hem along one of the long edges and crease it with your fingers or with a warm iron. Then turn it over again to make a double hem.

Pin the hem and baste it with long running stitches. Sew it with little hemming stitches that are very small and hardly show on the right side.

Hem the other long edge and the two short edges.

73

To make a napkin, cut a piece of cloth 16 inches long and 16 inches wide. Measure 4 inches from one side and pull out a woof thread. Weave a border along that edge. Then hem the edges as you did the placemat.

Making a Simple Loom

It is also possible to make a simple loom with a small box or lid and a handful of paper clips. The box or lid should be of stiff cardboard. It does not matter how deep the box is. In fact, the shallower it is, the easier it will be to handle.

Fasten a row of paper clips, each touching the one next to it, on two opposite sides of the box.

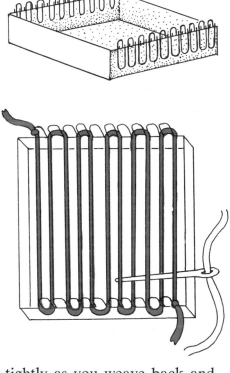

Now *dress* your loom:
Tie the end of the yarn to one of the paper clips on the end of the row. Wind the yarn for the warp back and forth from one side to the other, going around the paper clips.
Tie the yarn to the last clip.

Use a blunt-end needle for a shuttle. Thread the needle with yarn for the woof and begin weaving, right next to the clips.

Be sure not to pull the woof too tightly as you weave back and forth. If you do, it will draw the outside warp threads close together. Then you will end up with a woven piece that is narrower in the middle than it is on the ends. Take the finished woven piece off the paper clips.

74

Making a Scent Cushion

Weave two small pieces of cloth on your homemade loom. Sew the pieces together with overcast stitches. Leave one side open. Stuff the cushion with pine needles. Or you can stuff it with balls of cotton or a worn-out nylon stocking and some good-smelling leaves or herbs from the kitchen cupboard. Or sprinkle the cotton or the stocking with perfume. Sew up the open side.

The scent cushion can be used as a pincushion or tucked in a drawer or kept anywhere so that you can enjoy its pleasant smell.

Using a Weaving Square

You can buy small, inexpensive hand looms on which to learn something about weaving. One of these is a 4-inch square frame with groups of little pegs or pins on all four sides that are used for dressing the loom. For a shuttle, a long steel needle comes with the loom. You will find that the sides and corners of the loom are marked with numbers and arrows. These are the landmarks that show you how to wind the yarn on the loom. Although directions come with the loom, some people find them hard to understand. These instructions might make it easier.

Dressing a Weaving Square

Hold the loom with the side marked with the numeral 1 in front of you, the arrow next to the numeral pointing away from you. Call the side toward you A. The side opposite you is B. The side on your left is C.

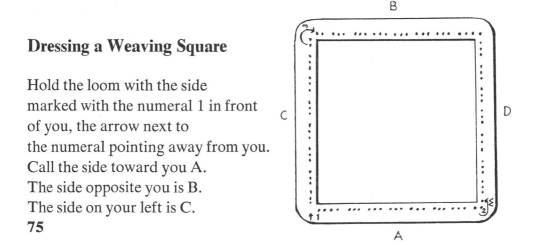

The side on your right is D.
Hold the end of the yarn in your
left hand. Starting at the numeral 1,
draw the yarn with your right hand
just inside the row of pins
along side C. Wind the yarn
around the first two pins on
side B, and bring the yarn back
to side A. Go between the
second and third pins of A
and tie the yarn with a knot.

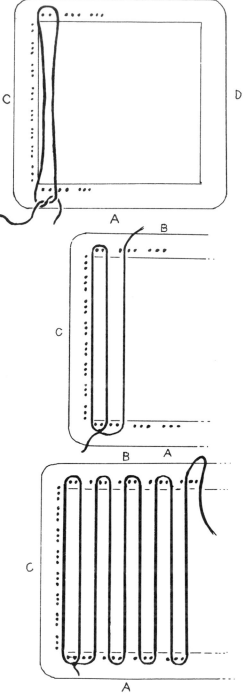

Then pull the yarn to the right
and wind around the next two pins
on side A and bring the yarn to B,
going between the first and
second pins in the second group.
Go to the right around the next
two pins in the second group.

Bring the yarn back to A,
going between the first and
second pins in the next group.
Keep on winding from A to B to A
until you come to the end
of the pins and the curved arrow
marked with the numeral 2.

Now begin winding the second layer of yarn, going across the first
layer.

76

Turn the frame so that side D is toward you. Go around the first two pins on side D and bring the yarn to the opposite side C. Go between the first and second pins. Wind the yarn around the next two pins. Bring the yarn back to side D. Continue winding from D to C and back until you reach the end of that row of pins and the arrow marked with the numeral 3.

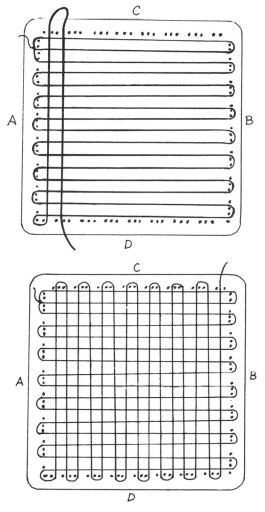

Then begin winding the third layer of yarn, across the second layer, and going in the same direction as the first layer.

Turn the frame again so that side A is toward you. Pull the yarn around the last pin on side C and the first pin of side B.

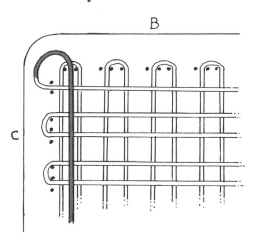

Go between the two pins on the
end of side B, by the numeral 3.
Bring the yarn toward you to
side A and go between the first
and second pins. Then wind the
yarn around the next two pins.
Go between the third and fourth
pins and bring the yarn back
to side B. Go around the first
two pins of the next group and
come back to side A.

You will see that, although
the yarn goes in the same direction
as the first layer, the yarn in
this layer fills in some of the
spaces between. When you have
finished the third winding,
you will have a thick "honeycomb"
of yarn. Now you are ready
to begin to weave.

Don't break off the yarn.
Wind the yarn loosely around the
outside of the loom 4½ times.
Then cut the yarn. Unwind it
from around the outside of the
loom and thread the free end
of it through the long needle.

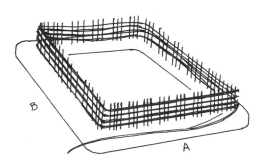

As in any kind of weaving, getting the loom ready is a complicated
process, but now you are ready to begin.

Weaving on the Weaving Square

Start weaving at numeral 2, going from side D on the right to side C on the left.
To start, go between the first and second pins on side D. Go over the first thread, under the next, over the next, and so on, over and under to the end of the row. Be careful not to miss any, for they are sometimes hard to see when you are working with three layers.

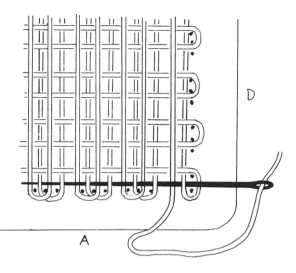

Pull the yarn completely through. Then turn the frame so that you can weave back. Go between two pins. One of the crosswise yarns of the second layer forms the second woof thread. You can use your needle or a crochet hook as a beater, to keep pushing the woof threads tightly against each other.

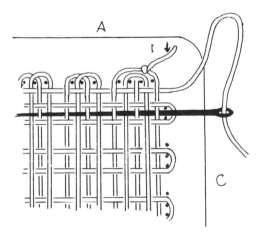

You will probably find that it helps to poke and prod at the yarn in both directions to keep it even.

For a change, try dressing the loom with one color yarn and weaving with another.

79

Making Things with Woven Squares

You can make many of the same things with woven squares that you made with knitted and crocheted squares. Use three squares to make a case for glasses (it will be a little wider and a little shorter than the one you knit), or nine squares to make a patchwork pillow cover. Make only one square to use as a coaster under a glass, or make a dozen squares for a doll blanket. Two dozen or more squares will make a scarf. It all depends on you and what you want to do and, of course, on how much yarn and time you have.

These woven squares can be decorated with embroidery stitches. Or you can make crocheted flowers to sew on.

Weaving on a Pillow

Not all weaving is done with yarn or thread, and not all weaving is done on a loom. For instance, you can weave an unusual pillow cover with ribbon or decorative tape, and you can weave it directly on the pillow!

If you have a pillow covered in a plain fabric that you like, try to find ribbon or tape that goes well with the fabric. The fabric will show through the spaces between the warp and woof.

Next, you must figure out how much ribbon or tape you'll need. Suppose that your pillow is 12 inches wide and 12 inches long. The ribbon you want to use is ½ inch wide, and you decide to leave ½ inch of open space between each strip of ribbon. That means you will need 12 pieces of ribbon for the warp and 12 more for the woof—a total of 24 pieces. Each piece should have an extra ½ inch on each end to turn under for a hem. So you'll need 24 pieces, each 13 inches long, which comes out to 8⅔ yards of ribbon.

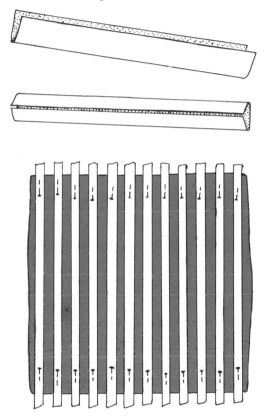

You can even use folded strips of cloth instead of ribbon. Cut the strips 2 inches wide. Fold them in half down the center and press with an iron or with your fingers. Open the strip and fold the outside edges toward the center. Fold again on the center line and press thoroughly with an iron. You don't need to sew them. Lay the 12 warp pieces in place, right on the pillow, with ½ inch between each piece. Pin each end.

When you are satisfied that the pieces are straight and evenly spaced, fold under ½ inch on each end and sew them to the pillow near the seam with small hemming stitches.

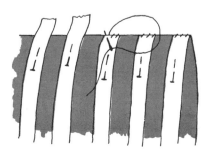

Then, using your fingers, weave each of the 12 woof pieces over and under the warp, leaving ½ inch between each piece. Pin them in place. Fold under ½ inch on each end and sew them with small hemming stitches.

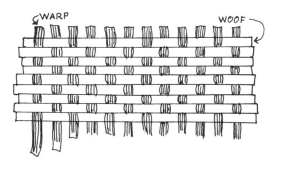

If you prefer, you can weave the woof pieces without leaving any spaces between. Then the fabric will not show through. You will need half again as much ribbon (13 yards instead of 8⅔).

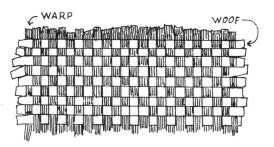

If you also arrange the warp pieces without spaces, you will need twice as much ribbon (17⅓ yards), and the pattern you create will be quite different.

Weaving a Wall Hanging

Sometimes it's fun just to experiment with different methods and to make something that has no purpose other than to be looked at and admired. Wall hangings let you do both.

Find a smooth piece of wood any size you want that will serve both as a loom and as a background for the hanging. Paint it, finish it with oil or varnish, glue on a piece of plain fabric, or leave it alone. (You might even decide to remove it when you've finished weaving.)

Then you'll need some small nails and a hammer. Pound in a row of nails along two opposite ends of the board, about an inch from the edge. Keep the nails fairly close together—less than ½ inch apart. If you want them to be even, you should measure with a ruler and mark with a pencil before you begin pounding.

But maybe you'd rather see how it turns out if the nails are not evenly spaced.

Dress the "loom" with a firmly twisted yarn or, better yet, with string for the warp. If you are keeping the warp straight and even, go around two nails at a time as you wind back and forth from one side to another.

Otherwise, go around one, two, or even three nails at a time.

It is with the woof that you can really begin to experiment. Try different weaving patterns: not just over one, under one, but over three or four at a time, under two or three. Then change to another pattern.

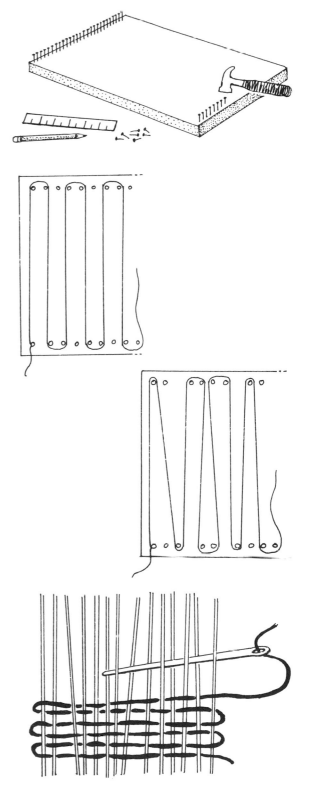

83

You don't always have to weave all the way across. Try weaving just partway back and forth for a few rows. Fill in the empty spaces with another yarn or leave them empty.

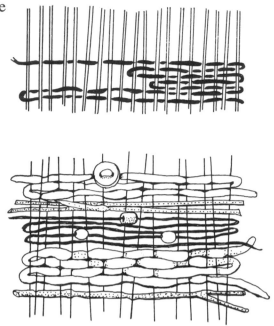

Use different kinds of yarn and string and weave in other materials, too, such as dried grass, small twigs, feathers, or wire. Try stringing beads, buttons, or even macaroni on the yarn as you weave it in.

Weave as though you were creating a painting. If you don't like an effect, pull it out and try something else. The only limitations are your imagination and the materials you can find.

When you're satisfied with the wall hanging, tie the ends of a piece of strong yarn or string or wire to two of the nails and hang it up.

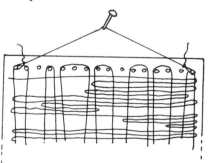

Or you can remove it carefully from the nails and hang it by one of the loops.

Then stand back and admire it.

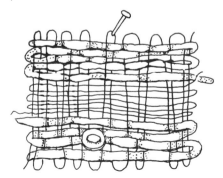

CHAPTER 4

Macramé

Macramé (pronounced *mak-ra-MAY*) is a method of making beautiful designs by tying ordinary string with simple knots. It has much in common with crochet. Both are French words. Both are forms of lace-making. And both use only the simplest materials. Macramé doesn't even require a hook; nimble fingers are enough.

It is a fairly new art that began in Arabia about seven hundred years ago. *Miqramah* is the Arabic word for "striped cloth," which was decorated with knotted fringe and braid. Samples of the beautiful handwork were carried by traders to southern Europe, and by the end of the fourteenth century, macramé was being done in Spain, Italy, and France. From there it spread through the rest of Europe and, eventually, to the United States.

Sailors became especially well known for their macramé. They found that knotting string into intricate designs was a good way to pass the time while they were away on long voyages. They also found that the interesting things they created this way made nice presents to bring home to their wives.

Macramé, like crochet, began as a decorative craft. It is still used mainly for decoration and for jewelry. But macramé can also be used for very practical items like belts and rugs.

85

What You'll Need

YARN: The yarn you've been using for crocheting, knitting, and weaving is too stretchy for macramé. But ordinary kitchen string or cord used for tying packages is excellent knotting "yarn." Smooth, light-colored cord is easier to handle and to see what you're doing as you go along.

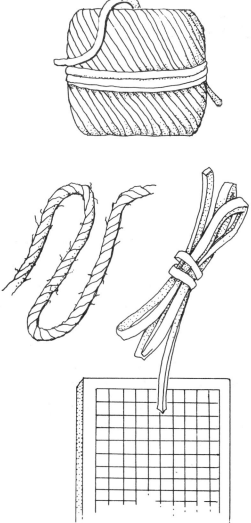

As you progress, you can try other "yarns": rough brown jute twine, leather shoelaces, heavy rug yarn, as well as the colorful kinds of macramé yarn sold in needlework and craft stores.

KNOTTING BOARD: A firm surface on which to pin the piece as you work on it makes the knotting easier. You can buy a knotting board, usually a piece of light-weight insulation board covered with paper and marked off in 1-inch squares.

But you can also make one yourself. It should be at least 1 foot long and 1 foot wide. If you have a piece of insulation board, such as Celotex, that is ideal. Cork is good, too. You can also tape together several layers of corrugated cardboard (the kind used for cartons).

Cover the material smoothly with brown wrapping paper and mark off the paper in 1-inch squares to help you keep your work straight and even.

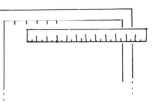

To work with a knotting board, hold it on your lap with the edge propped against a table. Or lay it flat on the table.

Not everyone uses a knotting board, especially for long, simple pieces like belts. You can anchor your work to a small block of wood tied to a doorknob. But it must be fastened to something that can withstand constant pulling and tugging as you tie the knots.

PINS: Special "T" pins are used to hold the finished rows of macramé in place on the knotting board as you continue working. Straight pins can also be used, but they often bend. Try using two straight pins together instead of one "T" pin.

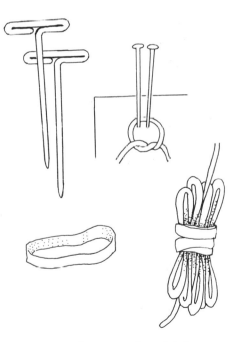

RUBBER BANDS: When the pieces of yarn are too long to handle easily, you can wind them up and fasten each with a rubber band.

You will also need a YARDSTICK, SCISSORS, and a BAG in which to keep everything.

87

Getting Started

Macramé is done by tying pieces of yarn together with two simple knots: the Half Knot and the Half Hitch. These two knots can be put together in many combinations to create other knots and to create many different designs.

Each piece of yarn is called an *end*. One length of yarn is doubled and tied to a *holding cord* to make two ends. You will need four ends to learn the basic knots.

For the holding cord, cut a piece of yarn 4 inches long. Tie an Overhand Knot at each end of the holding cord: make a loop with the cord and pull the end through.

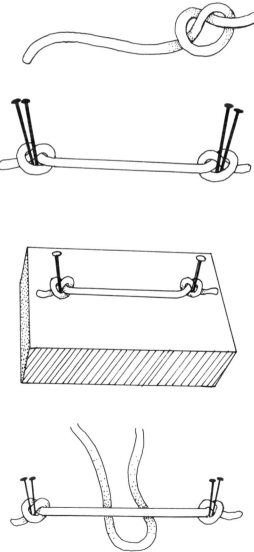

Fasten the cord near the top of the knotting board with pins. Put the pins through the knots at angles slanted away from you to hold the cord stretched tight.

Or nail the knots of the holding cord to a block of wood.

Then measure and cut two pieces of yarn, each 1 yard long. Fold one piece in half. Slide the loop formed at the center of the piece down behind the holding cord.

88

Bring the 2 ends of the
yarn down through the loop.
Pull the loop tight.

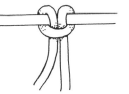

Tie on the second piece
right next to the first
in the same way. You will
have 4 ends, each about 18
inches long. Number the
ends from left to right,
1, 2, 3, 4.

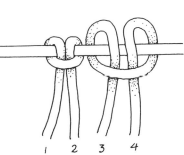

The Half Knot

Ends #2 and #3 in the center are called the *core ends*. The core
ends don't move, and the knot is made around them. Pin each core
end near the bottom edge of the knotting board so that it will stay
in place. (If you aren't using the knotting board, tie a piece of wood
or other weight to the ends and let them hang down.) The two
outside ends, #1 and #4, are the *working ends,* and they are used
to tie the knot.

To make the left-right
Half Knot, pick up End #1
and cross it loosely *over*
the core ends, forming a
wide loop on the left.

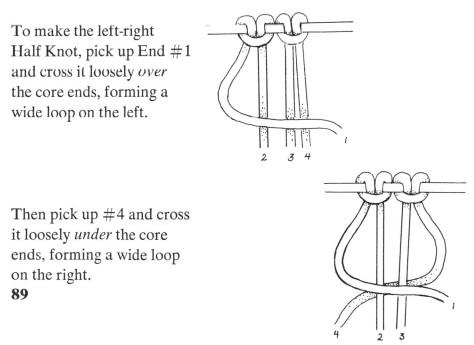

Then pick up #4 and cross
it loosely *under* the core
ends, forming a wide loop
on the right.

89

Pull #4 *up* through the left loop and #1 *down* through the right loop. End #1 is now in the place of #4 and #4 is in the place of #1.

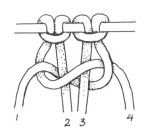

Draw the two ends tight. This completes the left-right Half Knot.

Keep on tying left-right Half Knots. Call whichever end happens to be on the left End #1, and the one on the right End #4. They will change places each time you tie a knot. A continuous series of knots forms a *sinnet*. As you work this series, you will notice that the sinnet has begun to twist to the right.

As you make the sinnet longer, it should twist around and around on itself. Loosen the core ends a little as you go so that the sinnet will twist freely.

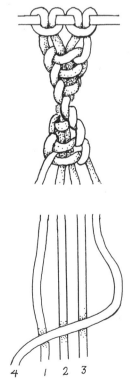

Next try making the right-left Half Knot. Pick up End #4 and cross it loosely *over* the core ends, forming a wide loop on the right.

90

Then pick up #1 and cross it loosely *under* the core ends, forming a wide loop on the left. Pull #1 *up* through the right loop and #4 *down* through the left loop.

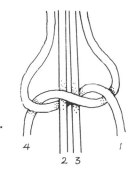

Draw the 2 ends up tight. This completes the right-left Half Knot.

Make a sinnet of right-left Half Knots. You will see that the sinnet twists to the left.

The Square Knot

Tie a left-right Half Knot. Then tie a right-left Half Knot. The two knots together make a Square Knot (sometimes called the Macramé Knot). Remember that each time you tie a Half Knot, #1 and #4 change places.

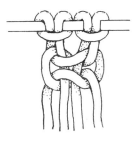

Make a sinnet of Square Knots. It is sometimes hard to remember which kind of Half Knot you are to tie next. But if you look carefully at the knot you just made, you will be able to decide.

If End #1—the one on the left—is coming out from beneath the loop that holds it down, you have just tied a right-left.

91

But if End #4—the one on the right—is coming out from beneath the loop that holds it down, you have just tied a left-right.

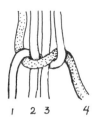

Measuring Yarn for Macramé

Each end should be at least four times longer than the piece you are going to make. But since each length of yarn is doubled to form two ends, you should cut the lengths at least eight times longer than the piece you are going to make. For instance, if you are going to make a piece 1 yard long, you'll need to cut 8-yard lengths to form 4-yard ends.

Thick yarn is used up faster than lightweight yarn because the knots are so much bigger. If you are using a thick yarn like rough jute twine, each end should be at least six times longer than the piece you are going to make, and you should cut the lengths of yarn twelve times longer than the piece you are going to make. It is *always* better to be generous than stingy when you cut the yarn, because it is so hard to hide the knot when you have to tie on a new piece.

The wider the piece you are making, the more ends you will need. To figure out how many ends to cut, tie a Square Knot with 4 ends of the yarn you plan to use. Measure the width of the knot. If a knot tied with 4 ends is ½ inch wide, for instance, you will need 8 ends to make an inch.

Winding the Ends

Long ends can be very awkward to work with, because they get tangled. Winding each end into a *bobbin* makes knotting easier.

Starting at the bottom, wind the yarn around and around your fingers until the unwound part is about 18 inches long.

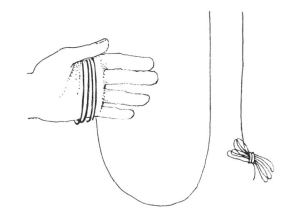

Slide the yarn off your fingers and fasten it with a rubber band.

Unwind a few inches of each end from the bobbin as you need it.

Making a Watchband

You can make a band for your watch by tying Square Knots in ordinary cord attached to a buckle.

The band will be more secure if you use a buckle with a tongue.

If you don't have that kind, a plain buckle can be used.

(And if you don't have a watch, you could make a fake one—or wear the strap as a bracelet.)

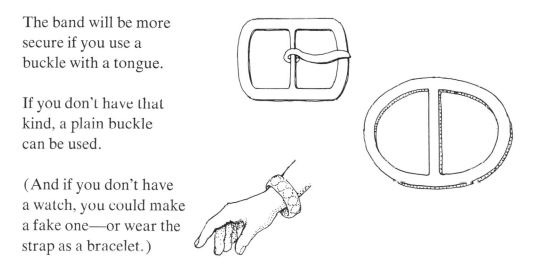

Measure around your wrist and add 2 inches to overlap—about 8 inches altogether. That means each end will measure 32 inches and each length of yarn that you cut will be 5 feet, 4 inches (64 inches). Cut a little extra to be sure.

The number of ends you will need depends on the width of the buckle and the thickness of the yarn. It should be a number that can be divided by 4. If you find that 8 ends work best, you will cut 4 lengths of yarn.

The shank of the buckle is the holding cord. Pin it on your knotting board. Tie on the 4 lengths to make 8 ends. Wind the ends into bobbins.

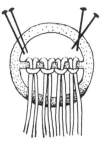

Row 1: Tie a Square Knot in the first 4 ends. (Before you tie each knot, pick out the 2 core ends and pin them down.) Tie a Square Knot in the next 4 ends. Pin the knots.

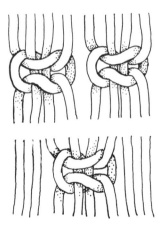

Row 2: Skip the first 2 ends. Tie a Square Knot in the next 4 ends. Skip the last 2 ends.

Repeat Row 1 and Row 2 to the end of the piece. As you work, move the pins along, always keeping the last two knots pinned down. The pins will make it easier to tie the knots. They also help to keep the finished piece straight and even.

When the piece is as long as you want it, tie each pair of ends in an Over-hand Knot: make a loop with the two cords together and pull the ends through the loop.

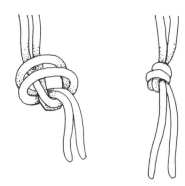

94

For sinnets, tie 10 Half Hitches, alternating left and right, in the first 4 ends. Then tie 10 Half Hitches, alternating left and right, in the next 4 ends.

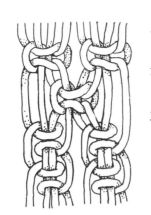

ROW 1
ROW 2
START OF SINNETS

Join the two sinnets by working Row 2.

Repeat the Square Knot pattern. Make two more sinnets. Continue this pattern for the length of the belt. Remember to pin the knots as you go. Keep track of the length of the belt. The last 6 inches should be worked in Square Knots so that it will buckle properly. Don't start a new sinnet if you can't complete it 6 inches from the end.

Tie each pair of ends in an Overhand Knot. Cut the yarn close to the knots, leaving a short tail on each end. Weave the tails in the back of the knots with a crochet hook.

The Double Chain Knot

In this knot, working ends change places with core ends for every Half Hitch. It is often used for sinnets and in making fringes and jewelry.

Tie 4 ends on a holding cord. Number the ends from left to right, 1, 2, 3, 4.

98

Cut the yarn close to the knots. Or, if you like, you can leave a short tail on each end. Use a crochet hook to weave the tails in and out of the knots on the wrong side.

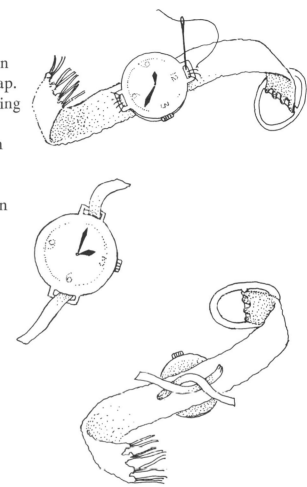

Mark the beginning of the 2-inch overlap. Center the watch between the buckle and the overlap. Attach the watch by sewing it to the strap with overcast stitches through the shanks of the watch.

Or wind a piece of ribbon over the two shanks and under the watch.

Pull the ribbon through the spaces between the knots in the band. Tie the ribbon on the wrong side, or sew the ends together.

The Half Hitch

The Half Hitch can be made in many different ways, and each variation has a different, tongue-twisting name. The names are harder to say than the knots are to tie.

Tie 4 ends on a holding cord. Number the ends from left to right, 1, 2, 3, 4. The two in the center are the core ends. Fasten them with pins.

95

Pick up End #1 and cross it loosely *over* the core ends, forming a wide loop to the left.

Then cross the same End #1 back *under* the core ends and pull it up through the loop.

Draw the end tight. That makes one left Half Hitch.

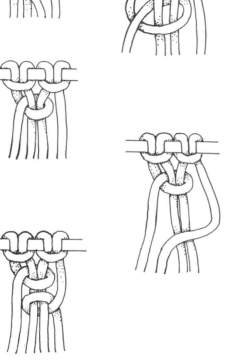

Now pick up End #4 and cross it loosely *over* the core ends, forming a wide loop to the right.

Then cross that same End #4 back *under* the core ends and pull it up through the loop. Draw the end tight. That makes a right Half Hitch.

When you tie a series of Half Hitches, first a left Half Hitch and then a right Half Hitch, they are called Alternating Half Hitches. These knots are often used for making sinnets.

Making a Belt

You'll discover the real pleasure of macramé as you begin to combine the knots. Try using sinnets of Alternating Half Hitches to connect sections of Square Knots to make a belt.

96

Use a wide buckle, if you have one, or two metal rings. C belt longer and pull the end of the belt through the sinr brown jute twine makes a handsome, casual belt, althoug can be a little hard to see as you are working. Bright-col looks pretty; so does plain cord.

Measure around your waist and add 4 inches for an ove 12 inches if you don't have a buckle). If your waist is 24 buckled belt will be 28 inches long. For lightweight yar each end will measure 3 yards, 4 inches (112 inches) and length of yarn will be 6 yards, 8 inches. Cut 6½ yards to

For thick yarn, like jute, each end will measure 4 yards, 2 inches), and each length of yarn will be 9 yards, 1 foot. (to be sure.

The number of ends depends on the width of the buckle thickness of the yarn. It should be a number that can be d If you find that 8 ends work best, cut 4 lengths of yarn.

Use the shank of the buckle as a holding cord and tie on the ends.

Or tie the ends around *both* metal rings.

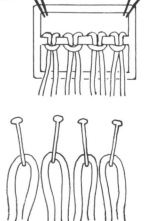

If you are not using a buckle or rings, loop each end around a pin instead of tying it to a holding cord.

Wind the ends into bobbins and fasten with rubber bands.
Row 1: Tie Square Knots in the first 4 ends, then in the ne
Row 2: Skip 2 ends, tie Square Knots in the next 4, skip
Repeat Row 1 and Row 2.
97

For the first knot, End #1 and End #2 are the core ends. Hold End #3 and End #4 together and tie a right Half Hitch.

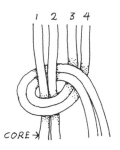

The 2 ends that were used to tie the first Half Hitch now become the core ends. And the 2 core ends are now the working ends. Use them together to tie a left Half Hitch.

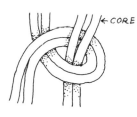

Continue tying right and left Half Hitches to form a chain.

Making a Bead Necklace

Beads are often a part of macramé designs. You can buy beads of different kinds and different sizes especially for use in macramé at craft stores. Or you can use what you have on hand. Beads from broken necklaces, buttons with shanks, and even short, straight pieces of macaroni (called *ditalini*) can be used in your work. Just be sure the holes in the beads and button shanks are large enough for the ends of yarn to go through. Put a dab of white glue on the cut ends of yarn and twist firmly. When they are dry, the yarn will pass more easily through the holes.

You can make a necklace of beads and yarn tied with Double Chain Knots. Cut 4 lengths 4 yards long (5 yards if the yarn is thick). For this project, you will start at the center and work toward each end.

99

Find the centers of the lengths and tie each two lengths together with an Overhand Knot.

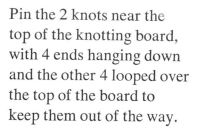

Pin the 2 knots near the top of the knotting board, with 4 ends hanging down and the other 4 looped over the top of the board to keep them out of the way.

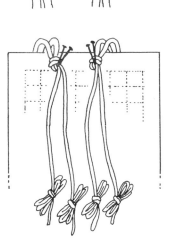

Wind the 4 hanging ends into bobbins.

As you make the Double Chain Knot, slide a bead onto the 2 ends that are the working ends before you tie the next knot.

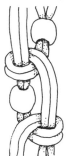

If you have plenty of beads (or buttons, or macaroni), use one between each knot. If you have only a few, tie several knots between each bead.

When the chain is 14 inches long, unpin it and turn it so that the other 4 ends may be knotted. Make the second half to match the first half.

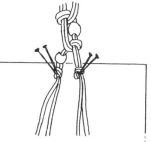

100

To join the ends of the chain
together, pin the last knot
of each half side by side
on the knotting board.
Tie them with a Gathering Knot
made this way:
Take the 4 ends on the
right as the working ends.
The 4 on the left become the
core ends. Put a pin to
the right of the working ends.
Make a loop to the right,
bringing the ends up and
around the pin.

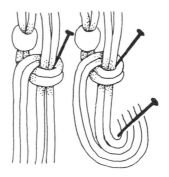

Lay the working ends *across*
the core ends. Then bring
them back *under* the core ends.
Pull the working ends up
through the loop.

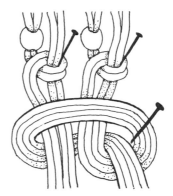

Take out the pin and draw
the ends tight. This very
secure knot is often
used for finishing.

Try on the necklace and trim
the ends to the length you
want. Put a bead or two
on each end or on each pair
of ends. Tie an Overhand
Knot above and below each
bead to hold it in place.

101

The Double Half Hitch

If you make two Half Hitches with the same end (both with End #1, for example), the knot is called a Double Half Hitch. There are several ways of working Double Half Hitches, and each can be used in different ways for different results.

In each kind, one end becomes the *knot-bearer,* on which the knots of each row are tied. It is important to keep the knot-bearer straight and even.

The Horizontal Double Half Hitch

Rows of knots are tied on a knot-bearer that goes straight across the piece. One or two rows can be used to separate sections of other knots. Several rows create a dense, even pattern.

Tie 4 ends on a holding cord. End #1 is the knot-bearer. Cross it straight over all the other ends, going in the same direction as the holding cord. Put a pin on the left, close to the ends. The knot-bearer goes around the pin, and the pin helps to hold the knot-bearer in place. Put another pin to the right of the ends as a guide. Hold the knot-bearer straight and tight with your right hand.

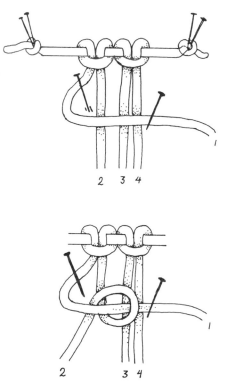

With your left hand, pick up End #2, bring it up over the knot-bearer, and pull it down and to the *left* through the loop that is formed.

102

Draw it tight. This makes a
Half Hitch. Tie a second
Half Hitch with End #2 for a
Double Half Hitch.

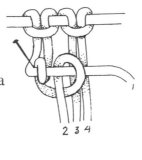

Tie a Double Half Hitch
on the knot-bearer with
each end.

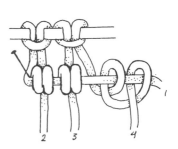

To make the return row, put a pin on the right just below the last
knot to hold the knot-bearer in place. Cross the knot-bearer over all
the ends, this time going to the left. Put another pin on the left as a
guide.

Use your right hand to tie
Double Half Hitches with
each end. Bring End #4
up over the knot-bearer.
Pull it down and to the
right through the loop
that is formed.

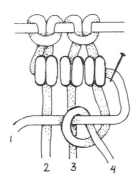

Making a Mat

Jute twine (or any kind of thick cord) can be used to make a
handsome and practical mat to put under plants or hot dishes. Tie the
twine with Horizontal Double Half Hitches and Alternating Half
Hitches.

To make a mat about 6 inches square, you will need to have 24 ends
(or a number that can be divided by 4). If you are using thick yarn
like jute, each end—except for the knot-bearer—should be 1 yard
long. The knot-bearer for this piece should be 2 yards long. That
means you will need to cut 11 lengths of yarn, each 2 yards long, and
1 length that is 3 yards long.

103

Cut a holding cord about
10 inches long. Tie an
Overhand Knot in each end
and pin it to a knotting
board marked off in 1-inch
squares as a guide.

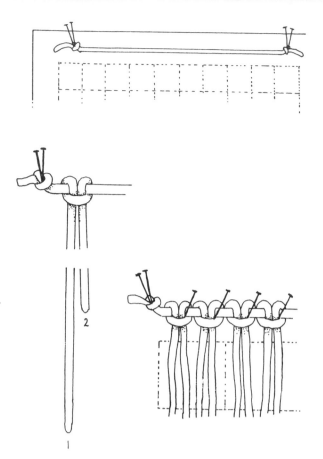

Fold the 3-yard length of
yarn so that one end is
2 yards long and one end
is 1 yard. Tie it on the
holding cord so that the
longer end becomes End #1.

Tie on the other ends and
space them so there are
4 ends of heavy yarn per
inch. Pin each knot.

Wind the ends into bobbins and fasten them with rubber bands.

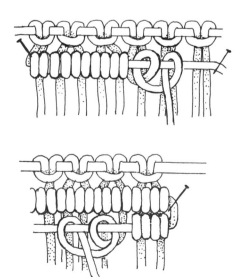

Use pins to hold End #1,
the knot-bearer, in place
across the ends. Tie a
Horizontal Double Half
Hitch with each end.

Use pins to hold the knot-
bearer for a return row.
Tie a Horizontal Double
Half Hitch with each end.
If you are using jute,
the piece will now measure
about 1 inch long.

104

Tie each group of 4 ends with Alternating Half Hitches. Make six sinnets about 1½ inches long. (You could also make the sinnets with Square Knots.)

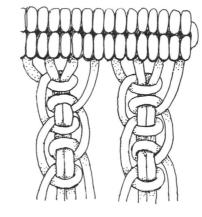

Use pins to hold End #1 in place as knot-bearer. Tie a Horizontal Double Half Hitch with each end. Then make a return row.

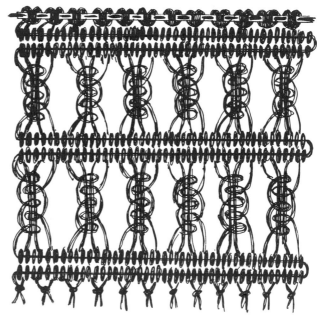

Make another series of 1½-inch sinnets.

Tie two more rows of Horizontal Double Half Hitches.

To finish, tie each 2 ends with an Overhand Knot. Cut the yarn, leaving tails. Weave the tails in the back of the knots with a crochet hook. Untie the Overhand Knots on the holding cord and weave in those tails, too.

The Diagonal Double Half Hitch

If you hold the knot-bearer at an angle across the ends instead of straight across them, you can create a number of interesting patterns.

105

Sometimes the diagonal row of knots goes from one side to the other and returns. Sometimes the diagonal row goes only to the center and meets a diagonal row coming from the opposite direction. These rows can cross and continue, or they can be kept separate. Experiment with some of the different ways of tying the Diagonal Double Half Hitch.

Cut 5 lengths of yarn, each about 1½ yards long. Tie 10 ends on a holding cord. Wind the ends in bobbins.

End #1 is the knot-bearer. Cross it over all the other ends at an angle, down and to the right. Put in pins as guides so the angle stays the same. Hold it with your right hand. Use your left hand to tie Double Half Hitches with each end.

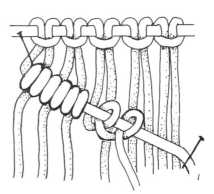

Remember to bring each end up over the knot-bearer. Then pull it down and to the *left* through the loop that is formed.

Then reverse the direction of the knot-bearer. Angle it down and to the left and put in pins as guides. Hold it with your left hand and tie Double Half Hitches with your right hand.

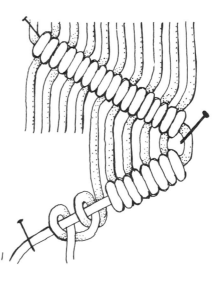

Remember to bring each end up over the knot-bearer. Then

pull it down and to the
right through the loop
that is formed.

This is one way to work the Diagonal Double Half Hitch. It leaves lots of open space between each row of knots and creates a lacy pattern.

You can also work rows of Diagonal Double Half Hitches close together to form a dense pattern. Begin with End #1 as knot-bearer and tie a row of Diagonal Double Half Hitches.

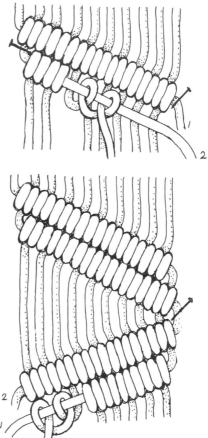

Then use the next end,
End #2, as knot-bearer
and tie a second row close
to the first one.
Pin the row carefully at
both sides to keep the piece
straight and even.

Each end in turn becomes the
knot-bearer for a row of
Diagonal Double Half Hitches.
The last knot in the row is
always tied with the end that
was knot-bearer in the row before.

Try making a few rows of Diagonal
Double Half Hitches working from
left to right. Then reverse and
make a few more rows of Diagonal
Double Half Hitches working from
right to left.

Still another way to use the Diagonal Double Half Hitch is to bring angled rows from each side to meet in the center. The rows are made close together.

107

With 10 ends on a holding cord, begin with End #1 as knot-bearer. Angle it down and to the right. Tie Diagonal Double Half Hitches with the next 4 ends.

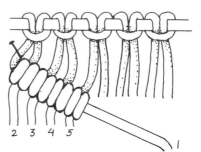

Remember to bring each end up over the knot-bearer. Then pull it down and to the *left* through the loop that is formed.

Pin the row and move the knot-bearer out of the way.

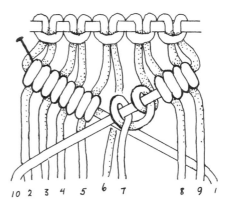

Then pin End #10 as knot-bearer in the opposite direction. Angle it down and to the left. Working from right to left, tie Diagonal Double Half Hitches on the knot-bearer with the next 4 ends.

Remember to bring each end up over the knot-bearer. Then pull it down and to the *right* through the loop that is formed.

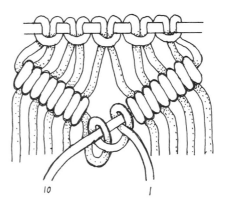

To join the rows, tie a Diagonal Double Half Hitch on the End #10 knot-bearer with the End #1 knot-bearer.

Sometimes you may find that the two rows of knots don't quite meet. With your fingers, slide the Diagonal Double Half Hitches along the two knot-bearers until they come together at the center to form a V.

108

To make the second row, start again on the left. Use the first end as knot-bearer and tie Diagonal Double Half Hitches with the next 4 ends.

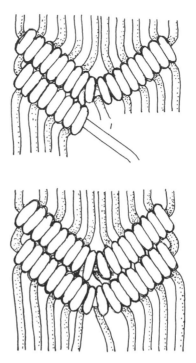

Then use the last end as knot-bearer in the opposite direction. Tie Diagonal Double Half Hitches with the next 4 ends. Join the two halves in the center by tying a Diagonal Double Half Hitch with the knot-bearer from the left.

Continue to tie as many rows of Diagonal Double Half Hitches as you want.

The Crossed Diagonal Double Half Hitch

You can also bring an angled row of Diagonal Double Half Hitches from each side so that they cross in the center to form an X.

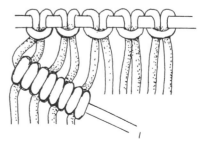

With 10 ends on a holding cord, begin with End # 1 as knot-bearer and tie Diagonal Double Half Hitches with the next 4 ends. Remember to bring each end up over the knot-bearer. Pull it down and to the *left* through the loop that is formed. Then

109

use End #10 as knot-bearer in the opposite direction. Tie Diagonal Double Half Hitches with the next 4 ends. Remember to bring each end up over the knot-bearer. Then pull it down and to the *right* through the loop that is formed.

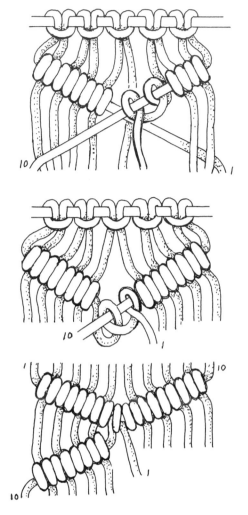

To join the two halves of the row in the center, tie a Diagonal Double Half Hitch with the End #1 knot-bearer on the End #10 knot-bearer. If the rows don't quite meet, slide the Diagonal Double Half Hitches along the knot-beams until they come together at the center.

Still working from right to left, tie Diagonal Double Half Hitches with the next 4 ends.

You now have a half row of Diagonal Double Half Hitches from the left and a whole row of Diagonal Double Half Hitches from the right. To finish the row from the left and complete the cross, pick out the first knot-bearer. It will be the sixth end from the left. Keep it angled down and to the right.

Use pins to hold it in place. Starting with End #7 and working from left to right, tie Diagonal Double Half Hitches with the next 4 ends. This finishes the X.

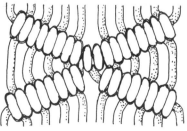

110

If you continue this pattern, a diamond-shaped design will be formed by the crossed rows.

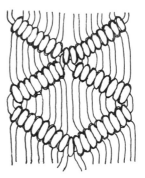

Making a Pair of Suspenders

A pattern of Crossed Diagonal Double Half Hitches can be worked quickly. It makes an unusual pair of suspenders to wear with jeans or a skirt.

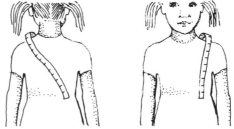

Measure the distance from the back of your waist on the right to the front on the left side, going over your shoulder. Add 2 inches.

Use bright-colored yarn, if you have it. You can also use two colors very effectively in this project.

Cut four lengths—two of each color—that are eight times as long as one suspender will be. For instance, if you measure 28 inches from back to front and you add 2 inches to that, the length would be 6 yards, 2 feet. Make it 7 yards, to be sure.

Cut one length of either color for the knot-bearer. Make it 8 yards long.

Loop each of the four lengths around pins to make 8 ends instead of tying them to a holding cord. The 4 ends in the middle should be one color, the 2 ends on each side the second color. (The knot-bearer

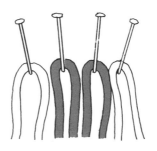

111

is usually one of the ends, but it can also be a separate piece of yarn.)

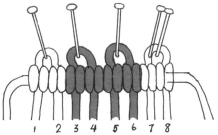

Take the length of yarn that is to be knot-bearer and find the center. Lay the yarn straight across the 8 ends, right next to the pins with the center between End #4 and End #5. Tie on the yarn with a row of Horizontal Double Half Hitches. That gives you End #1 and End #10, the knot-bearers. Wind the ends into bobbins.

Work a pattern of Diagonal Double Half Hitches. Pin carefully as you go along to keep the angles the same and the piece straight and even.

End with the row of Horizontal Double Half Hitches.

To finish, tie each pair of ends with an Overhand Knot. Weave in the tails. Make another suspender to match the first one. Find four buttons that will fit through the open spaces at each end. Sew the buttons in place on the waistband of a skirt or on a pair of jeans. Button on the suspenders in back, cross them, bring them over your shoulders, and button them in front.

112

Making a Vest

A macramé vest made of string and beads, if you have them, is quite an elaborate project, but it is a beautiful way to show off your skills.

First, you must take some important measurements and write them down.

Measure across your shoulders in back of your neck.

Measure from your shoulder to the middle of your chest.

Measure loosely around your chest.

Measure from the middle of your chest to your waist, or wherever you want the vest to end.

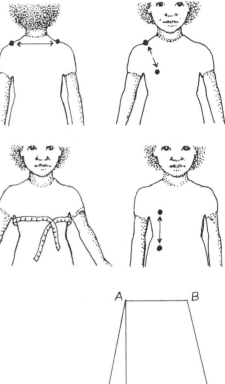

Now use these measurements to make this simple pattern with newspaper. The pattern is for one-half of the front of the vest.

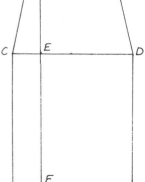

113

Divide the shoulder measurement by 3. If your measurement is 12 inches, line A-B will be 4 inches.

Divide your chest measurement by 4. If your measurement is 32 inches, line C-D will be 8 inches.

The measurement from your shoulder to the middle of your chest is line A-E. For instance, it might be 9 inches. The measurement from the middle of your chest to wherever you want the vest to come is line E-F. If you want it to end a few inches below your waist, the line from A to F might be 18 inches long.

When you have drawn the pattern, cut it out and fasten it to the knotting board with pins or tape. Or you can draw it directly on the knotting board. Mark it off in 1-inch squares as guides. (Don't worry if your board is not as long as the pattern. You can move your piece up as you finish a section.)

You will need quite a lot of yarn to make the vest. Make it with a medium-weight twine from the hardware store or with special macramé yarn that ties into Square Knots about ½ inch wide. If your measurements are close to those in the example, you will need about 480 yards of yarn. Read the label on the ball of twine or yarn to decide how many balls to buy.

To make the front:
Cut four lengths of yarn for every inch in the line A-B. If your pattern measures 4 inches, you will need 16 lengths of yarn to make 32 ends.

Measure the line A-F and multiply it by 8 to decide how long to cut each length. If A-F is 18 inches, each length will be 4½ yards.

Cut a holding cord 3 inches longer than the line A-B. Tie an Overhand Knot in each end. Pin the holding cord along A-B. Tie on the ends. Wind the ends into bobbins.

114

Tie a row of Square Knots
with every 4 ends across
the piece.

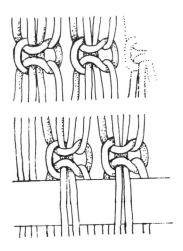

Start a second row about
¾ inch below the first
row. Slide a ruler, table
knife, or a piece of cardboard
cut ¾ inch wide
under the core ends and
over the working ends of
each Square Knot as you
tie it to keep the knots
an even distance from
the row above.

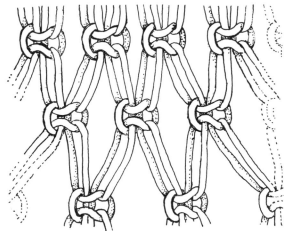

Skip the first 2 ends, tie
Square Knots with every
4 ends, skip the last 2 ends.

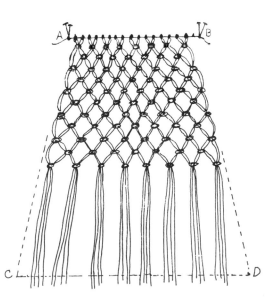

As you tie each row of Square
Knots, spread them apart
toward the slanted sides A-C
on the left and B-D on the
right. The knots will be a
little farther apart in each
row. Make the last row of
Square Knots just above the
line C-D.

115

Cut a piece of yarn 30 inches long for a knot-bearer. Starting 10 inches from the end of the yarn, tie it straight across the line C-D with Horizontal Double Half Hitches. Keep the ends of the knot-bearer free. Don't let them be worked into the pattern.

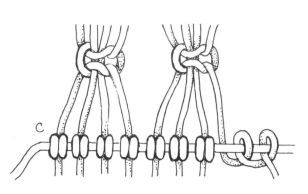

If your knotting board is not large enough to hold the entire piece, this is a good time to repin it with the line C-D at the top of the board.

Cut one length of yarn for every inch in the line C-D. If your pattern measures 8 inches, you will need eight lengths of yarn. Look at the length of the line E-F and multiply it by 8 to decide how long to cut each length. If E-F is 8 inches, for instance, each length will be about 2½ yards long.

Tie each length to the knot-bearer, between the Horizontal Double Half Hitches. That will give you 2 more ends between End #2 and End #3.

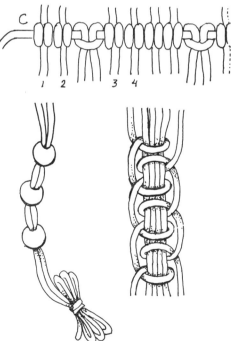

Make 2-inch sinnets with each 6 ends, using 4 ends as core ends. Tie Alternating Half Hitches or Square Knots. This is a good place to use beads. Slide them on the 2 ends that you just added before you wind the ends into bobbins.

116

Tie the first part of the knot.
Slide a bead into place.
Finish the knot. Begin another.

You don't need to use a bead in every knot or even in every sinnet. But you should plan the arrangement of beads so that you have enough to do at least the two sections of the front of the vest.

When the sinnets are finished, add another 30-inch knot-bearer with Horizontal Double Half Hitches. Keep the ends free.

Then with End #1 as knot-bearer, tie 11 Diagonal Double Half Hitches from left to right and return from right to left.

Next, use End #3 as knot-bearer and tie another 11 Diagonal Double Half Hitches and return. And so on across the piece.

If your piece is 8 inches wide with 48 ends, you will have four separate sections of Diagonal Double Half Hitches. The section will measure 2 inches or more long, depending on how steep you made the angles of the knot-bearers.

Then take the last end on the right and use it as knot-bearer for a row of Horizontal Double Half Hitches worked from right to left.

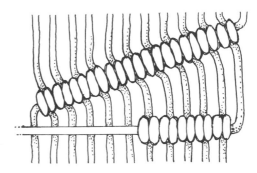

The rest of the vest can be
free-hanging fringe, unless
you wish to add another section
of knotting. When you have
finished, you can tie each
pair of ends with an Overhand
Knot (see page 88) just below
the last row of Horizontal
Double Half Hitches. Trim
the ends evenly.

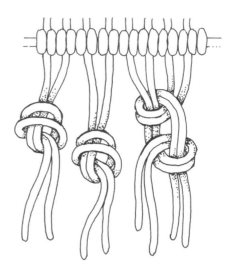

Or you can tie each group
of 4 ends with Double
Chain Knots.

This completes one-half of the front of the vest. Make a second half
to match it, making sure that the line C-D of Horizontal Double
Half Hitches of both halves and the row of Horizontal Double Half
Hitches below it match exactly.

To make the back:
Use the pattern from the
front to cut a new pattern
for the back. The only
change will be that the
line A-B is drawn longer
so that B-D is straight
instead of slanted. This
is for the *left* half of
the back.

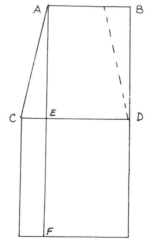

Cut the same number of lengths of yarn as you did for one-half of
the front. Each should be as long as those cut for the front. For the
holding cord, multiply the new A-B by 2 and add 3 inches. For
example, if the new A-B measures 6 inches, cut a cord 15 inches
long. Put a knot in the center and a second knot on the left end.
118

Pin the holding cord in place on the knotting board with the center knot at B. Tie the ends on evenly, spacing them along A-B.

Wind the ends into bobbins.

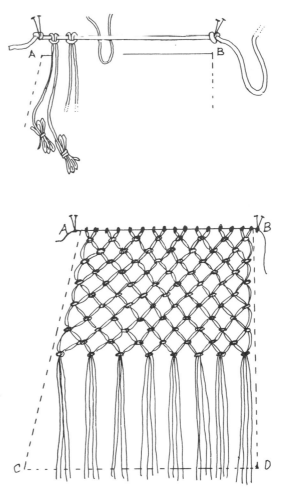

Tie the Square Knots the same way you did for the front sections. Spread them apart a little with each row so that the sides follow the slanted A-C line. Make the last row just above the line C-D.

Cut a piece of yarn 36 inches long for a knot-bearer. Starting 10 inches from the end of the yarn, tie the knot-bearer straight across the line C-D with Horizontal Double Half Hitches. Keep the ends free.

Add one length of yarn for every inch in the line C-D, tying it to the knot-bearer as you did in the front section.

Make sinnets, with or without beads, to match the front. Add a second 36-inch knot-bearer.

Tie a series of Diagonal Double Half Hitches to match the front, but don't tie the last row of Horizontal Double Half Hitches just yet.

Unpin the completed left half of the back. Turn the pattern over so that the slanted line A-C is on the right.

119

Pin the center knot of the holding cord at B. Make a knot at the end of the cord and pin it at A.

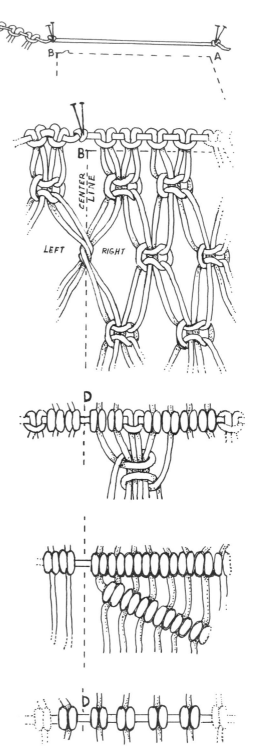

Make the right half of the back to match the left. On the second row of Square Knots pull the first 2 ends that are being skipped through the open space of the last knot on the left half. This helps to join the two halves together.

Use the second half of the knot-bearer from the left half of line C-D to continue the row of Horizontal Double Half Hitches.

Add more ends. Make more sinnets to match. Use the second half of the second knot-bearer from the left half to continue another row of Horizontal Double Half Hitches.

Continue the series of Diagonal Double Half Hitches from the left half.

120

If the last end on the right is long enough, use it as knot-bearer for a final row of Horizontal Double Half Hitches all the way across both halves of the back, unpinning and moving your work as needed.

If it is not long enough, cut another knot-bearer about 30 inches long and tie it on. Let the leftover ends on each side become part of the lower fringe.

Finish the lower fringe to match the front.

Sew the front parts to the back at the shoulders with overcast stitches.

Tie the sides with the remaining ends of the knot-bearers under the arms.

Use the other ends of the knot-bearers to fasten the vest in front.

121

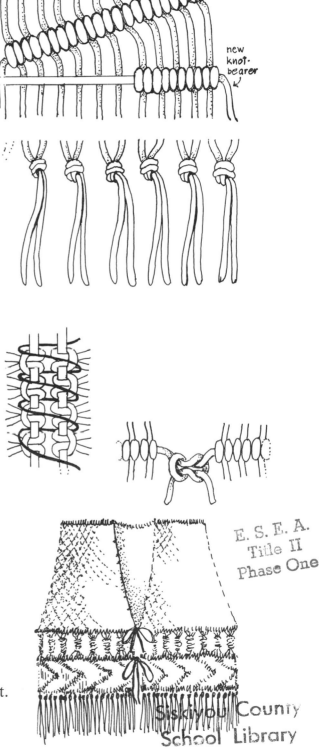

new knot-bearer

Making a Sampler Yarn Bag

A yarn bag, made up as a patchwork sampler, is a wonderful way to show off your new crocheting, knitting, weaving, and macramé skills. You can make up a dozen patches in some of the different stitches you have learned:

Single Crochet

Double Crochet

Garter Stitch

Stockinette Stitch

Seed Stitch

Block Stitch

Woven Square

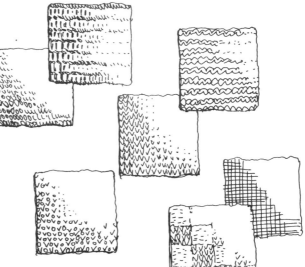

Make a total of twelve 4-inch squares using different colors of yarn.
Make some round crocheted designs to sew on as decorations.

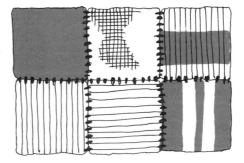

Sew together six different patches for each side of the bag. If your patches are each 4 inches square (of course, you can make them all shapes and sizes, if you want to), each side of the sewn-together piece will measure 12 inches long and 8 inches wide.

122

Now make a top for the bag with one of the ribbing stitches. Cast on enough stitches to make a top 8 inches wide. Knit in Ribbing Stitch for a few inches. Bind off. Knit a second section of ribbing like the first one.

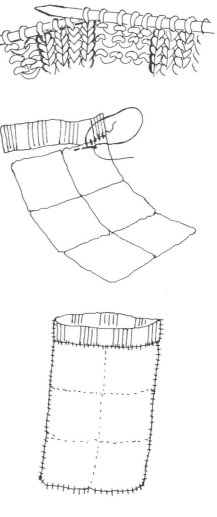

Sew a section of ribbing to one short side of a patched part. Sew the second section to a short side of the second patched part.

Then put the two parts together and sew around three sides. Leave the side by the Ribbing Stitches open.

Make a fringe of macramé along the bottom of the bag.

Cut sixteen lengths of thick yarn, each 2 yards long. Fold them in half to make 32 ends. Use a crochet hook to pull the loops through the last row of stitches along the bottom of the bag.

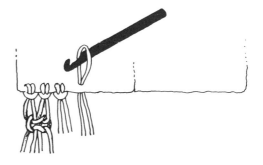

You could begin by tying some rows of Square Knots.

123

Then add some sinnets—
perhaps twisted sinnets
of Half Knots.

Add a section of Crossed
Diagonal Double Half Hitches.

Separate the sections with
Horizontal Double Half
Hitches.

Finish with plain fringe
tied with a Gathering Knot
for every 8 ends.

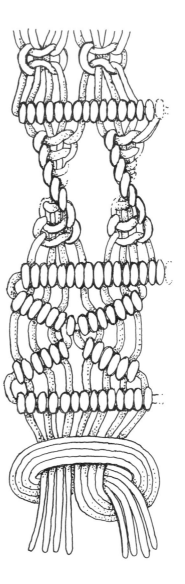

Chain two drawstrings of yarn,
each 22 inches long. Starting
at one end of the ribbing,
weave one drawstring in and out
of the ribbing with a crochet
hook, about an inch from the edge.

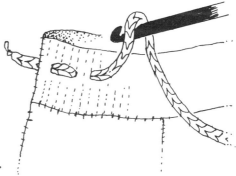

124

Go all the way around the opening.
Knot together the two ends
of the drawstring.

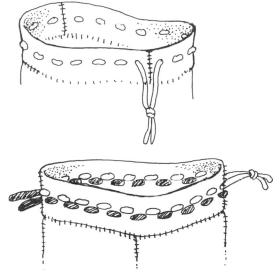

Starting at the other end
of the top of the bag,
weave the second drawstring
through the ribbing in the
opposite direction.
Knot the ends.

Keep your yarn and hooks and needles in the bag, along with one of
the many yarn projects you'll want to try, now that you know how.

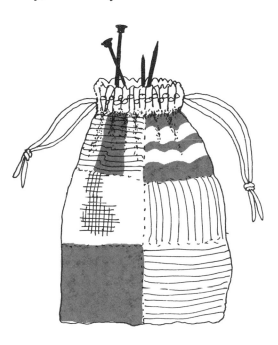

Index